MARGINS
OF ISLAM

Islam is a kaleidoscope of expressions shaped by different cultures. Local spiritisms flavor people's connections with the supernatural. Political histories and ideologies carve out other emphases. And all of these patterns are in flux, since change never stops. Lifelong learning is required from those who want to understand Islam. This book presents diverse Muslim lifestyles and worldviews in a readable, accessible, interesting form. Beyond description, authors explore particular bridges for communicating the gospel in various unique contexts. For updating and expanding one's knowledge, for interacting with creative minds, and for general enrichment, this book is a treasure.

—Miriam Adeney, PhD
associate professor of world Christian studies, Seattle Pacific University,
author of *Kingdom Without Borders: The Untold Story of Global Christianity*

Here are fourteen missiological case studies, written by practitioners who have lived for many years in a wide variety of Islamic contexts all over the world, and have wrestled with what it means to live out and communicate the Christian message. They take us far beyond simple theories about contextualization, and using all the skills of anthropology and sociology, help us to understand an extraordinary variety of different expressions of Islam. This book raises huge questions about how we should understand Islam, how we should teach Christians about Islam, and how we should communicate with Muslims. While it doesn't provide neat answers, it's a model of what's involved in reflecting seriously on long-term Christian engagement with Muslims.

—Colin Chapman
visiting lecturer, Arab Baptist Theological Seminary

Margins of Islam *sweeps away the reductionistic, yet pervasive, assumption that Islam is the same everywhere. As someone who has ministered to Turkic and Asian Muslims outside of the Arab world, this book is particularly helpful for me. Along with insightful explanations of different Islams from around the world, this volume provides a conceptual framework that will help readers understand and engage Muslims in any context.*

—Jayson Georges
author of *The 3D Gospel* and HonorShame.com

Humans and human societies are complex, yet simple categories too often frame our missiology and mission approaches, missing the changing, hybrid, at times puzzling realities of life. Margins of Islam *breaks this pattern, exploring diversity of expression across multiple settings in which Muslims live out their faith. Its missiological proposals offer a significant—and needed—contribution, intended for those who love and serve among Muslims, but with insights to be applied in numerous other settings.*

—David Greenlee, PhD
author and missiologist
director of missiological research and evaluation for Operation Mobilization

Water is H2O. But for the scuba diver, or surfer or marine biologist, it is much more. Is Islam confined to its creed and dogma? Those who swim in its waters experience it as much more. The authors invite us to dive among the coral reefs of Islam, observe its rich colors and bio-diversity, and feel the force of its currents and breakers. Rather than reducing Islam to a system of beliefs, they urge us towards incarnation—the risky venture of getting to know Muslims. Hybridity and liminality are the new buzz-words, but since its inception, Islam has intermingled with worldviews and cultures around the globe. This volume patiently unveils that reality, inviting Jesus-followers to encounter Muslims where they live, as they live. Thanks to Farah and Daniels for confronting us with the diversity of global Islam and implications for Christians who engage with it.

—Mike Kuhn, PhD
assistant professor, Arab Baptist Theological Seminary author of *Fresh Vision for the Muslim World*

Sixteen different scholar-practitioners illustrate how Muslims use and shape Islam to build distinctive worldviews and ways of life, and how a presentation of the gospel works best when it is grounded in the fabric of their social and emotional life. The critical contribution of this volume is the seminal idea of "adaptive missiology"—a missiology that begins with the assumption that each people group is so distinctive that no one "religious system" (i.e. Islam) can adequately define the nature of a local worldview and way of life. Therefore, a presentation of the gospel in each context requires personal relationship and learning essential to discern the local values, habits of life, and idolatries that characterize this particular expression of Islam, before a "unique and sufficient message of the Cross of Christ is proclaimed." This is an exceptional contribution to conversations on the global mission of the church to Muslims, and a must read for anyone engaged in such ministry.

—Sherwood G. Lingenfelter, PhD
senior professor of anthropology, provost emeritus, Fuller Theological Seminary

I so enjoyed Margins of Islam. *With numerous missiological insights in each article, this book is a bounty of practical wisdom. It challenges "reductionist" views—both of the gospel and of ministry to Muslims. Praise God for this crucial contribution to the global conversation on ministry in the Muslim context.*

—Werner Mischke, DD
author of *The Global Gospel*

In the venerable tradition of Clifford Geertz who taught us decades ago that Muslims in Java and Muslims in Morocco believed the same things about God and humanity yet practiced their faith in radically different ways, editors Gene Daniels and Warrick Farah have gathered together sixteen mission workers to Muslim peoples who extrapolate Geertz's fundamental insight to mission practice. The result is a book of invaluable wisdom about doing Christian mission in Islamic contexts.

—Terry C. Muck, PhD
scholar of religion, comparative missiologist, and theological educator
co-author of *Christianity Encountering World Religions*

Contrary to persistent stereotypes, Islam is not monolithic and unchanging. Here—at last!—is a book that takes seriously the bewildering diversity among Muslims worldwide and explores responsibly the missiological implications of these diverse contexts. This is a terrific book which deserves a wide readership.

—Harold Netland, PhD
professor of philosophy of religion and intercultural studies, Trinity Evangelical Divinity School

As long as Muslims are outside of saving faith in Jesus Christ, there is need for a flow of writings on how to reach them. In recent years there have been a plethora of books written on the topic. "Why another?" some skeptically may ask. Because this collaborative volume brings to us both balance and up-to-date cutting edge missiological observations on the world of Islam in a fresh way. This book will quickly become a standard textbook for understanding the varied dynamics of this non-monolithic religion.

—Marvin J. Newell, DMiss
senior vice president of Missio Nexus
years of service among Muslim-majority peoples in Indonesia

Our world is comprised of a Muslim mosaic, not a monolithic Islam. The religion may have its pillars, but radically different expressions. Daniels and Farah have done a great service in the Kingdom by reminding us of this fact! Margins of Islam takes readers on a global journey revealing the multiple expressions of the Islamic faith. This book gives us solid evidence of what we have known, but seldom allowed to influence our mission practices. We no longer have any excuse to train others to reach all Muslims in the same way. This book challenges us to know our contexts and allow such insight to shape contextualized strategies and methodologies.

— J. D. Payne, PhD
pastor, missiologist, podcast host, blogger, and author of *Apostolic Church Planting*

Margins of Islam *is an extraordinary collection of articles that points to the inappropriateness of a simplistic analysis of the rich diversity in global Islam, while providing windows into how serious Christians might engage Muslims with dignity, honor, and grace. The seasoned experience of the contributors from a wide variety of contexts provides a depth of reflection that makes this collection a rich resource for missional engagement in the contemporary world.*

—Perry Shaw, EdD
professor of education, Arab Baptist Theological Seminary
three decades of ministry in the Middle East, author of *Transforming Theological Education*

As children we often prefer neatly divided plates to keep the apple sauce out of the peas. As we grow up, we give up our desire for clear boundaries between the food groups and learn to enjoy a good biriyani mixed full of grains, vegetables, spices, and yes, fruits and nuts. Likewise, the global diversity of Muslims stubbornly resists our attempts to label and categorize. Margins of Islam *helps us learn to witness for Christ within a fluid Muslim world while discontinuing our over-reliance on externally defined juxtapositions.*

—Keith E. Swartley
editor of *Encountering the World of Islam*

In a marvelous tour de force, Margins of Islam *exposes the widely held, but false assumption that the house of Islam is a monolithic religious entity which either resists or responds to missiological strategies. Collectively, these authors offer up case studies and rich and textured "on the field" experience which reflects the true variegated diversity of Islam. This book is contextual missiology at its finest.*

—Timothy C. Tennent, PhD
president, Asbury Theological Seminary, professor of World Christianity

This text is a masterful collection of representative examples of various types of Muslims around the world and aspects of the gospel that resonate with their concerns be they Sufi, secular, ethnic, Western, youth, or other types of Muslims. Every witness to them should profit from it.

—J. Dudley Woodberry, PhD
dean emeritus and senior professor of Islamic Studies
School of Intercultural Studies, Fuller Theological Seminary

Margins of Islam: Ministry in Diverse Muslim Contexts
© 2018 by Gene Daniel and Warrick Farah

Scriptures marked (NIV) are taken from THE HOLY BIBLE, NEW INTERNATIONAL VERSION® NIV® Copyright © 1973, 1978, 1984, 2011 by International Bible Society® Used by permission. All rights reserved worldwide.

Scriptures marked (ESV) are taken from The Holy Bible, English Standard Version® (ESV®) Copyright © 2001 by Crossway, a publishing ministry of Good News Publishers. All rights reserved.

Published by William Carey Publishing
(formerly known as William Carey Library Publishers)
10 W. Dry Creek Cir | Littleton, CO 80120 | www.missionbooks.org

William Carey Publishing is a ministry of Frontier Ventures
1605 E. Elizabeth St | Pasadena, CA 91104 | www.frontierventures.org

ISBN's: 978-0-87808-066-3 (paperback)
978-0-87808-067-0 (mobi)
978-0-87808-068-7 (epub)

Melissa Hicks, managing editor
Andrew Sloan, copyeditor
Mike Riester, cover and interior design

Printed in the United States of America
22 21 20 19 18   2 3 4 5   BP 1000

Library of Congress Cataloging-in-Publication Data
Names: Daniels, Gene, 1963- editor.
Title: Margins of Islam: missiology in diverse Muslim contexts /
    Gene Daniels and Warrick Farah, editors; foreword by David Garrison.
Description: Littleton: William Carey Publishing, 2018.
Identifiers: LCCN 2018040957| ISBN 9780878080663 (pbk.) | ISBN 9780878080687 (epub)
Subjects: LCSH: Missions to Muslims. | Islam.
Classification: LCC BV2625 .M2974 2018 | DDC 266.00917/67—dc23
LC record available at https://lccn.loc.gov/2018040957

MARGINS OF ISLAM

Ministry in Diverse Muslim Contexts

FOREWORD BY
DAVID GARRISON

GENE DANIELS | WARRICK FARAH
EDITORS

Contents

PART 3: REFRAMING MISSIOLOGY

Contributors

Patrick Brittenden, DPhil

Brittenden has lived in North Africa for over twenty years. His primary interests are teaching, evangelism, and indigenous church planting. His passion for the church, mission, and education come together in a doctorate he is completing at Oxford University on the contemporary Muslim-background church of Algeria. Patrick was formerly an executive leader of PALM (a training ministry of Pioneers International) and is currently a consultant supporting the development of local MBB training approaches and encouraging the growth of North African churches.

Arthur Brown, DMin

Brown has been ministering in the Middle East since 1991 and a resident in Lebanon since 2005. Until 2017 he taught in the areas of Youth Ministry and Applied Theology and was Associate Director [Youth] at ABTS' Institute of Middle East Studies. Arthur is involved in a number of regional and global networks, developing contextually appropriate youth work, and helped establish the *khebz w meleh* interfaith youth project in Lebanon. Arthur is now BMS World Mission's Regional Leader for Europe, the Middle East and North Africa, and has recently relocated to the UK. He has contributed chapters to a number of books.

Gene Daniels, DLit et Phil

Daniels is a missiologist whose specialty is qualitative research with Muslim-background believers (MBBs). He is also a college instructor and mission trainer who conducts classes and training events both in the US and in the Muslim world. Previously Gene and his family were church planters among Muslims in Central Asia for twelve years. He is the author of three books and numerous articles, all on Christian mission. Gene and his wife, Linda, who have four grown children, currently live in Little Rock, Arkansas. Gene Daniels is a pseudonym.

Ted Esler, PhD

Esler is the president of Missio Nexus, an association of agencies and churches representing over forty thousand Great Commission workers worldwide. A Minnesota native, Ted worked in the computer industry before becoming a church planter in Sarajevo, Bosnia, during the 1990s—about which he wrote the book *Overwhelming Minority*. In 2000 Ted became the Canadian director of Pioneers, and three years later he moved to Orlando to join Pioneers USA's leadership team. He was appointed the president of Missio Nexus in 2015, and he also serves on the board of other ministry organizations. Ted is married to Annette, and they have five children.

Warrick Farah, DMiss

Farah is a missiologist serving with One Collective (https://onecollective.org) in the Middle East, where he coaches team leaders working in community transformation and discipleship. He also serves as Assistant Professor of Missiology at an evangelical seminary that trains Arab world leaders for ministry in the region. Focusing on MBBs, Warrick's research on conversion, theological paradigms of witness, and insiderness has been published in journals such as *EMQ*, *IJFM*, and *Global Missiology*. You can follow him on his blog at muslimministry.blogspot.com. Warrick Farah is a pseudonym.

David Garrison, PhD

David has a PhD in historical theology from the University of Chicago. He is a veteran of more than thirty years as a missionary pioneer. His books include *Church Planting Movements* (2004) and *A Wind in the House of Islam* (2014). Garrison currently serves as executive director of Global Gates, and as Church Planting Consultant in the Professional Services Group of Missio Nexus.

CG Gordan, MS

Gordon is a veteran cross-cultural communicator and student of missiology. He has worked and ministered in East, Central, and South Asia for the past three decades. CG and his team are presently training and mentoring Christian cross-cultural communicators from Asia. He earned a master of science degree in sociolinguistics from Georgetown University. CG Gordon is a pseudonym.

Robin Dale Hadaway, ThD

Hadaway has been the missions professor at Midwestern Baptist Theological Seminary in Kansas City, Missouri, for twelve years. Previously he and his wife, Kathy, served in church planting and administration with the International Mission Board, SBC, in Northern Africa, Tanzania, and Brazil for eighteen years. Robin worked with a Muslim unreached people group in Northern Africa and later served as the director of Eastern South America, supervising 350 missionaries. He also has been a senior pastor, a businessman, and an officer in the US Air Force. Robin and Kathy have three grown children.

Kevin Higgins, PhD

Higgins is the president of William Carey International University, and the coordinator of work among Muslims for Global Teams International. He has ministered to Muslims in the US, Africa, and South Asia since 1980. Kevin is now focused on mentoring leaders in several mature and emerging movements to Jesus in Muslim contexts, stretching from the Horn of Africa to East Asia.

Alan Johnson, PhD

Johnson has worked in Thailand for twenty-nine years with the Assemblies of God, USA, connecting with the national Thailand AG organization. He has done ethnographic studies in a Bangkok slum community, studying social influence processes. Alan is also the author of *Apostolic Function in 21st Century Missions*.

Michael A Kilgore, DMiss

Kilgore has over twenty years of broad experience in Southeast Asia. He has worked as a seminary lecturer, an advisor to church-planting teams, a trainer of national tentmaker missionaries, an English teacher, and a humanitarian aid organizer for marginalized refugees. This last role led to Michael being imprisoned and deported. Along the way, he and his wife have raised three children in Southeast Asia—all of whom yearn to return. Michael A Kilgore is a pseudonym.

Enoch Jinsik Kim, PhD

Kim is assistant professor of communication and mission studies at Fuller Theological Seminary, where he is in charge of the Korean Language Doctor of Missiology program and teaches various other subjects. Prior to that he served among Chinese Muslims for sixteen years. Enoch is the author of one book and many articles on mission.

Yakup Korkmaz, MA

Korkmaz has been a church planter in Turkey since 2002. He trains both missionaries and nationals in the area of Muslim evangelism and apologetics. He has also been involved in the reconciliation movement between Armenians and Turkish Christians. Yakup has written several evangelistic and apologetic books in the Turkish language, as well as a cultural guidebook for missionaries who work in Turkey. He is married and has two adopted children. Yakup Korkmaz is a pseudonym.

Rick Kronk, PhD

Kronk and his wife spent their first sixteen years of marriage in Europe with Christar as church planters among North African Muslim immigrants. In addition to field-based ministry, Rick has been involved in training future workers among Muslims globally as director of Christar's summer training called "Manarah." He is the author of *Dreams and Visions: Muslims' Miraculous Journey to Jesus*. Rick is currently Professor of Mission at Toccoa Falls College.

Warren Larson, PhD

Larson served with Christar for twenty-three years in Pakistan. While church planting was his main task, he also served as director of a reading room, administrator of a Bible correspondence school, and field director of Christar. Warren is former director of the Zwemer Center for Muslim Studies at Columbia International University. He teaches online courses to equip workers and edits the Zwemer website. His book on Islamism was recognized as one of the fifteen most significant books on missions in 1998. Due to his understanding of Islam, Warren has been quoted widely in both Christian and secular publications. He and his wife live in Vancouver.

Phil Rawlings, MA

Rawlings is codirector of the Manchester Centre for the Study of Christianity and Islam, based at the Nazarene Theological College, where he teaches undergraduate and postgraduate courses on Christian engagement with Islam. He was a local church leader for nearly twenty years in a majority Muslim area of Manchester, where the church ministered to the local communities, sharing faith and building relationships. Phil is now the "interfaith officer" in three areas of inner-city Manchester, where his vision is to see new churches planted in majority Muslim areas of the city. He continues to live in Manchester with his wife and four children.

Evelyne Reisacher, PhD

Reisacher is associate professor of Islamic studies and intercultural relations at Fuller Theological Seminary. Her current research interests include exploring gender issues in Islam and Muslim-Christian relations. Before coming to Fuller, Evelyne ministered with *L'Ami* in France for twenty years, facilitating the relationship between churches and North African immigrants and developing courses, teaching tools, and seminars for sharing the gospel cross-culturally. She trained Christian leaders and church members in Europe, North Africa, the Middle East, and Southeast Asia. Evelyne has written one book and edited two books, in addition to contributing to several others. Her many articles and blogs focus on Muslim-Christian relations.

Foreword

David Garrison, PhD
author of *A Wind in the House of Islam*

If the body of Christ only knew what the body of Christ knows, it would know a lot! Christians around the world are engaging Muslims at a level and breadth that is unparalleled in human history. What are the lessons we are learning? And perhaps more importantly, are we sharing and applying those lessons with one another and with the broader body of Christ for the sake of Christ's kingdom?

For too long Christians who seek to understand the Muslim world, and indeed their own Muslim neighbors, have limited themselves to the study of Islam's core teachings found in the Qur'an and perhaps, if they are ambitious, the Hadith. Only after diving into the Muslim world, or the worldview of their own Muslim neighbors, do they come to realize that Islam and its 1.8 billion adherents are much more complex than they had imagined.

Indeed, Islamic texts only provide a shared historic touchstone to the sprawling faith that now commands the allegiance of nearly one quarter of the world's inhabitants. In many cases the five pillars of Islam—the *shahada*, the alms, the *hajj*, the daily prayers, and the Ramadan fast—serve as little more than points of departure for the majority of the world's Muslim population into complex worldviews exhibiting myriad expressions that have taken shape as Islam has expanded into every corner of our world.

If we are to engage Muslims in a meaningful way with the gospel of Jesus Christ, we must go beyond textbook analysis of creeds and ritual practices. We must understand and engage them as they understand themselves, with all of the complexity that journey entails.

Margins of Islam takes us into that complex world, enabling us to penetrate the fears, hopes, dreams, and aspirations of Muslims who need to know how the gospel of the kingdom can meet them where they are and bring them to the foot of the Cross. The authors of this book invite you to join them on this journey of discovery, as they faithfully bring Scripture to bear upon the worldviews of the world's largest non-Christian population.

As such, this book is not exhaustive, nor does it pretend to be, but it should serve as a welcome intermediate course for any and every Christian seeking to engage what may very well be the body of Christ's greatest challenge in the fulfillment of the Great Commission.

Introduction

Gene Daniels, DLit et Phil

The Muslim world today consists of 1.8 billion people,[1] the majority of whom live in a great swath of humanity stretching from West Africa through the Middle East and all the way to Southeast Asia. They are born into more than three thousand distinct cultures and speak about that many different languages. Furthermore, millions of Muslims also now live outside the traditional "Islamic world," North Africans in France and South Asians in the UK being just a couple of examples. With this kind of staggering diversity, how does one meaningfully prepare for practical ministry to Muslims?

One tried and true way is through studying classic texts such as Samuel Zwemer's *Islam and the Cross*, Phil Parshall's *The Cross and the Crescent*, or perhaps *Answering Islam* by Geisler and Saleeb. Unfortunately, these excellent books share a common weakness with most other missiological books on Islam; they approach Muslims as if they were a monolithic bloc because they all follow the same religion. While this has a simple logic to it, it also carries certain implications. When our missiological lens is shaped primarily by religious affiliation it causes us to focus on doctrine, scriptures, and other orthodox elements of Islam. In other words, this causes us to focus on the things of which distinct boundaries and categories are made.

Consequently, learning about Islam tends to mean the study of things like the Qur'an, the five pillars, perhaps throwing in a few hadiths for good measure. Most assume this will show us what true Islam is, thus keeping the boundary lines clear between what is Islam and what is not. However, when we apply our neat religious categories across cultures we often end up with portraits of local people that they would not themselves recognize. Even with the best of intentions, missionaries sometimes create our own understanding of "Islam" that is quite different from on-the-ground realities, thus distorting mission into a pursuit of hypothetical ghosts of Islamic orthodoxy.

Most of us default to hard-and-fast boundaries because that is what we were taught beginning in elementary school. Since our earliest years we were trained to look at a map and think, "Here is Texas and over there, across that line, is Mexico." We later carry that same mental construction into adulthood when we read that in 2017 the poverty line in the United States was $24,600 for a family of four. Boundaries like this are simple, clear, and easy to comprehend. They work great for introducing children to maps and perhaps even work for the very grown-up field of economists, but these hard boundaries are less and less useful the closer we get to human experience—the place where authentic Christian mission takes place.

---

[1] According to a 2015 Pew Research Center estimate; see "Muslims and Islam: Key findings in the U.S. and around the world," accessed June 21, 2018, http://www.pewresearch.org/fact-tank/2015/12/07/muslims-and-islam-key-findings-in-the-u-s-and-around-the-world/.

As an example, let us revisit that boundary the US government calls the "poverty line." In 2017, it fell at exactly $24,600 for a family of four. Thus, if your neighbor is earning $25,000 per year, their little family is doing just fine—right? But what about things like past-due medical bills or a gambling addiction—Don't they play a role in the financial health of the family? In other words, it's not quite as simple as a boundary line between poverty and non-poverty would lead us to believe. The binary nature of the government's poverty line offers a clear demarcation for statistical purposes, but it not as helpful when we get close to actual people. And more importantly, the official poverty line might even obscure reality because it is rooted in the abstraction we call economics. Human experience is more dynamic and organic than such abstractions are able to portray.

This points to the reason for the book in your hands. In order to develop effective mission strategy and practice in the Muslim world we need a better way to think about the lived experience of Muslims than through a prism of categorical religious boundaries. A more natural way of thinking, the one we will use in this volume, is looking at you right now from the text on this page or screen. In one sense, the "page" in front of you is composed of a number of lines of text. However, in another very real sense that same page extends to the actual, physical cutoff of the paper or the screen. In between the end of the text and the physical limit of the paper is the slightly irregular space we call a margin.

Or another image that can help us understand the "margins" of human landscapes in Islam is the physical margins around a field of wheat or some other crop. Just like in human landscapes, the spaces at the edge of a field are an uneven mix of the intended crop along with weeds and wildflowers. Both of these illustrations are easy to picture, but they may leave you wondering how this idea of "margins" connects with the great diversity of the Muslim world and better mission practice? The answer lies in the following direction.

Most of us like to think in terms of hard boundaries because they establish clear lines and help us "know" things, such as who is Buddhist as opposed to who is an atheist, or who is Muslim rather than Hindu. But in assuming this high degree of categorical clarity we sacrifice a great deal of quality, accuracy, and depth of understanding about human experience. These seemingly precise religious boundaries do not work well for us in mission because biblically based ministry is not about engaging the *religion* of Islam; rather it is about engaging *people* who are Muslim. Thus a more missiological way of thinking about many parts of the Muslim world is akin to looking at the margins of a wheat field—a ragged, uneven place where many plants grow together and even compete with the intended crop. We believe this is much better than thinking in terms of religious blocs like the geopolitical boundaries between nation-states, where encyclopedic definitions tell us where one begins and another ends.

Of course, seeing people through the lens of Islam is not completely antithetical to seeing them through a lens as Muslims, but it is important to recognize that they have vitally different points of reference. The first focuses on doctrine and scripture, the elements which comprise the orthodox core of that faith. In contrast, the latter focuses on the behaviors and worldview of those who consider themselves part of a local community who call themselves Muslims. In theory these two spheres are the same—formal doctrines of the religion are supposed to be reflected in the actual beliefs of its practitioners. Yet as this book will show, there is often a very significant difference between formal doctrine and living practice in many contexts of the Muslim world today.

If we think missiologically, this departure from Islamic orthodoxy can take several shapes. Sometimes it is simply an advanced state of nominalism. For example, the Pew Forum (2012) studied the religious attitudes of Muslims in thirty-nine countries and found that a significant percentage of Muslims in some countries say they seldom or never attend prayers at the mosque.[2] However, that does not mean these same people are not fiercely proud and protective of their identity as Muslims. In many of the same countries where *jumah* (Friday) prayers were seldom practiced, a large majority of Muslims also said that religion is very important in their lives (ibid.). Considering the centrality of *jumah* prayers to orthodox Islamic faith, this contradiction points to a significant difference between orthodoxy and the local idea of what it means to be a Muslim.

Another form these margins of the Muslim world can take is seen in Michael Kilgore's chapter on Muslims on the island of Java in Indonesia (chapter 10). He paints a picture of people who recognize they have blended imported Islamic practice into their traditional belief system, but still consider it to be a valid composite. Considering that Indonesia is the world's most populous Muslim country, we cannot simply dismiss such people as "not really Muslim."

This is a reminder that by referring to these Muslims as on the *margins of Islam*, we do not mean they are *marginalized*—certainly not in their context. For example, as strange as it might seem to us, many Muslims are functional atheists. They do not demonstrate any form of belief in Allah, but they still maintain connection to the *ummah*[3] because it is their natal community and they see no reason to openly leave. Therefore, they remain "Muslim" in the eyes of their community. Additionally, in many parts of the world people find no contradiction between being Muslim and practicing various kinds of occultism and animism, not only side by side but deeply intertwined. Situations like these can be very disorienting to new missionaries who come to the field with their own clear religious categories in mind.

---

[2] Examples include Uzbekistan (77 percent), Azerbaijan (75 percent), and Tunisia (44 percent).
[3] Ummah is Arabic for community or nation and is often used for the world-wide community of Muslims.

The "margin" of folk Islam mentioned above is one that is widespread enough that most have at least heard of it. But the margins explored in this volume will take many forms. Some are primarily ethnic in nature, as in the Muslims of Thailand (chapter 14). Other margins are significantly shaped by intellectual issues, such as the Gülen movement in Turkey (chapter 6). Still other contexts are hard to classify, such as Islam in France (chapter 5) or "glocal" Muslim youth (chapter 16).

Despite this enormous range of diversity, all of these contexts are united by important commonalities. For example, they all claim a real and vital connection to the core—they all consider themselves to be part of the ummah. In other words, for many their self-identity as Muslims takes precedence over the practice of orthodox Islam. That is why this book takes an *emic* perspective, meaning how people perceive *themselves* is more important that how we might classify them from the outside.[4]

Related to that, it is also missiologically important to understand each of these contexts through the lens of how they do, or do not, relate to official, orthodox Islam. I remember something that happened many years ago when we were fairly new missionaries in Almaty, Kazakhstan. A local friend invited us to dinner, and afterward another missionary couple kindly offered us a ride home since it was dark and cold. On the way, the husband explained that he was working with Kazakh college students. Then he said, "We have been here two years and just realized that Kazakhs are Muslims. No one told us they were Muslims before we left home. We just came here to reach college students. Do you have any resources to help us learn how to work with Muslims?"

It is true that Kazakhs are often more animist than orthodox, with urban youth adding a noticeable layer of secularity to the mix. Therefore, a book explaining the five pillars of Islam would not have been particularly helpful to this couple. Nevertheless, their sending agency did them a huge disservice by completely ignoring the ways in which a Muslim heritage still deeply impacts the lives of these young people.

Of course, there are limits to how much any religion can stretch. At a certain point a group's beliefs or practices move so far from the core that they become recognized as a distinctly different faith. A perfect example of this from the world of Islam would be the Baha'i—a group that originally began as a renewal movement within Islam but eventually embraced a completely universalistic view of world religions to the degree that it took its own separate place among them (Smith 1996). Since the Baha'i have moved completely off even the furthest margins of the Muslim field, we will not consider them in this volume. But they are the exception that proves the rule. Though being "Muslim" is an elastic concept in the self-perception of many communities, the Baha'i demonstrate that eventually hard boundaries do come into play.

---

[4] The emic perspective is often understood by contrasting it with an etic perspective, which uses as its starting point concepts and theories generated outside of the context being studied.

Certainly there are many places where being Muslim is much more than culture and where adherence to Islamic orthodoxy is the rule. These are contexts where classic Islamic studies are critical to the task of developing good missiology. Since there are already numerous good books on this part of the Muslim world, we will only touch on this in chapter 1, "Who Represents Islam?" by Evelyn Reisacher. And even then, the goal is not to assume what Islam is or is not, but to describe the difficulty Islam itself has in trying to define a core.

This space we are calling the margins of Islam, the region between orthodoxy and recognized separation, is indeed wide; but more importantly, it is ill-defined. This volume will explore fourteen of these margins, not because they are particularly special but because they are representative of the diversity in the Muslim world. The contributing authors all write from the position of personal experience in that particular context. Just as there are many different academic disciplines that contribute to missiology—theology, anthropology, sociology, history—each author will approach their task from a slightly different perspective. Yet in their varieties of approaches, each chapter will have several common elements interwoven, all designed to help the reader in practical ways:

- A "thick description"[5] of the context
- Exploration of *commonalities* the context shares with classical Islam
- Description of the ways the context is *different* from classical Islam
- Specific ways the context influences mission strategy
- Reflection questions

This volume was written for the student of mission as well as the missionary practitioner in the field. Our hope is that by painting pictures of ministry in some of the different margins of the Islamic world, we will help readers grapple with whatever context they may find themselves trying to engage with the gospel. This is particularly important because too much of contemporary evangelical mission practice is based on "universal" models of ministry—in other words, ministry that is stripped of its context. In this volume, we have provided the reader with several examples of approaches to ministry that are just the opposite, clearly rooted in their context—in these case studies from the "margins" of Islamic orthodoxy. We hope this will allow readers to envision ways they too might bear much fruit in their own Muslim context.

References

Geertz, Clifford. 1994. "Thick Description: Toward an Interpretive Theory of Culture." In *Readings in the Philosophy of Social Science*. Edited by Michael Martin and Lee C. McIntyre, 213–31. Cambridge, Massachusetts: Massachusetts Institute of Technology.

Pew Forum for Religion in Public Life. 2012. "The World's Muslims: Unity and Diversity." Pew Research Center. Accessed April 22, 2013. http://www.pewforum.org/uploadedFiles/Topics/Religious_Affiliation/Muslim/the-worlds-muslims-full-report.pdf.

Smith, Peter. 1996. *A Short History of the Baha'i Faith*. ONEWorld Publications.

---

[5] "Thick description" is a key term in the anthropological theory of Clifford Geertz (1994). It refers to explaining a culture through many details and interpretation of those details. It stands in contrast to a "thin description," which gives facts alone without interpretation.

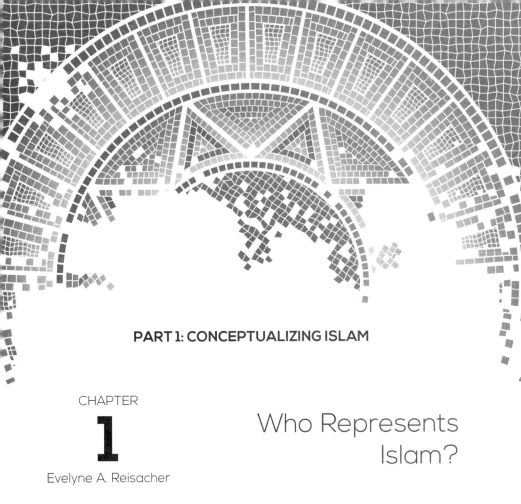

PART 1: CONCEPTUALIZING ISLAM

CHAPTER

1

Evelyne A. Reisacher

Who Represents Islam?

The other day I had coffee with friends from church when one of them, Ryan, asked me urgently, "Evelyne, I thought I had a decent understanding of Islam, but I am now increasingly skeptical about what I know." He explained his confusion at encountering a multiplicity of Muslim voices and customs during his travels. For example, he did not know how to integrate narratives about a peaceful Islam when confronted with violent jihad in the news. He also wondered why, in Saudi Arabia, women do not drive, while in Pakistan they do and even pilot planes. He was also puzzled to see Muslims worship through songs and dances in some parts of the world, while others fiercely condemn such practices. He ended with, "Could you please tell me who represents Islam?"

My first reaction was to say that it is impossible to respond to this question in a few sentences—Islam spans fourteen centuries and is now found everywhere in the world. But I understand Ryan. I had the same desire when I started engaging with Muslims several decades ago. I searched for *the* book or teaching that would reveal the true essence of Islam. I signed up for Muslim-awareness seminars in churches. In a few sessions they taught me the articles of faith and rituals of Islam, with occasional references to the *sharia*.[1] I trusted I had found the "real" Islam—that is, until I started interacting with Muslims in my own neighborhood and then around the world. I eventually came to the same conclusion as Ryan: How could all those various expressions of Islam I encountered neatly fit in one representation of Islam?

But working through Ryan's question is a necessary exercise for everyone engaging with Muslims. Indeed, I believe that his question is timely and highly relevant. First, because my friend Ryan is not the only one confused. Christian leader Steve Bell contends that Christians today "are deeply unsettled and divided—to say the least—about what Islam is" (2011, 250). It is, therefore, important to provide the church with resources to help its members sharpen their thoughts on this issue.

Second, scholars and religious leaders have debated this question since the beginning of Islam without reaching a consensus.[2] Some claim there is a universal Islam, and others believe Muslims are so diverse that it is impossible to find a definition that would satisfy everyone. Christians who want to engage Muslims with the gospel must therefore learn to appreciate the many nuances portrayed in this book.

Third, the response to the question of who represents Islam has significant impact on Muslim-Christian relations. In effect, if Christians do not take this question seriously, they may misrepresent Islam and Muslim societies. This could negatively impact their capacity to understand Muslims and respectfully witness to them. It could even lead to communication breakup, mistrust, and conflicts between Christians and Muslims.

Given the weight of these issues, I feel even more compelled to respond to Ryan. In this chapter, I will answer his query by addressing three questions that usually frame the debate around who represents Islam: (1) Is it good enough to state that there is one Islam? (2) How does one address the diversity of Muslim societies? (3) Who decides who is an authentic Muslim?

In my discussion, I will briefly introduce a number of theories and concepts proposed by scholars of Islam who have dealt with those questions, hoping that my readers will then be better equipped to minister in the diverse world of Islam today.

---

[1] *Sharia* is Islamic canonical law based on the teachings of the Koran and the traditions of the Prophet, that is the Hadith and Sunna.

[2] Professor of Jewish Studies and Islamicist, Aaron W. Hughes (2013), writes, "The struggle to define the real Islam is not just a modern phenomenon carried out by Western interpreters of the religion. It is a phenomenon that dates back to the earliest sources of the tradition as various groups struggled to understand Muhammad and his message in the light of various legal, religious, and intellectual paradigms that they themselves both inherited and created" (3).

One Islam?

Since Muslims share common symbols, beliefs, and practices, it is common to hear believers and scholars of Islam say that there is only "one Islam." Introductory books on Islam provide examples of what universally binds Muslims together. As an illustration, let us briefly consider the first two tenets of Islam, the oneness of Allah (*tawhid*) and the prophetic legacy of Muhammad. These two beliefs are summarized in the *shahada*, or Muslim confession of faith, which is a two-phrase sentence stating that there is no other divinity than Allah, and Muhammad is his messenger. Every Muslim must say the shahada to be considered Muslim. It serves as the password[3] to Islam for those who convert. It is also an identity marker that helps differentiate between Muslims and non-Muslims.[4] Swiss Muslim scholar Tariq Ramadan talks about "the *shahada* that every Muslim, in order to be recognized as such, must pronounce before God and the whole of humankind, and by which he establishes his identity" (2003, 73). This confession of faith unites all Muslims. It is on the basis of those commonalities that some scholars, such as the anthropologist Akbar Ahmed, argue that there is only "one Islam" (1986, 58).

But can there be such a straightforward response? Perhaps we could unpack this a bit by looking at some of the different ways Muslims understand the shahada that they recite. First there is the issue of wording. The two-part shahada, as currently spoken, is not recorded in the Qur'an but in the Hadith.[5] In early Islam, other variants of the shahada included confession of both Muhammad and Isa.[6] Given these nuances, it is quite possible that early Muslims did not all share the same fundamental confession. Would they all have been considered authentic Muslims?

Second, there is the issue of meaning. It is well attested that words can have several meanings depending on the context in which they are used. This raises the issue of the many debates about the nature of Allah (Cumming 2012) and the identity and role of Muhammad. Volume after volume have been written by Muslims about the meanings of these critical terms. Not only do Islamic theological schools hold diverging views, many individual Muslims do not align with any "official" view as they connect with Allah in their own unique experience. Which of these diverse views of Allah and Muhammad, while pronouncing the shahada, represents real Islam?

---

[3] One author calls it the "key to Islam, as well as its cornerstone" (Selim 2015, 83).

[4] In times of conflict, for example, some Muslim groups have used it to differentiate between non-Muslim enemies (who do not know how to recite the shahada) and the kin in religion who, when asked, can recite the confession of faith and are freed.

[5] See Qur'an 3:18 for an example of a verse containing only the first phrase. Likewise, in the Hadith there are examples of the first phrase standing on its own (Sunan an-Nasa'i, The Book of Forgetfulness, Book 13, Hadith 175).

[6] *Isa* is the Qur'anic name for Jesus. See for example Ṣaḥīḥ al-Bukhari, book 60, Hadith 106, "The Prophet said, 'If anyone testifies that None has the right to be worshipped but Allah Alone Who has no partners, and that Muhammad is His Slave and His Apostle, and that Jesus is Allah's Slave and His Apostle and His Word which He bestowed on Mary and a Spirit created by Him, and that Paradise is true, and Hell is true, Allah will admit him into Paradise with the deeds which he had done even if those deeds were few.'"

Third, what if reciting the shahada alone is not sufficient to define who is a Muslim and who is not? This confession only refers to two articles of the faith (regarding God and the last prophet of Islam). What of the Muslims who say it but do not believe the other ones?[7] Or what about still other Muslims who may recite the shahada but don't follow the other four prescribed rituals.[8] Would they still be considered Muslims? Or inversely, would Muslims who follow other rituals but do not recite the shahada represent Islam?

Fourth, non-Muslims may also weigh in on the definition of who represents Islam. Unfortunately, many non-Muslims today seem to identify "authentic Muslims" as people who practice violent jihad and want to go back to seventh-century Islamic laws. Yet this would mean that Muslims with a different view are not "true" Muslims and therefore do not represent Islam. But this begs the question, "Do non-Muslims even have the right to decide who is and who is not a Muslim?"

Finally, there are those who never recite the shahada and still claim they are Muslims. We may call them cultural Muslims, or nonpracticing Muslims. They still feel part of the Muslim community, but their self-identification as Muslims is not based on their piety. Does their lack of religious practice give us the right to say that they are not valid representatives of Islam?

For brevity's sake, this discussion has only highlighted one well-known Islamic practice, the shahada. But the same discussion could be undertaken concerning other aspects of Muslim faith or practice, such as the belief in angels, fasting, or the giving of alms. Under every seemingly common term or practice in the Muslim world lurks great contextual diversity, and thus the reason for this volume. For those who wish to share the good news of Jesus with Muslims, it is simply not enough to say there is "one Islam" and let it go at that. We have to be willing to explore the multiple shades of meaning and different facets of expression within Islam. In the next section, I will introduce a scholarly debate which will help us do exactly that.

What Kind of Diversity?

Beyond question, Islam has generated a plethora of theological debates (as all religions do). These in turn have created many different interpretations of the Qur'an, the Hadith, and other important texts. For those who doubt the diversity of Islam, it would suffice to take them on a stroll between miles of bookshelves in libraries that specialize in Islamic studies. You will discover countless commentaries, with sometimes complementary, sometimes conflicting views on Islamic texts. Esposito and Mogahed are right to say that "While many people commonly speak of Islam and Muslims in broad, all-encompassing terms, there are many *interpretations* of Islam

---

[7] For example, the beliefs in angels, holy books, the day of judgment, or predestination.

[8] The other rituals besides the *shahada* (confession of faith) are *ṣalat* (prayer), *ṣawm* (fasting), *zakat* (almsgiving), and *hajj* (pilgrimage).

(emphasis added)" (2007, 1). We could also add to this all the individual opinions that have not been reported in scholarly works and circulate daily in mosques, families, and the public sphere of the Muslim world.

Other reasons for this diversity are related to the wide range of social, cultural, and political contexts Muslims live in. In the later pages of this volume you will read of settings as widely divergent as the secular Muslims of Bosnia to Sufis in Africa whose practice is infused with African traditional religions. If someone were to take one snapshot of the worldwide Muslim population, it would not come as a uniform portrayal but rather a collage of kaleidoscopic diversity. This leaves us with a real challenge of how to find terminology that will best express diversity without denying common beliefs. The rather eclectic listing of words and phrases below demonstrates some of how scholars have wrestled with this, and will hopefully convince my friend Ryan that no one can respond, in a single sentence, to the question of who represents Islam.

Let us start with the prominent Islamicist Ignaz Goldziher, who did not believe in a monolithic Islam. He claimed it was a mistake to look at Islam as a monolithic whole and believed that the dynamics of its diversity were evident in Islam from its earliest history (Lukens-Bull 2014, 1073). Then we have Professors Herbert L. Bodman and Nayereh Esfahiani Tohidi, who entitled their book *Diversity within Unity* (1998) to recognize the diverse cultural and social processes that shape the lives of women in Muslim societies in the Middle East, Africa, and Asia. Another noted scholar, Hughes (previously quoted), uses the phrase "version of Islam" and talks about "various constructions of Muslim belief and practice" (2013, 247). He later adds, "It is more appropriate to speak of an overlapping set of Islams that run the gamut from the mystical to the militant or from the so-called orthodox to the so-called heterodox" (407). We could also look to Professor of International Politics, Raymond William Baker, who talks about the "many incarnations of Islam" in his latest book, entitled *One Islam, Many Muslim Worlds* (2015, 195). Yet another scholar, Vartan Gregorian, uses his own imagery when he titles his book *Islam: A Mosaic, Not a Monolith* (2003).

Of course, this list could go on and on since every scholar of Islam must eventually come to terms with this question of diversity. While most highlight diversity without denying common beliefs and practices, some have even dared to claim that there is not one single Islam but several. Anthropologist Abdul Hamid El-Zein, for example, suggested "that the term *Islam* be replaced by *islams*" (1977, 228).

This brief review has highlighted the fact that scholars are well aware that one cannot talk about one Islam without emphasizing at the same time the great diversity that exists in Muslim societies. It is impossible to talk about oneness without mentioning diversity. These two aspects are essential when we describe the Muslim world. We have seen that scholars express this diversity in manifold ways. They talk about many versions, incarnations, constructions, and worlds of Islam. They identify overlapping sets of Islam. They say that Islam is like a mosaic. They state that Islam is not monolithic.

I encourage you to continue to collect such phrases in your readings of scholarly works on Islam. You will be surprised at the manifold ways in which scholars acknowledge the diversity found within Islam and Muslim societies. On the spectrum ranging from one Islam to many islams, we find a multitude of different descriptions and wordings of the Islamic diversity. Instead of comparing and contrasting all the different expressions, which would require much more space than this short chapter, I would rather encourage my friend Ryan to begin trying out those expressions when describing Islam and Muslim societies and also collect new ones in his ongoing study of Islam.

Intersection between Oneness and Diversity

Although important, concluding that Islam has many different expressions is not enough to address the core of the question raised in the opening paragraph: "Who represents Islam?" The next step is to find out how the oneness of Islamic expression and the diversity of Muslim societies intersect. It is key to establish this link in order to bring sense to what may sometimes look like a very chaotic relationship. I list here a few ways in which theologians, anthropologists, and sociologists of Islam have attempted to describe the link between commonalities and differences, with the hope that it will continue to bring greater clarity to this debate.

First, there are those who claim a complete separation between faith and culture. In other words, they do not believe that faith can be influenced by culture or vice versa. To explain this approach, Bowen takes the example of female prohibition to drive in Saudi Arabia. According to him, some Muslims define that practice as Saudi culture and not Islam. But for the Saudi jurists who write the laws that ban women from driving, it is Islamic and not cultural (2012). Scholars in this train of thought seem to be saying that culture and faith, like oil and water, never mix. But this binary model of complete separation between faith and culture seems to contradict the diversity that one can easily observe throughout the Muslim world.[9] So while some Muslim groups may postulate an ideal Islam, even *that Islam* would entail diversity when exported to different contexts.

The second model describes the relationship we discuss as one between a "great" and a "little" tradition. Robert Redfield was the first scholar to identify these two categories, suggesting that all world religions could be divided into a "great tradition" and a "little tradition."[10] Lukens-Bull expounds on Redfield's model, saying, "The great tradition, the orthodox form of the cultural/religious center, is that of the urban elite. It is the religion of the reflective few and is cultivated in schools and temples and is 'consciously cultivated and handed down.'" He goes on to explain that there

---

[9] The issue of if and how culture shapes faith is not limited to Islam. Down through history many Christians have also acted as if there is only a single Christian culture that can be universally exported without changing.

[10] See, for example, Redfield's *Peasant Society and Culture* (1956).

are many other expressions that have been used to describe the great tradition, such as "'textual traditions,' 'orthodoxy,' 'philosophical religions,' 'high traditions,' and 'universal traditions'" (2014, 1005).

Lukens-Bull continues to reflect on the work of Redfield:

> The little tradition is the heterodox form of the cultural/religious periphery. The little tradition incorporates many elements of local tradition and practice. The little tradition is the religion as it is practiced in daily life by ordinary people. … Little traditions are also referred to by the terms "local tradition," "low tradition," and "popular religion" (ibid.).

Many scholars have adopted that model in past decades. They have written books and developed courses on the premise that there is orthodox Islam and then there is popular or folk Islam. Sometimes this creates a false assumption that the two are completely separate. Some Islamic theologians also separate the two and fiercely condemn little traditions (or popular Islam) as heretical.[11] Unfortunately, this binary attitude veils the fact that there are many nuances in little traditions which connect to the great tradition, and that it is not so easy to separate the two. If we decide to use this categorization, we would need to not only acknowledge the two traditions but make sure that we study the ways they are interconnected.

A third way scholars have looked at the concept of Muslim identities is to describe the diversity they observe in Muslim societies. For example, Hughes writes, "There exist many types of Muslim groups or communities, all of whom have constructed identities for themselves based on their particular understanding of the tradition, which they subsequently deem as the best or the most authentic." He adds, "We should thus be cautious of upholding one particular Muslim identity as the most authoritative" (2013, 393).

Hughes goes on to say, "Muslim identities are shaped by a host of factors that are dependent on various contexts. It accordingly becomes problematic to speak of *a*, let alone *the*, 'Muslim identity' (or 'Jewish identity' or any other)" (ibid., 407). He further explains, "Any attempt to understand Islam must involve an appreciation of both the religious teachings and the diverse cultural forms of the tradition" (ibid., 447). The question of identity has fascinated not only Hughes but many anthropologists and sociologists of Islam, who understand that Islam is not just a textual tradition but involves individuals and communities who thrive in specific sociocultural contexts. Identity theory and research offers a whole range of concepts that could help us understand the diversity we observe in Muslim societies.

Finally, anthropologist Talal Asad acknowledges both the universal and local forms of Islam, but refuses to place them in a dichotomy; instead, he offers a model to combine them into what he calls a "discursive tradition." That is, Islam as it is lived is the product of an ongoing "discourse" between universal and local forms, and its

---

[11] One of those schools is Wahhabism.

past and present (1986, 14). To follow Asad's model, my friend Ryan would have to ask how individual Muslims at a given time and in a given context interpret and apply religious texts as they have been passed down in history and will continue to be in the future, and how they are being shaped to fit in an ever-changing world. This idea of a "discursive tradition" then becomes a useful model to describe the continuity of Islam in various cultural contexts.

All these scholars have one main thing in common: Each adopted the view that one cannot understand Islam without this ongoing conversation between the past and the present, the universal and the local. The challenge lies in identifying ways in which faith intersects with culture without falling into the trap of binary thinking. We have encountered in this section several models that allow us to interpret the diversity we observe in Muslim societies. Each of them represents a solid attempt to cut through the confusion that exists in the minds of many people when they encounter Islam in a given context. They also show that this process can only take place when theologians are in conversation with anthropologists and sociologists of Islam.

Who Decides Who Represents Islam?

In order to define who represents Islam, one final question has to be explored: "Who decides?" Do Islamic authorities decide, or the rank and file Muslims of the world? To go further, is it only Muslims, or do outsiders like ourselves have a voice in answering the question?

Hughes takes up this issue when he writes, "There is always a danger in defining an 'authentic' (or, alternatively, 'real,' 'essential' or 'fake') representation. In any such attempt, we must always ask ourselves: who decides what criteria to use, and what gets to count as a true (or false) expression of faith?" (2013, 247). In this section we will briefly look at key actors in this debate.

It is common for religious leaders to seek to define what is normative in their faith. They want to protect their followers from altering the divine revelation, misunderstanding the path of salvation, neglecting divine commandments, etc. Consequently, the task of most commentators, scholars, and jurists will be to underline what is authentic Islam and denounce what is not authentic. But throughout history there has never been universal agreement on what is normative. For example, recently the leadership of ISIS (Islamic State of Iraq and Syria) claims to represent the authentic Islam, while other Muslims fiercely contend they do not. Each expression of Islam imagines itself to be what was taught by the prophet Muhammad himself (ibid., 207).

Then we also have to consider the role of what is in many places official, government-sanctioned Islam, which is usually the product of theological schools. A recent example of this was an attempt by a group of senior religious scholars from around the world to establish a consensus, called the Amman Message,[12] between

---

[12] See the summary of the Amman Message at http://ammanmessage.com.

Sunni, Shi'i, and Ibadi religious leaders about who is a Muslim. Although this meeting, organized by King Abdullah II of Jordan, may be a good attempt to gather a large part of the Muslim community worldwide, it was quickly clear from online discussions that government-defined Islam is something that not all Muslims will universally endorse.

Religious leaders and scholars who define the normative and official Islam usually rely heavily on the study of sacred texts. But I hope this chapter has already made it plain that the work of theologians and jurists alone cannot define Islam. We also need the anthropologists and sociologists because they look at Islam with different methodologies. They study Islam through studying people. In other words, the social sciences put a human face on the study of Islam. Anthropologists and sociologists study local contexts and investigate the lives of real people, groups, societies, and networks. They explore the experiences of everyday Muslims from around the world through interviews, focus groups, and participant observation. They examine "ordinary lives" (Bowen 2012, 3) and study Islam "as lived religion" (Marranci 2008, 428–29).

Recently, Esposito and Mogahed gave voice to the "*silenced* majority" and showed the "actual views of everyday Muslims" through a Gallup study that involved tens of thousands of interviews around the Muslim majority world (2007).[13] That study shows, for example, how Muslims divergently understand concepts like sharia and democracy. These subtleties would not appear in theological texts on the same topics.

By using empirical research, anthropologists and sociologists help to guard us against generalizing representations of Muslims. While theologians study the tenets of Islam to understand Muslim piety, sociologists and anthropologists look at specific practices and views, at everyday life. As Muslim anthropologist Akbar Ahmed (2010, 5) explains, "An anthropologist is like a camera. He takes a snapshot of society at that moment in time."

This approach also unveils the complexities of religion. For example, Muslim theologians and jurists may claim, based on Islamic texts, that Islam does not support religious female leadership. But sociologists could counter this by offering case studies of the recently formed women's mosque in Los Angeles[14] or the growing religious roles of Muslim women in various parts of the Muslim world (Masooda and Kalmbach 2012).

Another important aspect of anthropological and sociological studies is that they include voices of individual Muslims, who therefore contribute to the definitions provided by scholars and experts. Thus Muslims may self-define as Muslims not because they recite the shahada (as the religious texts would teach) but because they are born into a Muslim family or have Islam on their birth certificate, or simply because they "feel" Muslim, even if they do not practice. Although many Muslim theologians may

---

[13] This is how the two authors describe their research: "This book is the product of a mammoth, multiyear Gallup research study. Between 2001 and 2007, Gallup conducted tens of thousands of hour-long, face-to-face interviews with residents of more than 35 nations that are predominantly Muslim or have substantial Muslim populations."

[14] See http://womensmosque.com.

disagree with the process of self-identification of Muslims, the latter still provides useful information on the current state of Islam, which is especially important for missiology.

As this section has shown, there is not one single body that decides who represents Islam, but many. The question for my friend Ryan, and all of us who care about reaching Muslims, is to decide whether we want to rely only on the views of normative and official Islam or if we also will try to understand the wider community of Muslims outside religious circles. All forms of Islam may not be normative or authoritative, but "normative" is not who we are trying to reach with the gospel. Without these wider perspectives, Ryan will not understand what he observes in various contexts of the Muslim world.

Conclusion

I began this chapter with a question from my friend from church, Ryan, who wanted to understand who actually represents Islam. I have argued that the best way to answer this pressing question is to borrow three questions that scholars of Islam use in their research: (1) Is it good enough to state that there is one Islam? (2) How does one address the diversity of Muslim societies? (3) Who decides who is an authentic Muslim?

Reviewing the theories and concepts developed by scholars on those questions allows us to draw the following conclusions. First, Ryan's question is complex. Even scholars cannot answer it in a nutshell. Unfortunately, too many Christians want a simple and straightforward answer on which they can build their approach to ministry. But the contention of this volume is that effective ministry among Muslims cannot be done without diligent study of the specific contexts in which one wishes to minister.

Second, we have noted that yes, there are beliefs, practices, and traditions that Muslims share together universally. However, can this be called "one Islam"? I would be reluctant to answer affirmatively unless another phrase is attached that somehow expresses the diversity of Islam, as many scholars presented in this chapter have done.

Third, this study reveals that Islam is not static; it is constantly fluctuating as new people and contexts embrace it. This renders the ongoing conversation between theologians, anthropologists, and sociologists necessary. Theologians may be the protectors of the sacred texts that they try to preserve and hand down to other generations. But anthropologists and sociologists, while also taking these texts into account, remind theologians that Islam is not just a faith tradition but also a living tradition. This is why the reflection on who represents Islam must be open-ended.

Fourth, missionaries should not be confused by the diversity we see in Muslim societies. Instead they should carefully study expressions of Islam in their context as lifelong learners so they will be better able to communicate with the Muslims in their lives.

Finally, this chapter has presented numerous models of how scholars intersect common beliefs and practices with multiple interpretations, expressions, and dynamics of Islam. I have not covered all the models of this complex process.

However, those presented provide a start to those who wish to approach the question of "Who represents Islam?"

I hope that at the end of this chapter Ryan will be less confused—although I have not given him the two-sentence response he was looking for. Instead I hope to have shown that the response depends on at least three factors: who makes the decision, the way unity and diversity intersects in the manifold contexts of Muslim societies, and that the voice of every Muslim helps shape the definition of Islam.

Reflection Questions

1. Suppose Ryan asked you, "Does ISIS represent true Islam, or are they not even Muslims?" How would you answer?

2. Considering what you have learned in this chapter, compare two experiences you have had in different Muslim contexts. How do you explain both the similarities and the differences?

References

Ahmed, Akbar S. 1986. *Toward Islamic Anthropology: Definition, Dogma, and Directions*. Herndon, VA: The International Institute of Islamic Thought.

———. 2010. *Journey into America: The Challenge of Islam*. The Brookings Institution.

Asad, Talal Asad. 1986. *The Idea of an Anthropology of Islam*. Washington, DC: Center for Contemporary Arab Studies, Georgetown University.

Baker, Raymond William. 2015. *One Islam, Many Muslim Worlds: Spirituality, Identity, and Resistance across Islamic Lands*. New York: Oxford University Press. Kindle edition.

Bell, Steve. 2011. "Approaching Muslims with Grace and Truth." In *Between Naivety and Hostility: Uncovering the Best Christian Responses to Islam in Britain*. Edited by Steve Bell and Colin Chapman. Crownhill, UK: Authentic. Kindle edition.

Bodman, Herbert L., and Nayereh Tohidi, eds. 1998. *Women in Muslim Societies: Diversity Within Unity*. London: Lynne Rienner Pub.

Bowen, John R. 2012. *A New Anthropology of Islam*. Cambridge: Cambridge University Press.

Cumming, Joseph L. 2012. "Ṣifāt al-Dhāt in al-Ashʿarī's Doctrine of God and Possible Christian Parallels." In *Toward Respectful Understanding and Witness among Muslims: Essays in Honor of J. Dudley Woodberry*. Edited by Evelyne A. Reisacher. Pasadena, CA: William Carey Library. Kindle edition, 3021–4316.

El-Zien, Abdul Hamid. 1977. "Beyond Ideology and Theology: The Search for the Anthropology of Islam." *Annual Review of Anthropology* 6: 227–54.

Esposito, John L., and Dalia Mogahed. (2007). *Who Speaks for Islam? What a Billion Muslims Really Think*. New York: Gallup Press.

Gregorian, Vartan. 2003. *Islam: A Mosaic, Not a Monolith*. Washington, DC: Brookings Institution Press.

Hughes, Aaron W. 2013. *Muslim Identities: An Introduction to Islam*. New York: Columbia University Press.

Lukens-Bull, Ronald A. 2014. "Between Text and Practice: Considerations in the Anthropological Study of Islam." In *Defining Islam: A Reader*. Edited by Andrew Rippin. New York: Routledge. Kindle edition.

Marranci, Gabriele. 2008. *The Anthropology of Islam*. Oxford: Berg Publishers.

Masooda, Bano, and Hilary Kalmbach, eds. 2012. *Women, Leadership, and Mosque: Changes in Contemporary Islamic Authority*. Boston: Brill.

Ramadan, Tariq. 2003. *Western Muslims and the Future of Islam*. Oxford: Oxford University Press.

Redfield, Robert. 1956. *Peasant Society and Culture*. Chicago: University of Chicago Press.

Selim, Ali Shehata Abdou. 2015. *The Concept of Coexistence in Islamic Primary Sources: An Analytical Examination*. Cambridge: Cambridge Scholars Publishing.

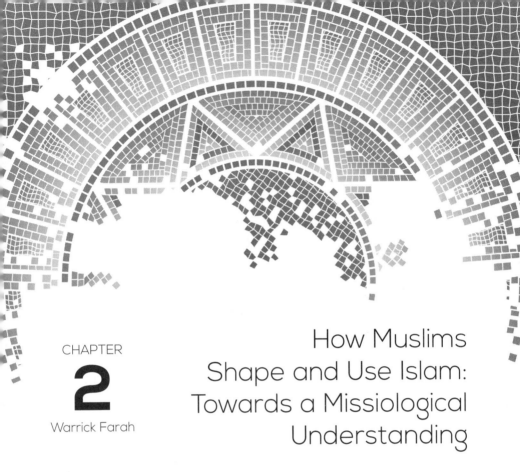

How Muslims Shape and Use Islam: Towards a Missiological Understanding

"I know Islam better than this Muslim does," I remember thinking to myself many years ago during a discussion with a friend in the Middle East. Trying to score an apologetic point, I interpreted a verse from the Qur'an to demonstrate, I hoped, how the gospel was a beautiful alternative. Yet my Muslim friend had never heard of the "Islamic" idea I insisted came from the Qur'an. After repeated mistakes like this one in various contexts, I came to realize my error: The "Islam" I assumed Muslims practiced existed *only in my mind*.

Understanding Islam from the top down—beginning with the Qur'an, the life of Muhammad, the Hadith, and the caliphate—has a privileged place in the history of Christian engagement with Muslim peoples. We want to understand the people we are trying to engage, and thus it makes perfect sense to study the official texts and history of Islam to better understand their worldview. But this top-down approach suffers from a serious weakness—many Muslims are nominal, doctrinally aberrant, or know little about the formal creeds of their community. Christians in the West tend to homogenize Muslims (or limit Islam to only one expression) as a simple way to describe who they are and what they believe. This is especially noticeable since 9/11, when "Islam" became an incessant topic in Western media. Christian books about Muslims written from this top-down perspective have proliferated since that infamous day.

Understanding the core texts of the Islamic tradition is indeed valuable, but a complementary perspective on Islam is also vital because we need to better understand how Muslims themselves live within their own contexts. It is only by examining how different Muslims live and what they believe that we can appreciate the great diversity in Islam today and thus develop mission strategies that are fitting for various contexts across "the world of Islam." This brief introductory chapter demonstrates that Islam is not a simple cloning machine, but a multifarious[1] set of interpretations and practices that Muslims use in various ways in different contexts to meet diverse needs. This chapter also plays a specific role in this book, as it lays out a theoretical framework to aid in studying the following chapters on specific Islamic contexts.

Conceptualizing Islam

In the previous chapter, Evelyne Reisacher aptly demonstrated that the question "Who represents Islam?" is, to a certain extent, unanswerable. The derivative issue, "What is Islam?" is also a tricky question without a simple answer. A recent book, titled by this very question (Ahmed 2015), has generated much discussion from scholars of Islam, culture, and religion.[2] Ahmed has persuasively critiqued previous definitions of Islam while offering a new conceptual paradigm for making sense of the complexity.

He argues that attempts to define Islam are plagued by two common errors. The first error is to place Islam in a ridged framework that is unable to account for the diversity of Muslims around the world who often contradict one another. The second error is to claim that there is no such thing as Islam, but instead only islams imagined by each Muslim. One consequence of this second error makes labeling something "Islamic" practically meaningless. Ahmed argues that useful conceptualizations of Islam must account for internal contradictions and yet also the historical coherence of the human phenomenon. With this in mind, Islam can be defined as a process of "meaning-making" undertaken by Muslims as they interact in their context with the revelation given to Muhammad.[3] In a flexible yet specific definition like this, it is also necessary to understand the history of Islam and the sociological influences that affect our conceptualization.

---

[1] "Unless Western analysts, policy-makers, academics and secular Muslim governments acknowledge the important differences within Islam and the justification of some grievances, then the reasons both behind the broad Islamic resurgence and rise of Muslim terrorism cannot be grasped. This can only be achieved by learning to understand the fluid and multifarious nature of Islam, what it can offer and mean to individuals, communities and nation-states, and the significance of the ensuing ideologies and actions within those contexts" (Sutton and Vertigans 2005, 14).

[2] See http://marginalia.lareviewofbooks.org/islam-forum-introduction

[3] This is my abbreviated summary of Ahmed's complicated proposal.

The Formation of Islam and the Globalizing Ummah

Historically, Islam has continually evolved as new communities entered the ummah. These transformations occurred because, in general, Islam lacks an institutional authority able to make pronouncements concerning the parameters of Islamic legitimacy. This contributes both to the flexibility of the Islamic tradition as well as to the pattern by which some Muslims claim the "mantle of Islam" while denouncing all others (Berkey 2003, 83).

On the margins of Islam, when new communities became Muslim, they looked to local religious scholars, not some "official" Islam, to find answers to their practical and spiritual questions. Of course, in many cases the local religious scholars were also representatives of official[4] Islam, yet even then their texts were always mediated by human interpretation (consciously realized or not). The result is that localized traditions of Islam were birthed in each locale, each different and at the same time officially "Islam."

Richard Bulliet calls this understanding of Islam a "view from the edge" and argues that it best explains where Muslims have found sources of religious authority as Islam expanded. It is these local interpreters of the Qur'an and especially the hadith[5] that have legitimized Islam as they addressed the contextual concerns of newly emerging Muslim communities:

> The nature of Islamic religious authority and the source of its profound impact upon the lives of Muslims—the Muslims of yesterday, of today, and of tomorrow—cannot be grasped without comprehending the historical evolution of Islamic society. Nor can such a comprehension be gained from a cursory perusal of the central narrative of Islam. The view from the edge is needed, because, in truth the edge ultimately creates the center. (Bulliet 1994, 12)

Islam has become a global faith partly because diverse cultures were incorporated and subsequently codified into its official texts during its early expansion. Frequently, new forms of Islam were synthesized from this interplay between the margins and perceived sources of Islamic authority. Bulliet argues that early Islamic religious authority was based on local hadith interpreted (and fabricated) by locally prominent families of religious scholars. It was not until the eleventh and twelfth centuries that these hadith were either accepted or rejected as weak (1994, 114).

This "view from the edge" perspective also sheds light on how Islam continues to operate today. "Muslims have repeatedly voiced their needs and discovered leaders who have been responsive to the times and circumstances of their petitioners.

---

[4] By "official" I mean either traditional, orthodox Sunni Islam (which is still far from uniform) or the state-sponsored Islam of that time and locale.

[5] Many (considered to be authentic) hadith were clearly late forgeries that reflect the culture and needs of that age. There is even a hadith that claims Muhammad said, "After my departure the number of sayings ascribed to me will increase in the same way as sayings have been ascribed to previous prophets" (Goldziher 1973, 2:56). Gabriel Said Reynolds notes, "Evidently, this hadith was forged by someone who hoped to convince Muslims to stop forging hadith" (2012, 89).

Today the process continues, because it has come, through historical development, to be an integral part of Islam" (ibid., 204). For some Muslims Islam can be about legalistically maintaining the Islamic status quo, but for many others it means turning to local interpretations that meet their felt needs.[6]

This emergence of new forms of Islam is most obvious in the West as Muslim immigrant parents struggle to transmit their religion to their children. This "second generation" (those who do not abandon their faith altogether) attempts to make Islam relevant through constructing new identities in the context of sociopolitical experiences and transnational networks.[7] Increasingly, globalization is facilitating the creation of types of Islam that are more open and inclusive than the previous iterations inherited from the nation-states of their Muslim parents (Leonard 2009). As Brad Gill observes from the book *Globalized Islam: The Search for a New Ummah* (Roy 2004), a new ummah is arising. "The un-orchestrated cacophony of a 'globalized Islam' is eroding and transforming old authority, and a traditional ummah is feeling the torque of modern civilization" (Gill 2015, 60). Yet this "torque" goes in both directions, and at times even serves to reinforce traditional patterns of authority. In fact, some fundamentalist expressions of Islam have arisen to protest what they perceive to be Islam's compromise with the West.

Globalization exhibits this fundamental duality; its interconnectedness fosters both a sense of what is shared and what is different. "Thus even as globalization can enhance for Muslims their sense of membership and belonging in the global ummah, it may also nurture their sense of being distinguished in important respects from many other Muslims" (Kibria 2011, 4). Because this global ummah today is reactive and evolving in various ways and in various contexts, our analysis of Islamic peoples needs to correspond with these changing realities.

The Sociology of Islam

While a top-down view is important to understand the Islamic tradition, it is equally important to understand Islam sociologically as something that, as Armando Salvatore (2016) says,

> shapes social reality not via a ready-made institutional solution (such as a shari'a frequently misconstrued as a legal code ready to be applied) but *by empowering social actors to draw on a civilizational reservoir to creatively shape solutions to social problems based on the specific circumstances of a locale and of the age.* (Salvatore 2016, 13, *emphasis mine*)

This sociological understanding of how religion works in society helps us go beyond the inherent limitations of a reductionist understanding built solely upon studying the main texts and history of Muslims. Fortunately, the bottom-up view also

---

[6] Many expressions of Islam operate between these two poles, and even those who wish to maintain the status quo are doing so out of a felt need. Islam, as it is lived out, is always a discourse between past and present. See Reisacher's previous chapter in this volume, "Who Represents Islam?"

[7] For example, the "transglobal hip hop umma" (Alim 2005).

helps us better understand how the Islamic textual tradition actually works because it takes seriously the interpretive lenses of Muslims as they deal with the Qur'an and Hadith in their contexts. Simply put, it brings us closer to the practical theology of Muslims, rather than the theology they theoretically hold.

Like all religious movements, Muslims participate in a dynamic process as they continually shape and reshape their version of Islam to meet felt needs or negotiate identities. For example, the rise of ISIS (Islamic State of Iraq and Syria) has made this process front-page news as their self-proclaimed leaders "partake in processes of social innovation" while laying claim to some supposed true Islam (ibid., 14). ISIS has displayed proficiency in creating both alternative ideology and practice in a way that matches the characteristics of other successful social movements (Sutton 2014). Therefore, while the overwhelming majority of the world's Muslims reject ISIS's interpretation and practice of Islam, their legitimacy as "Muslims" cannot be easily dismissed.[8] The rise of ISIS exemplifies the principle that "it is not Islam that shapes Muslims, but rather Muslims who, through discourses, practices, beliefs and actions, make Islam" (Marranci 2008, Kindle 489).

In other words, "Islam" does not have a life of its own. Islam does not simply establish itself as a coherent entity on a people as if it had a will or power in and of itself. Its long history and traditions do carry a great deal of weight. However, that weight is socially received—not enforced. Muslims use Islamic texts, traditions, rituals, and practices to find meaning and structure in their environment. But in doing this they are selective—they choose which parts of the greater Islamic tradition to use, which parts to modify for themselves, and which to ignore. Additionally, they often incorporate practices found in other non-Islamic traditions into their lived experience (such as folk religion or Western democracy). This results in the "little tradition" of local Islam, to share a term with Evelyn Reisacher in the previous chapter.

As Christians, we reject certain Islamic beliefs and practices,[9] just as the gospel critiques all cultures. But the missiological task of engaging a culture begins with simply seeking to understand Muslims on their own terms—that is, how they understand their own faith and practice in a particular context. Armed with this understanding, we will be better equipped for mission in various Muslim contexts.

---

[8] Martin Accad argues that given the diversity of Islam today, even Muslims who claim ISIS is un-Islamic "need to understand ISIS for what it truly is: a deeply religious, fundamentalist, 'restorative' ideology, with long and deep roots both in history and in decades of radical preaching in certain types of mosques across the world" (2015). Also commenting on the dangers of associating ISIS with some form of ideal Islam, Colin Chapman argues against assuming that everything Muslims do can be understood simply by looking at their texts, where political and historical context have no relevance (2017, 7).

[9] I agree wholeheartedly with the Lausanne Covenant, article 10, which states that the gospel "evaluates all cultures according to its own criteria of truth and righteousness, and insists on moral absolutes in every culture." It is imperative to measure all religions, including Christianity, by the revelation of Jesus Christ (Tennent 2010, 223).

Islam as One Thread in the Braided Rope of Muslim Society

While recognizing the varieties of Islamic expressions in the world today, there is indeed a core, shared understanding of what it means to be Muslim. We might point to belief in the singularity of Allah's divine being or the prophethood of Muhammad to describe this core. Yet while there is such a thing as *Islam*, there are also many *islams* that draw from this heritage. In contrast to the widespread misunderstanding that all Muslims are identical, my point is to demonstrate that Islam is not a type of machinery that duplicates clones from one culture to the next. Although this should be self-evident to the Christian who knows many Muslims, our missiological approaches often assume this reductionist approach.[10] "Many people wholeheartedly committed to reaching Muslims have made the mistake of treating Islam as a monolithic system and proposing 'one size fits all' solutions to the challenge of effective outreach among Muslims" (Waterman 2017).

We need to move on from this tendency to generalize the faith and practice of Muslims, especially considering the historical formation of Islam and globalizing influences previously discussed. Rather than asking, "What is the message of Islam?" it is more appropriate to ask, "What do the Muslims I know believe, love, and practice? And why do they think, feel, and act in these ways?" This change of perspective on Islam moves us from the top-down to the bottom-up approach.

In light of the issues discussed in this chapter and the inadequacies inherent in missiological approaches that homogenize Muslims, how then should we think of Islam in relationship to Muslim societies? I propose we consider viewing Islam *as one strand in the braided rope of society*. When we look at a Muslim people, the entire rope (their society) is not Islam; it is only one of the threads. The rope includes many more strands intertwined together: politics, culture, history, geography, rituals, values, language, etc. The Islam strand is visible constantly, as it is part of the "whole warp and woof of society" (Goldsmith 1976, 318). Many Muslims claim that Islam is indeed a comprehensive code that deals with all matters of life. However, depending on how complex or strong the rope is, or how important it is to identify as a Muslim in that context, Islam is not all we see. This is particularly noticeable when we look at Muslim societies on the margins of the Islamic world.

Here are some characteristics and advantages of this metaphor of Islam:

1. Islam is something people use and weave into the fabric of their society. It fulfills a purpose and meets certain needs. The specific weave of the rope shows creativity and design.

---

[10] Against this type of reductionism, some Christian missiologists go so far as to say that we should try to avoid using religious categories such as "Muslim" or "Christian" to describe an ethnic or cultural group (Ramachandra 1999, 41). It is not possible to tie any of the major world faiths to any particular culture. Even considering the Arabization that often comes along with Islamization (due to the supposed untranslatability of the Qur'an), we should be very cautious when referring to Islam as a civilization (Sutton and Vertigans 2005, 129ff.).

2. You can isolate Islam and examine it as distinct from society, but when you do the rope unravels and no longer serves its intended function. The thread is not the rope; it doesn't serve a function apart from the other threads.[11]

3. When you look at the rope in its entirety, it is nearly impossible to follow the strand of Islam. Instead, the threads only make sense in relationship to the others. Human societies are irreducibly complex.

4. Each rope (Muslim society) is configured differently. And each strand (form of Islam) varies in strength and purpose in each rope. Some strands are even micro-braids themselves, with "Islam" braided in (e.g., Islamic finance versus conventional finance).

5. Both Muslims and non-Muslims can recognize a commonality of the Islam strand and are able therefore to group Islamic ropes together, decide what is not an Islamic rope, or instead classify some ropes on the margins of Islam.

How can this "strand in a rope" analogy aid in forming a missiological understanding of Islam? As described at the beginning of this chapter, the Islam that existed only in my mind was symptomatic of my view of Islam during my early years living among Muslims. I assumed Muslims believed the things I thought Islam taught. But when I started to listen and enter the challenge of exploring my Muslim friends' faith, I discovered that the search for true Islam was not only illusive but also irrelevant. Instead, I decided to build my understanding of Islam on my friend's understanding because that is what Islam was to *him*, and in the context of genuine dialogue and witness that is what is most important.

My study of Islam from the top down was relevant only as I sought to simultaneously learn from the bottom up. Only then was I able to discern the particular strand of Islam in the complex rope of Muslim society. I also began to see the many factors other than Islam which contribute to the formation and expressions of Islam. This empathetic attitude of a learner has helped me gain more authentic relationships with Muslims, a more accurate understanding of Islam in Muslim societies, and a more attentive audience for the transforming hope of the gospel.

Conclusion

In missiological approaches to understanding Muslims, we have over-homogenized Islam by describing it from the top-down: its texts and its history of the caliphate. While this may be good enough for general purposes, it is not a sound missiological approach. Today, especially considering the impact of globalization on the multifarious nature of Islam, a bottom-up perspective is necessary for us to truly engage Muslims, particularly those living on the historical and cultural margins of the Islamic world.

---

[11] I recognize that the ability to separate "religion" from other parts of society is a secular modernist notion with roots in the Protestant Reformation and in the Enlightenment (Nongbri 2013). My intention is not to be dichotomistic but to provide a visual analogy that explains how and why Islamic contexts differ.

Coincidently, this perspective also helps us properly understand both the historical and current globalizing evolution of Islam.

For all that Muslims worldwide may have in common, it is still inadequate to consider Islam a single, coherent entity. Just as religion (including secularism) functions in all societies, Muslims shape Islam for various reasons to fit the needs of their context. Islam cannot be properly explained simply by referencing some supposedly monolithic "Islamic worldview."

Discussing the major lesson learned from the seminal work *Islam Observed* by Clifford Geertz (1968), Terry Muck summarizes, "Even though you know the basic theoretical and theological teachings of a religious tradition, don't be surprised at the radically different manifestations of that religion in different cultures. In other words, don't assume you know until you observe" (2016, Kindle 2532). Effective Christian engagement with Muslims requires us to be more aware of these contextual differences because unique forms of Islam require unique approaches to Muslim peoples.

At this point you may be wondering, "So what practical impact does this understanding of Islam have on my missiology?" In various ways, the following chapters demonstrate what it means to shape missiology from the margins of Islam, not by focusing on some normative Islam, but on Muslims themselves in their context. As you read, you should become more prepared to engage the Muslims in your Islamic context.

Reflection Questions

1. To what degree has your view of Islam included both top-down and bottom-up approaches? Do you think your view of Islam matches the form of Islam actually practiced in your (current or future) context? Explain.

2. Think about some of the books or articles you have read on Muslim ministry in the past. Have any of those authors over-homogenized Islam? Was this helpful to you at the time, or did it obscure important realities in your context? Why or why not?

References

Accad, Martin. 2015. "Beating Back ISIS." Accessed January 2, 2017. https://imes.blog/2015/02/20/beating-back-isis/.

Ahmed, Shahab. 2015. *What Is Islam?: The Importance of Being Islamic*. Princeton, NJ: Princeton University Press.

Alim, H. Samy. 2005. "A New Research Agenda: Exploring the Transglobal Hip Hop Umma." In *Muslim Networks from Hajj to Hip Hop*. Edited by Miriam Cooke and Bruce B. Lawrence. Chapel Hill, NC: The University of North Carolina Press.

Berkey, Jonathan. 2003. *The Formation of Islam: Religion and Society in the Near East*, 600–1800. New York: Cambridge University Press.

Bulliet, Richard W. 1994. *Islam: The View from the Edge*. New York: Columbia University Press.

Chapman, Colin. 2017. "Christian Responses to Islamism and Violence in the Name of Islam." *Transformation: An International Journal of Holistic Mission Studies* 34 (2).

Geertz, Clifford. 1968. *Islam Observed: Religious Development in Morocco and Indonesia*. Chicago: University of Chicago Press.

Gill, Brad. 2015. "Editorial." *International Journal of Frontier Missiology* 32 (2): 59–60.

Goldsmith, Martin. 1976. "Community and Controversy: Key Causes of Muslim Resistance." *Missiology* 4 (3).

Goldziher, Ignác. 1973. *Muslim Studies*. Albany, NY: Aldine Publishing Company.

Kibria, Nazli. 2011. *Muslims in Motion: Islam and National Identity in the Bangladeshi Diaspora*. Piscataway, NJ: Rutgers University Press.

Leonard, Karen. 2009. "Transnational and Cosmopolitan Forms of Islam in the West." *Harvard Journal of Middle Eastern Studies* 8:176–99.

Marranci, Gabriele. 2008. *The Anthropology of Islam*. Oxford: Berg Publishers.

Muck, Terry. 2016. Why Study Religion? *Understanding Humanity's Pursuit of the Divine*. Grand Rapids: Baker Academic.

Nongbri, Brent. 2013. *Before Religion: A History of a Modern Concept*. New Haven, CT: Yale University Press.

Ramachandra, Vinoth. 1999. *Faiths in Conflict?: Christian Integrity in a Multicultural World*. Downers Grove, IL: InterVarsity Press.

Reynolds, Gabriel Said. 2012. *The Emergence of Islam: Classical Traditions in Contemporary Perspective*. Minneapolis: Fortress Press.

Roy, Olivier. 2004. *Globalized Islam: The Search for a New Ummah*. New York: Columbia Universtity Press.

Salvatore, Armando. 2016. *The Sociology of Islam: Knowledge, Power and Civility*. West Sussex, UK: Wiley.

Sutton, Philip W. 2014. "The (New) Invasion of Iraq." Accessed January 2, 2017. https://www.polity.co.uk/giddens7/blog/default.aspx?tag=215.

Sutton, Philip W., and Stephen Vertigans. 2005. *Resurgent Islam: A Sociological Approach*. Malden, MA: Polity Press.

Tennent, Timothy. 2010. *Invitation to World Missions: A Trinitarian Missiology for the Twenty-first Century*. Grand Rapids: Kregal.

Waterman, L. D. 2017. "Different Pools, Different Fish: The Mistake of 'One Size Fits All' Solutions to the Challenge of Effective Outreach among Muslims." Accessed January 28, 2017. http://fuller.edu/Blogs/Global-Reflections/Posts/Different-Pools,-Different-Fish—The-Mistake-of—One-Size-Fits-All—Solutions-to-the-Challenge-of-Effective-Outreach-Among-Muslims/.

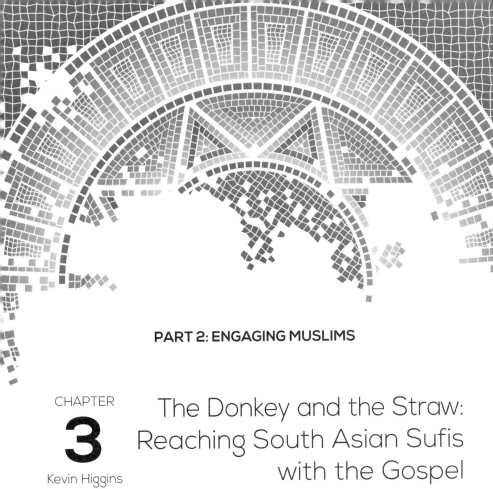

CHAPTER

3

Kevin Higgins

The Donkey and the Straw: Reaching South Asian Sufis with the Gospel

Several years ago we gathered more than twenty Muslim-background believers from two different movements in South Asia. Both are self-described "insider movements," and we met to pray, listen to stories from the field, learn, and encourage each other. The room was crowded and humid as we took large chunks of time to let each person share their story. I was encouraged by the spiritual depth and conviction of these godly followers of Jesus.

The next day, during meals, I had two conversations. In each case a leader from one movement lowered their voice and said, "Brother Kevin, those other guys are not really 'insiders'; they can't fit in with their people."

"Why?"

One says, "They sing."

Another says, "No, it's because they don't sing."

What was going on? One group came from a context in which the influence of the Salafi vision of Islam predominated. In their area, mullahs told Muslims to destroy shops that sold music CDs. These brothers saw the use of music as a foreign (Western Christian) insertion based on a misunderstanding of Islam. The other group was from a Sufi influenced context. Singing was integral to their devotion and worship. These brothers saw the rejection of music as a foreign (Western Christian) insertion based on a misunderstanding of Islam.

Contexts matter, as you already know. And one context that seems to be ripe for further engagement is the so-called higher Sufi Muslim world.

Four Difficulties

I open by confessing to four difficulties I have wrestled with. First, I am accustomed to writing about missiology most often from the context of my own hands-on, field experience and work. Mine has been with Wahabi Sunnis and with so-called folk Muslims. My work with so-called "high" Sufis is still a new dimension of my ministry, so I must confess to a very limited sample size of actual experiences.[1]

A second difficulty is best illustrated by a comment a believer from a Sufi background made to me when I told him I was interested to know more about "high" Sufism. His response was simple: "It doesn't exist."

I almost agree. There is a sort of Westernized and popularized—and dare I say, "New Age"–shaded—Sufism that I hear some Westerners refer to. That type of Sufism does not actually exist outside of that small circle. But there is a sort of continuum that runs from what we might refer to as "folk," or popular, Sufism as practiced at many of the shrines of Asia to the Sufi schools that follow actual *tariqas* (see below) and teachers and truly seek a closer experience of God and not merely an immediate miraculous solution to a problem. Determining where folk and high Sufism begin and end is no easy task.

That task would be easier if I could begin with a clear definition. But exactly here another difficulty is encountered. What is Sufism? The Sufis themselves find this difficult to explain. More accurately, Sufis freely and quite happily declare that it is an impossible (if not irrelevant) question. As one of the more widely known advocates of the Sufi way has written, "The more the dogged searches of the western world have tried to dig out the secrets of the Sufi, the more hopelessly complex the task has seemed to be" (Shah 1964, 18).

The reasons for this are many, but at the heart is the fact that understanding Sufism is ultimately not an objective exercise best undertaken in an attempt at a detached, academic spirit. Rather it is only known and discovered by "participation, training,

---

[1] The distinction between "high" Sufism and so-called "folk" Sufism is something that only emerges in the abstract. In practice the lines are not so clear. One person's "orthodox" or "mainstream" is another person's "fringe," and vice versa.

and experience" (ibid., 19). In other words, if I aim to describe Sufism in a way a Sufi would actually recognize and accept, I cannot do that through an academic article. No minor problem for an author of such an article.

Finally, Sufism's self-understanding is that it is the "nut" or essence inside the "shell" of every religion (including Islam). As such, any discussion of how a Christian, missional approach to Sufis should take shape must take into account the fact that many of the normal discussions of communication of the gospel for Muslim ministry will not readily apply. Sufis will most likely see our evangelism as an uninitiated and surface-level exercise in the more superficial dimension of religion: an example of the shell (Christianity) rather than the nut (direct experience of God).[2]

In spite of these four difficulties, I will venture an attempt. I begin with a brief overview of Sufism. I will give at least a portrait of some commonly mentioned themes, beliefs, and practices. I will include only a brief glimpse of historical background to Sufism. I will proceed from that to make a number of observations about the challenges and opportunities that Sufism presents to Christian witness and witnesses. I believe that the opportunities are inherent in the challenges. They are perhaps two sides of the same coin. In order to help in the process of application and exploring the implications of the observations made in the course of this chapter, I have included some questions for reflection. And finally, I plan to end with a conclusion. That may seem obvious, but as I began to write I was not sure yet what form that might take. Perhaps the Sufis would approve.

A General Overview of Sufi Viewpoints and Practices

I do not have the space for a full description of the rise of Sufism and its development within Islam. I will rely here upon the succinct yet fairly comprehensive overview found in the work of the Pakistani Muslim teacher and author, Fazlur Rahman. While Rahman gives room for the possibility that later Sufism may have been partially shaped by outside influences such as Christianity or "gnosticism" (which he leaves undefined), he also makes clear that the roots of the Sufi way are to be found within the earliest sources of Islam: the Qur'an and Hadith—that is, within the life and example of Muhammad himself (1979, 128–29).

Other authors have also speculated about various outside sources of influence, including the opposite direction by which Sufism influenced Christianity, for example. But there is general consensus that the roots of Sufi thinking and practices are found in the life of Muhammad (Rahman 1979; Guillame 1956; Esposito 1998; Lapidus 1988).

The question of sources is an example of the difference between the way an academic and primarily Western audience might approach this topic versus how a

---

[2] Or as one famous Sufi parable describes it, the Sufi is the "linguist," whereas adherents of different religions talk past one another using different languages to speak of the same reality. See Shah's brief retelling of the parable of the grapes (Shah, 23–24).

Sufi might. As one Sufi has said, asking about the history and possible sources of Sufism is like focusing on the origins of a Mongolian carpet that now sits on your floor. The most important point is not where it was made or where it came from, but where it is now and what use you are making of it.

Further complicating the attempt to define Sufism is the vast variety of "orders" or "schools," or to use the Sufi word, *tariqas* (literally, "path" or "method"). Rahman lists twenty-three, which he says is merely a list of those he felt to be most important. These are marked by differences in rituals, practices, beliefs, organization, and general outlook (1979, 157). At the same time, these different orders interact with each other. And they do so to such an extent that it is possible "for a single individual to belong to several fraternities at the same time" (ibid., 158).[3]

Having made these disclaimers, however, it is possible to give some outline or contours of what emerge as common Sufi practices and approaches. I will list several summaries from different authors and then try to synthesize them. Rahman suggests that the core qualities that distinguish Sufism are a deep trust in Allah; the central place of focus as the relationship between Allah and humans (in contrast to the focus of law and *fiqh* in Islamic jurisprudence); an "ascetic pietism" and devotion; the practice of *dhikr* (literally, "remembrance," or "making mention," but in devotional contexts referring to the practice of repetitive recitations of various words or verses from the Qur'an, or the names of Allah, etc.); gathering in "circles" for devotions; more-than-typical emphasis on the beliefs about a "Mahdi" (an almost messianic end-times figure); the concept of a *tariqa*, or path, taught by a Sufi master, or pir (ibid., 129–57).

Esposito summarizes the Sufi way as "annihilation (*fana*) of the lower, ego-centered self" and cultivating the state in which one can be said to "abide or rest (*baqa*) in God" (1998, 107). According to Esposito, this is typically a journey of three stages: renunciation, purification, and insight (ibid., 107).

Each Sufi leader (sometimes called a *shaykh*, or *pir*) passes on to their disciples a path that will lead them through these stages. Esposito cites an example of some of the Sufi practices he finds typical of such a tariqa, which may help the reader understand what is being referred to:

> The disciple should keep his garments clean and be always in a state of ritual purity. … One should not sit in a holy place gossiping. … At dawn a disciple should pray for forgiveness. … Then in the early morning he should read the Koran, abstaining from talk until sunrise. … Between the two evening prayers, he should be occupied with his

---

[3] This raises interesting questions about a current debate in missiology related to the issue of religious identity and belonging, though this is beyond the scope of this chapter. Two recent books are excellent resources on this issue of identity: Kathryn Kraft, *Searching for Heaven in the Real World: A Sociological Discussion of Conversion in the Arab World* (Eugene, OR: Wipf and Stock Publishers, 2012); and David Greenlee and Bob Fish (eds.), *Longing for Community: Church, Ummah, or Somewhere in Between* (Pasadena, CA: William Carey Library, 2013).

recollection (dhikr) and the special litany (wird) which is given to him by his master. … The Sufi should welcome the poor and needy and look after them. (Nicholson 1967, 46; cited in Esposito 1998, 106)

Esposito also mentions the special place of music for the Sufis. This takes the form of songs to or for God in most cases, though there are examples of songs for and about Muhammad. Perhaps the most famous examples of this musical dimension would be the "whirling dervishes" of Turkey who combine music and dance as a form of spiritual exercise aimed at fostering communion with God. The Sufi most associated with the dervishes, and one who has been somewhat well known in Western circles, was Jalal al-din Rumi (Esposito 1998, 108).

A very popular form of such music in South Asia is the *qawwali*, a song which can last twenty minutes or longer as it builds from a slow start to a state of "ecstasy" (Harvey 2009, 134). I once attended a large gathering at a shrine in South Asia (going there for the purpose of intercessory prayer), and as it happened, we arrived on the night of a large celebration. The singing of qawwalis was a major feature of the evening, and when the crescendo of ecstasy began to increase, it became very much akin to some charismatic worship events I have attended: raised hands, closed eyes, intensely focused devotion and praise, clapping, and some dancing (although not much in this case).

These attempts to summarize Sufi approaches and practices would not be complete without mention of another feature. One reason for the controversies within Islam about Sufism and Sufis stems from the fact that some Sufis, while in the state of ecstasy sometimes achieved during the above practices, have made statements about their experiences that have been declared dangerous, questionable, and heretical by other Muslims. And in some cases, Sufis have repeated such statements later when not in states of ecstasy.

Examples include statements such as "Glory to me. How great is my majesty," uttered by Abu Yazid, and "I am the Truth," spoken by Al Hallaj. Hallaj was later crucified (Esposito 1998, 102). This seems to have been due to suspicions of Christian influence, which came about because of Hallaj's frequent references to Jesus, whom he apparently viewed as a great Sufi master. Such utterances exhibit the deep intuitive experiences some Sufis have claimed. During such experiences, some Sufis have felt so near to God that it seems to them that they have become united or even "one" with God.

This introductory section has aimed at simply giving a broad picture of the difficulties in defining and describing "typical" Sufism on the one hand, while on the other hand seeking to at least paint in broad strokes some generally common characteristics. These latter include intense devotional practices, an emphasis on purity of soul and life, the quest for direct experience of God and deep relationship with God, and a general perception that ritual forms and rational theology alone do not constitute true religion.

In part as testimony to this last point, and in part as a fitting summary of this section, I close this introductory discussion by quoting the words of perhaps the most famous of all the Muslim Sufis, Al-Ghazali. But before we hear his words, it is important to know a bit about the man who spoke them.

Born in Iran in the eleventh century, Ghazali mastered Islamic law, theology, and philosophy and became a famous and much sought-after scholar and teacher. However, at the height of his fame and reputation he experienced what can only be described as a spiritual crisis. By his own admission, he felt lost. In his own words:

> The best of my activities, my teaching, was concerned with branches of knowledge that were unimportant and worthless. ... My motive in teaching ... was not sincere desire to serve God ... but I wanted widespread recognition. ... I stood on an eroding sand bank ... worldly desires were trying to keep me chained ... while the herald of faith was summoning, 'To the road! To the road! ... Your intellectual and practical involvements are hypocrisy and delusion.' ... I turned to the way of the mystics. ... I saw clearly ... that I had gone as far as possible by way of ... intellectual application, so that only personal experience and walking in the mystic way were left. (Esposito 1998, 104)

Challenges and Opportunities

I will address several challenges, which are at the same time opportunities. I am focusing here primarily on the messenger rather than the message, though I do not want that to be taken to mean that I don't think the message is important—far from it. But I focus on the messenger because it seems natural to begin with the personal challenges and opportunities that working closely with Sufis might present to me and to others who desire to share the gospel, challenges and opportunities that could affect my own growth in the Lord, before turning to the (in some ways easier) question of the message.

Parables and meaning: A different way to think of "storying"?

I mentioned earlier in this chapter that it is typical for the Sufis to make use of stories. "Storying" is also a recent emphasis in Christian mission, and we might assume that this could serve as an easy bridge for communication. However, the challenge is that Sufi stories are different in nature and application when compared to the typical use of storying as a methodology in Christian mission. Stories for Sufis are not necessarily told to make a rational point. So they are not like most Christian sermon illustrations. And they are not used step by step to build conceptual background for a theological point, as is the case with various ways of employing "chronological Bible stories."

In many cases, the stories Sufis tell seem to have no apparent spiritual point at all. This is particularly true of the stories that have gathered around the figure of Mulla Nasrudin. In many instances, Nasrudin stories are told merely as jokes, and yet they were originally devised to serve an entirely different purpose. Far from being stories told to make some difficult point clearer, the original intent seems to have been, in part at least, to actually "halt for a moment, situations in which certain states of mind are made clear" (Shah 1964, 63).

In other words, Nasrudin tales are often intended to slow comprehension rather than to aid it. And this serves as a challenge to much of the rational, intellectual, conceptual aims of typical evangelical approaches to communication of the gospel. Yet it is precisely in this challenge that we are presented with an opportunity. The opportunity is as much for the Christian as for the Sufi. By that I mean that there is a definite affinity between the Sufi use of stories and Jesus' use of parables, and in seeking to understand the Sufis on this point we too have an opportunity to discover afresh something of Jesus' mind and heart.

While it is a common assumption among Christians that Jesus used parables in order to illustrate and illuminate and make clear, it is at least equally true—if, indeed, not truer—that Jesus used parables for the opposite purpose: to obscure and thereby test, in one sense, to see who was curious enough to seek further and to press in more intently to understand and learn.

When the disciples and some others come to Jesus and "asked him about the parables," it is to them that Jesus replies, "The secret of the Kingdom of God has been given to you," while the others, those who did not come to ask, "Everything is said in parables" (Mark 4:10–11.[4] Why? So that they may be "ever seeing but never perceiving" (4:12).

The communication of Jesus, and of the Sufis, is often both allusive (pointing elsewhere) and elusive (difficult to actually define). And yet it is effective. For the Christian seeking to share the gospel with Sufi Muslims this presents a challenge to our typical assumptions about needing to be clear and logical. And it presents us with the opportunity to learn more of the mystery to be discovered in the ways God works to draw people to the Way.[5]

The mystical quest—and evangelical spirituality

When I was a new believer, I was discipled by people who were older in the Lord than I was. They did a wonderful job, and one brother in particular spent an hour each week with me. We prayed together, looked at Scripture, and he frequently talked with me about the importance of my daily "quiet time" with the Lord. I was diligent. And I put into practice the model I was taught, which centered a good deal around the study and application of the Bible. The goal was to Pray, Read, Observe, Apply, Pray, and then Tell someone what I learned: PROAPT.

There was nothing wrong with this approach or outline, and I benefited spiritually as my knowledge of Scripture blossomed. But the model betrays a particular—and, compared to the wider body of Christ—narrow set of assumptions about spiritual life and formation.

---

[4] All Scripture references in this chapter are from the *New International Version*, unless stated otherwise.
[5] In addition to Jesus' own use of parables, I am reminded too of the stories of the lives of the desert fathers and their enigmatic stories and tales, which are very much akin to those told by and about the Sufis.

One of my Muslim friends is a believer in Christ from a Sufi background (personally and through his family). His experiences in Christian spirituality have thus far led him to conclude that Christians do not walk deeply in the things of God. His experience of evangelical worship has been that it is "busy," noisy (referring to the worship music he has experienced), contrived, and shallow. The models of personal devotion he first received were dry and stale and seemed to offer no encouragement or opportunity for actual experience of God.

This is a potential major challenge for evangelical witness, and yet again an opportunity for both the Sufi and the Christian. Many other models of spiritual life are available within the global and historic body of Christ:

- The Orthodox use of the Jesus prayer, with the aim of growing in the ability to pray from the heart
- The spiritual exercises of St. Ignatius of Loyola, which foster, among other things, a particular use of the imagination
- The various traditions of meditation, "mental prayer," contemplative prayer, in much of the Roman Catholic tradition
- Praying the daily offices in the Anglican tradition
- Praying the Psalms
- Lectio divina[6]

Some items in the selective list above suggest not only a different approach to prayer but also how we engage the Scriptures devotionally as well. In addition to actually praying the Scriptures (for example, the Psalms) and the use of something like lectio divina, mining the treasures of Christian spirituality in history will also draw attention to how certain texts of Scripture have been used by saints and leaders in the past.

The example that springs first and foremost to my mind is the Song of Solomon. A cursory look at modern commentaries on the Song will reveal that this book of the canon has been through a wide variety of interpretive uses and approaches in the hands of different commentators. The trend historically was to view the Song as an allegory or extended metaphor for the intimate relationship between God and the soul (or, in some cases, the church). The tendency in more recent times has been to emphasize the awareness that whatever else the Song may be, it is first and foremost an actual love song about the romantic, and in places erotic, love between a man and a woman.

But might such an approach be in danger of throwing out the baby with the bath water? Perhaps the more mystical application of the Song need not be completely rejected. Perhaps the mystical tradition has seen more than recent approaches prefer to allow.

---

[6] By *lectio divina*, I am referring to any number of models for small groups engaging Scripture in a prayerful, meditative, and more experiential way. Typical of this approach is to open with prayer; read a selected text out loud several times; allow for silent meditation and time for the Scripture to soak in, as it were; and then sharing of responses to the text—responses which focus more on what the participants sense is happening within them as they are listening to the text and to the Lord. This is not suggested as a model to replace exegesis and other forms of Bible study and theological reflection, but as a resource in addition to such examples.

I am not in any way suggesting that we should jettison all that has been gained relative to solid exegesis and sound hermeneutics relative to our approach to canonical texts such as the Song. At the same time, the saints of God who found the Song (and the Psalms as well) to be so descriptive of the soul's relationship to God, and found these texts so crucial in their spiritual lives and prayers, may still have something to teach us.

In seeking to communicate the gospel with Sufis, Christian witnesses will also be challenged to examine their own spirituality, and in so doing have the opportunity to discover more of the riches within the body of Christ and grow personally as well.[7]

The Holy Spirit and Sufism

Engaging Sufism offers the Christian witness another challenge and opportunity relative to the work of the Holy Spirit in the lives of believers. I don't want to oversimplify this by jumping immediately to comparisons between Sufism and, say, the Pentecostal or charismatic movements of the last fifty years or so. In speaking with churches, I have at times referred to the Sufis as the charismatics in Islam (and hastened to add all sorts of correctives to that statement!). However, I do not want to suggest the idea that the points of connection between charismatic Christian experience and Sufism are limited to the more widely known phenomenon such as ecstatic worship or even the apparent similarities between charismatic prophetic speech and some of the Sufi declarations made while claiming to be speaking not only under God's influence but indeed in the first-person divine voice—as God actually speaking. (I refer the reader back to al-Hallaj, mentioned earlier, as an example.)

I will address just two points in this section. First, anyone working to seed the gospel among Sufis will be forced to address their views of miracles and the work of the Spirit in healing, deliverance, etc. Thankfully, the recent charismatic movements within the Christian world, including mainline denominations, has served to give mission works a greater awareness of and experience of these realities. The challenge, then, is to expect this and be ready for this in ministry to Sufis, if one has not become familiar with the miraculous in their ministry experience.

This is, again, also the opportunity. That is, this challenge offers us the opportunity to grow in this facet of ministry. It also may serve to illumine some of the stranger occurrences in the biblical account of miracles. Sufis report all sorts of bizarre miracles, which may leave the Christian worker incredulous to say the least.[8] But studying the Bible with Sufi friends and seekers will likely result in our Sufi friends seeing stories that we may pass over: Phillip's transportation to Azotus, the sun stopping in Joshua, floating ax-heads, etc. This may be an opportunity for us, as witnesses, to see passages of familiar Scriptures in new and fresh ways.

---

[7] One excellent resource is Basil Pennington's short book, *Centering Prayer* (New York: Image Books, 1982).

[8] One famous miracle told in one part of South Asia recounts the event in which a great saint turned into a bird, flew into the sky, turned and flew down, and was able to bury or burrow himself into the ground. End of story; no apparent point to the miracle.

This brings me to a second point. Most of us who serve as evangelical witnesses for the gospel have (I assume) a more or less solid theological grasp of biblical truths related to the Holy Spirit: Trinitarian teaching and the Spirit's role in sanctification, for example. And although Christians are divided about many aspects of this, there are at least schools of thought which agree to some extent about topics such as spiritual gifts. There is less agreement about the nature and meaning of terms like "baptism in the Spirit," but wide agreement within certain denominations at least (i.e., large groups who at least agree with others within their group, if not consensus through the whole body). However, the challenge I see in all of this is that so few of us, myself included here, seem to have anything like an authentic experiential grasp of so much of what we read in Scripture about the Spirit.

I know, based on my reading of the text, that the Spirit cries out "Abba, Father" (Gal 4:6). I know and believe this. But I have a strong sense that Paul has tasted something deeper than I have grasped and that he writes from that deeper experience, assuming his readers know what he is talking about.

Similarly, I know, based on my reading of the text, that the "Spirit intercedes… in groans too deep for words" (Rom 8:26). But again, I sense that Paul is writing from an experience that I can only suppose I understand. I see texts such as "… who has blessed us with every spiritual blessing in the heavenlies in Christ" (Eph 1:3) in a similar light. Certainly, we cannot "make" ourselves experience such things. And I firmly believe that my trust by faith that these realities are just that—realities—is sufficient for my walk and life in many respects.

And yet when I read of the sorts of spiritual experiences the Sufis report and promise to those who pursue the Path, I realize that my Sufi friends may well be looking to me and to my spiritual life not just for spiritual truths to be understood rationally and then accepted by faith. They are likely looking to see if the gospel, and if my life, offer anything like the spiritual realities they have heard promised by their own tariqa.

I want to be quick to add that I am not suggesting that such experiences are all legitimate. I know that Satan can parade as an angel of light and that there are counterfeit spirits and spiritual experiences. But I would be less than honest if I did not also suggest to myself and others who seek to bring the gospel to Sufis that doing so will in fact challenge our life in the Spirit, or the sometimes shallowness of it.

Thus, while I am not suggesting that all Sufi experiences are legitimate or spiritually healthy, I am suggesting that we should face the opportunity in this "challenge" and examine our own experiential grasp of the depths of all that God in fact offers us in Christ.

Rethinking discipleship (and formation) and leadership in "movements"

A final challenge, in which I also see an opportunity, is in the area of discipleship and leadership. Sufi movements are entirely built around what Christians call discipleship. In Sufism, a disciple (a *murid*) follows the teaching and path and example of their master, their *pir*, or *shaykh*. They do so because they have become convinced that the master can in fact lead them further in their search for God, and lead them to deeper experience of God. And what does the leader offer? What sort of guidance and direction?

Typically, the guidance given will be much more specific and detailed than most Christians might be used to or comfortable with. Just one example is the *dhikr*, or method of prayer and recitation, that masters might instruct their disciples to use.

This will normally include the phrase or phrases or litany of prayers to use in doing *dhikr*, such as repeating the Muslim creed, or repeating one or more or all of the ninety-nine names of God, or repeating a certain combination of them, etc. It will typically also include when to repeat these, and how many times, and in which order or combination.

So one challenge is that the method of discipleship is so different. A second challenge is that leadership is selected differently: based on whether the leader can actually lead another to a deeper experience of God, which presumes that this leader, himself or herself, has such a deeper experience to offer. Yet again, it is in the challenge that I see the opportunity. This challenge may enhance our own discipling of others by adding a dimension of specificity that I, at least, often minimize or even denigrate as potentially legalistic and overly directive. And yet, I have also found disciples among MBBs wanting more specific direction.

Another opportunity I see, as Christian witnesses engage this aspect of Sufism, is that yet again we may be challenged to reexamine our own spiritual depth: What do I really have to offer my disciple? What has my own experience, truly and honestly, been of the intimacy and healing and new life in Christ I claim to offer? Have I, in fact, walked the path to the place where I am claiming to lead my disciple?

Conclusion

When I began to write I was not sure what shape my conclusion might take. I have decided to end without trying to tie everything together. Instead I will pass along a story about Mullah Nasrudin.

Nasrudin was living near the border area between two countries. Every day he crossed the border, with a donkey cart loaded heavily with straw. The border guards began to notice that Nasrudin was adding to his house and improving his lands. They came to suspect that he was profiting somehow by his daily border crossings, and they assumed he must be smuggling something.

Every day they inquired and searched. They probed every grain of straw and every possible hiding place on or under the cart. They searched Nasrudin's clothing. They even explored potential secret hollow places in the wood. But nothing was ever found except the cart, the straw, and the donkey.

Years later when the border guards had retired and Nasrudin had grown old, it so happened that Nasrudin found himself sitting next to one of the guards at a dinner to which they had both been invited. They soon recognized each other, and while sharing stories of the old days the guard asked Nasrudin, "Now I am no longer a guard and there is nothing I can do, so you are safe and free to tell me. What were you smuggling on all those journeys across the border?"

Nasrudin's reply was simple. "I was smuggling donkeys."

As we consider the many challenges that face us when seeking to communicate the gospel to Sufis, we might be well served to keep this story in mind. Among the challenges, perhaps right in front of us are also opportunities. May we have wisdom and insight to look beyond the straw and the cart and find the donkey.

Reflection Questions

1. How has your own spiritual journey prepared you for interaction with, and a sympathetic understanding of, Sufi friends? How widely, and deeply, have you imbibed the spiritual treasury of Christian tradition? Is there anything you feel prompted to do in this area, and if so, what and why?

2. How might your vision for and practice of leadership development and discipleship be shaped by the Sufi (and in many traditions, Christian) practices of spiritual formation, "spiritual direction," and the role of a spiritual guide and mentor in the life of another? How might you seek that out for yourself? Include it in your way of developing and discipling others.

References

Esposito, John L. 1998. *Islam: The Straight Path*. 2nd ed. New York: Oxford University Press.

Greenlee, David, ed. 2015. *Longing for Community*. Pasadena, CA: William Carey Library.

Guillame, Alfred. 1956. *Islam*. New York: Penguin Books.

Harvey, Graham, ed. 2009. *Religions in Focus: A New Approach to Traditional and Contemporary Practices*. Oakville, CT: Equinox Publishing.

Kraft, Kathryn. 2012. *Searching for Heaven in the Real World: A Sociological Discussion of Conversion in the Arab World*. Eugene, OR: Wipf and Stock.

Lapidus, Ira M. 1988. *A History of Islamic Societies*. Cambridge: Cambridge University Press.

Rahman, Falzur. 1979. *Islam*. 2nd ed. Chicago: University of Chicago Press.

Shah, Idries. 1964. *The Sufis*. NY: Anchor Books.

"Sufism." In *The Oxford Dictionary of Islam*. Edited by John L. Esposito. *Oxford Islamic Studies Online*. http://www.oxfordislamicstudies.com/article/opr/t125/e2260.

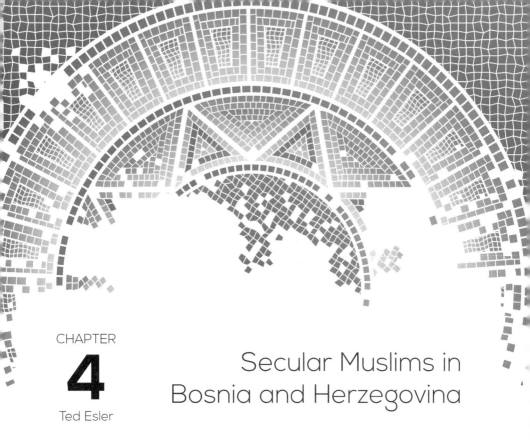

CHAPTER

4

Ted Esler

Secular Muslims in Bosnia and Herzegovina

At the outset of the decade of the 1990s, Bosnian Muslims were regarded as some of the most secular of all Muslims. The unity and representation of multicultural, multireligious harmony displayed at the 1984 Olympic Games testified to the homogenizing influence of the Yugoslavian dream of a nonreligious, nonsectarian, ethnically diverse, united Balkan state. Islamic expression in Sarajevo in 1992 was regarded by most as historical, architectural, and cultural. One third of all marriages in Bosnia and Herzegovina (hereafter just called "Bosnia") were mixed between different religions.

However, like an iceberg on a collision course with an unaware ocean liner, the unseen and deeply embedded ethnic and religious worldviews of the Croats, Serbs, and Bosnian Muslims were hidden beneath the surface. When nationalistic leaders masterfully stirred the historic rivalries between these three groups, Europe's most serious war in a half-century erupted.

The Bosnian War proved that beneath the secular veneer lay a deeply embedded Islamic worldview. Sarajevo today is significantly different than it was in 1990. It is an undeniably Muslim city, and a revival of its Islamic population has pushed secularism back into a corner.

Had it not been prodded and poked into existence, would this form of Islam in Bosnia have reemerged? To be sure, the reasons for the armed conflict were many, prompting the infamous statement, "Yugoslavia is the despair of tidy minds" (Beeson 1982, 228). Yet the rapid rate at which Islam reconstituted itself into what was known as a secularized culture was astounding and calls for a reappraisal of what we mean when we use the phrase "secular Islam."

A good example would be Ahmed, a young secular Muslim man living in Sarajevo when the war broke out. His life had been consumed by Western popular music. He had long hair, wore Levi's, and was working hard to learn English so he could consume more Western pop culture. During the war, he was drafted into the Bosnian army and fought numerous battles. At the end of the war he was a confirmed Muslim. He saw the Croatians and Serbs as Christian combatants against the Bosnian Muslims. Islam became a part of his response as a Bosnian. Ahmed entered the war with what appeared to be a secular mentality, but became a confirmed Muslim during the conflict.

Perhaps the comparison and contrast between prewar Bosnia, with its more or less secular culture, and the Islamic Bosnia following the war can shed light on what is meant by this strange combination of terms: a secular Muslim. This odd-sounding phrase is a poor description for the increasing number of people with Muslim backgrounds who do not practice Islam or embrace its central teachings—in their public behavior—but who, nevertheless, privately or unconsciously hold to a similar worldview as those who do. Many of the same secularizing forces that have created a post-Christian worldview in the West are at work among some Muslim peoples. However, it does not follow that they will take the same path as their Western counterparts in losing their religion.

The Two "Bosnias"

Bosnia, as a part of Yugoslavia before the war, was a prosperous place. Many people had homes in the city and *vikendicas*, or weekend homes, up in the mountains. A lucky few would travel to the Adriatic coast. Unlike most Communist countries, Yugoslavia was not hidden from Europe behind the Iron Curtain. Yugoslavs freely traveled to and from Germany, Austria, and other parts of Europe for both vacation and work. They were provided with a liberal education. Religion was tolerated in Yugoslavia more so than in other Communist bloc countries.

Yugoslavia was also a Communist country. The leaders, while somewhat tolerant, gave little encouragement to people of faith. The 1984 Olympics, held in Sarajevo, were seen as a triumph of multicultural, multireligious society. This was reflected in the behavior of its citizens. A young Yugoslav from Bosnia was just as likely to follow U2's Bono as any other European young person might. It would be easy to assume that theirs was a culture without a strong religious worldview.

Yet soon after the end of the Bosnian War an abrupt change occurred. Despite the overwhelming presence of the international community (particularly through the presence of NATO forces initially and, soon thereafter, the European Community's rebuilding efforts), Bosnia turned toward the East, not the West. Alija Izetbegovic, the new founding president (sometimes referred to as the George Washington of Bosnia), was the founder of the Muslim political party and was himself a devout believer. Islamic institutions quickly rose up and reestablished their presence in Bosnia.

Today the Saudi-funded King Fahd Mosque is emblematic of the many new mosques that have been built throughout the capital city of Sarajevo. There are over half a dozen new madrassas (Qur'anic schools) in the city (Bilefski 2008), and bearded men walk the streets with their wives firmly in lockstep behind them. Streets have been renamed after Muslim heroes. Hundreds of millions of dollars have been spent by Islamic nations to recast Bosnia as an Islamic state, with even some competition between Iranian Shi'ites and Saudi Sunnis.

Researcher Emira Ibrahampasic, in a study of the religious observance of Bosnian women, notes that many Bosnians see this resurgence as a *return*. She writes, "General consensus among devout and observant Muslims defines reislamization as *povratak Islamu* [a return to Islam]—the adoption of proper Islamic rites and duties in daily life, most notably the 5 pillars of Islam" (2012, 77).

The question becomes, "A return from what and why?" A common result of war is widespread social crisis; thus, many Bosnians were compelled to search for a meaningful structure to rebuild their lives. It seems the lifeways of their ancestors were the most accessible, and perhaps the most logical, path to take. Also, the war shattered the illusion of a shared secularist society, thus requiring Bosnians to reinforce ethnic boundaries, and a visible, public expression of Muslim identity served that purpose well. Therefore, in the former, secular Bosnia, it was sufficient for religious convictions to dwell under the surface. In the new Bosnia, these convictions needed to assert themselves, thus affecting behavior.

Secular Muslims versus Nominal Muslims

Islam and contemporary Christianity have fundamentally different approaches to how they see the state's relationship with religion. Foundational to the secular state with a Christian history is the concept of the "separation of church and state." In contrast, Islam has, for most of its history, seen government as a part of its religious expression. Even in secular states where Islam is widely practiced and the government is not considered to be controlled by clerics, we find that Islam has a preferred status in the culture and political system.[1]

---

[1] Turkey provides another example of a *povratak Islamu*, a return to Islam. Current events indicate that Islam may become a bigger influence in the Turkish future.

The term *secular Muslim* takes the issue away from the state/religion context and describes it as a worldview. It juxtaposes two opposites into one descriptor. It no longer refers to nation states but a person's religious beliefs. It is a phrase borrowed from the experience of the Western Christian, predominately in Europe.

Westerners should be cautious about utilizing Western models of worldview in an Islamic context. The popularized view of secularization holds that societies inevitably progress through change that emphasizes rationality and modernization, ultimately leading to a decline in religion in all spheres of life. Even though this is a popular theory, it has not held up to academic scrutiny.[2] Sociologists have put it this way, "The growth of Islam across the world highlights the inadequacies, Eurocentrism, and Christian-centeredness of the secularizing theory" (Sutton and Vertigans 2005, 173).

This suggests that a better label for Bosnians who are not practicing Islam might be "nominal Muslim" instead of "secular Muslim." It better describes the intrinsic worldview as rooted in their Muslim heritage, while at the same time highlighting that the behavior is not reflective of that deeper worldview.

It might, for example, refer to a Bosnian named Adnan. Like his fellow countrymen, he was almost certainly "raised Muslim" and would affirm the shahada (statement of belief in Islam), but is unlikely to attend the mosque regularly or to consider religion as very important to his life.[3] However, he does have an extensive library of Western movies and video games on his computer. And he enjoys soccer, with his favorite team being Manchester United. If pressed, he would call himself a "Muslim," yet Adnan does not know even the most basic Islamic teaching. But it is important to note that he certainly has not embraced an agnostic or atheistic position either.

Secularism has no shahada or "sinner's prayer" that inducts the believer into its ranks. There is typically no moment of conversion, but it is the result of a long process in which layers of belief are replaced with layers of unbelief or, most often, a view that religious ideas are irrelevant. For reasons beyond the scope of this discussion, Christian cultures seem to make room for secularism in ways that Muslim cultures do not. Underlying even the most nominal Muslim's worldview is the ever-present background of upbringing, family ties, and identity, which are never irrelevant. Even though surface behaviors may be lacking, there most often continues to be a deeply embedded Islamic influence.

From a Western perspective, nominalism may appear to be a drift into secularism, but that is a limited understanding of what is happening in the Muslim context. We should not presume the secular Muslim has an indifference toward religious things, as there is with secularism in the West.

---

[2] For a full treatment of this topic, see Stark 2015.

[3] Pew Research Center (2012). Ninety-six percent of Bosnian Muslims affirm the shahada, but only 36 percent say that religion is very important to their life.

For example, imagine that Selma is a twenty-two-year-old woman from Paris. Her family immigrated from Bosnia when she was a young girl. She attended a French school that celebrated the secular, anti-religious sentiment of the Enlightenment. Her friends were a mix of immigrant children and local French schoolmates. Selma's parents divorced, and she was raised in a single-parent home with her mother, who essentially was unwelcome in the local Muslim community due to her ex-husband's influence.

As Selma watches inflamed Muslim agitators flip and burn cars across Paris, she does not feel a part of their movement. She does not speak the language of her native country well and knows little about the Qur'an. The most significant impact that Islam has had on her life has been through the yearly Ramadan festival, which was celebrated in her community and home. At the same time, she is not fully French. Her dark complexion, the location of her neighborhood, and her modest dress all remind the locals that she is a Muslim immigrant. As a college student, she fears being asked about her nationality, while simultaneously avoiding contact with the more devout Muslims who may judge her.

When Selma visits Bosnia, she observes a resurgent Islam. Her female relatives wear hijabs, practice the prayers, and attend the mosque. Her nominal level of observance begins to change, and she becomes more devout as she participates in these activities with her relatives. She hears sermons about the need for Islamic renewal and begins a journey toward deep devotion to Islam.

In this example, we see a woman who came from one of the most secular nations in the world today. But was Selma secular? Not in the sense that many of us might think. Socially, her identity as a Muslim was mostly latent in the secular environment she grew up in, and the Islam she knew exerted little influence on her outward behavior. Yet Selma's growth in Islam is common with some second-generation immigrants who, for various reasons, desire to reconnect with their heritage when given the chance. Thus, when Selma entered an environment in which Islam was routinely observed, those dormant Islamic traditions were kindled.

The Secularization Theory

Sociologists have argued for a theory of secularization in which these forces inexorably march societies toward a less religious worldview. Inglehart and Norris state, "The death of religion was the conventional wisdom in the social sciences during most of the twentieth century; indeed, it has been regarded as *the* master model of sociological inquiry" (2006, 3). This rush to judgment regarding the collapse of religion has been widely discredited by demographic observations and the growth of religions globally. Researcher Philip Jenkins, for example, has made the claim that the twenty-first century will be more religious than the twentieth (2011). Certainly the resurgence of Islam has also contributed to the realization that our future might be more religious, not less.

Sociologists have long sought to understand the secularization process. Initial conclusions have been largely discredited, yet there is some helpful insight in these studies. Bryan Wilson, one of these early researchers, defined secularization in very simple terms as the decline of social significance of religion (1982). José Casanova has noted three distinguishing characteristics of secularization: a decline of religious beliefs and practices, privatization of religion, and differentiation of the secular spheres (2006, 6–7). We will look at each of these in turn.

In Bosnia, the prewar culture was considered to be secular because of the decline of "religious beliefs and practices," as Casanova (2006) describes. Certainly, the roughly forty-five years of Communism played a significant role in this decline of *practice*. Others have additionally suggested that material wealth may lead to a decline in religious observance, and the former Yugoslavia was a relatively affluent East European nation (Pew Research Center 2015). Our fictional Selma was led toward nominalism by the circumstances of immigration to a non-Islamic environment.

The privatization of religion is often understood to be an outcome of pluralism. It might happen when two people of different, and potentially opposing, worldviews encounter each other. Often the result is to avoid the worldview differences. On an individual level, for example, a white male British factory worker might have a colleague on the job who is an immigrant from Muslim Pakistan. In order to have a productive work relationship, neither party discusses their spiritual worldview—it becomes private. On a macro scale, laws regulating religious expression that are "fair" for all inevitably push religion from the public square. This is the paradox of pluralism; differences only exist below the surface in "safer" arenas, such as home and mosque. This phenomenon has accelerated as immigration has grown—particularly in Europe, the most secular of global regions.[4]

The war changed the privatization of Bosnian religious experience and pushed it into a more open aspect of Bosnian identity. The sides were identified by both ethnic and religious identity. In fact, it is hard not to see the war as religiously motivated at some level. After the war concluded, religion could no longer be private. Job opportunities, education, and a host of cultural "gates" were either opened or closed based on one's religion.

The extent to which religion will dominate Bosnia in the future is a matter of debate. A recent court decision made it illegal for women who work in the court system to wear a hijab while fulfilling an official duty for the court (Bhutia and Porter 2016). This led to large protests against this accommodation to non-Muslim citizens (the hijab was considered to influence the court's neutrality). Nevertheless, before the war this issue would never have surfaced because so few women wore the hijab. Thus, the war has had a significant influence on the extent of public expressions of religion.

---

[4] For a discussion on the incompatible nature of Islam and private religious practice, see "Believing Without Belonging: Just How Secular Is Europe?" Conference Proceeding Transcript, Pew Forum 2005. Accessed August 11, 2015. http://www.pewforum.org/2005/12/05/believing-without-belonging-just-how-secular-is-europe/.

It is also worthwhile to note the resistance to secularization that Muslim immigrants have shown in Europe. A 2006 survey indicated that most European Muslims identified first with Islam and only secondarily with their country of residence. The authors summarize their findings by stating, "Religion is central to the identity of European Muslims … they tend to identify themselves primarily as Muslim rather than as British, Spanish, or German" (Pew Research Center). These issues of identity reveal a deeper connection to an Islamic worldview despite the secular context in which immigrants live.

Thus, the secularizing theory, while applicable to peoples rooted in a Western worldview, has little application for Muslims. It may be better to call these nonobservant Muslims nominal, not secular. This term better captures the distinction between a lack of behavior versus a lack of belief.

Sharing Jesus in the Bosnian Context

The Bosnian War led to many nominal Muslims rediscovering their faith. If one strolled down the main streets of Sarajevo in 1990 there would be virtually no women wearing traditional Islamic clothing. Today it is common. Islam has risen from a discarded religion to one of great prominence in the daily life of most Bosnians. How does one swim upstream in this sea of advancing Islam?

We should remember that the Bosnian experience is not a singular example of a culture in great distress that returned to its Islamic roots. Despite the resurgence of Islam in Iran and North Africa, Christian efforts in both of these places are also experiencing success. Globally it appears that while Islam is revitalizing there is a corollary interest in Jesus on a scale not seen before.

It could be that these efforts may have the reverse effect of their desired outcomes: Secular Muslims may be encouraged to rediscover their Islamic roots. This could also shed some light on how best to reach secular Bosnia Muslims with the gospel.

Secularism Is Not a Worldview

In a 2011 Pew Research study, evangelical leaders viewed secularism as the single greatest threat to evangelicalism globally. Leaders from North America, Europe, and Latin America all ranked the threat higher than consumerism, sex, violence, and Islam.

Yet secularism alone is not a hegemonic religious worldview—it does not seek to answer life's questions, gather people of like views together, rally support around a singular leader or set of beliefs, or follow other conventional manifestations of religion. Rather, it simply exists as the absence of a religious worldview. It always pairs with some other belief system. Perhaps this should cause us to reconsider giving secularism the status of "worldview"[5] at all. It is primarily the absence of religion, not a cohesive belief system. Thus, while it offers a challenge to Christianity, it is not at

---

[5] Secular humanism has arisen as a formal religion for secular followers. It has attempted to form itself as a religious movement. However, the vast majority of people whom we would consider to be "secular" would not affiliate themselves with secular humanism.

all similar to the challenges brought about by Islam, Buddhism, Hinduism, and other systems of belief. It might be more productive to consider the effects on people and culture that secularism introduces.

Loss of Community

Rising secularism brings about a number of changes that threaten the status quo of the culture in which it is growing. These changes are not necessarily causal; it is a chicken-and-egg question as to whether these create secularism or vice versa. These effects can be particularly devastating to traditional Muslim societies.

The most obvious of these is a breakdown of the traditional family. In almost all countries that have gone through a Christian to secular transformation, the traditional family structure has suffered. Falling birth rates, a reliance on social welfare systems instead of family, singleness, and liberal sexual mores are all a part of this endemic loss of family life in secular cultures. Eberstadt writes, "In Western Europe, nearly one home in three (32%) is already a one-person unit, while in autonomy-prizing Denmark the number exceeds 45%" (2015).

Additionally, individualism in secular societies is also a challenge to more communal cultures. A focus on the individual is, of course, a key feature of the Enlightenment. These two realities from secular culture (the demise of the traditional family and individualism) often combine to cause a crisis of identity for most religiously minded people and particularly for those coming from a Muslim background.

In working with largely nominal Muslims in Bosnia, I found that the loss of family and community ties have already led them to the conclusion that a religious worldview holds more promise than a secular worldview. This may be one reason why Islam so quickly reinserted itself in the Balkans. People did not need an apologetics course to see that faith should be a part of one's life. They sensed the loss of community and sought to rediscover it in the mosque.

Jesus' ministry has much to say about the family and its importance. Jesus himself knew what it was to be forsaken and could identify with a person struggling with loneliness (Matt 27:46). His unblemished record of holiness speaks to those living in an age when nobody is considered righteous. These are all significant ways that Jesus' life speaks to a secular culture, Islamic or otherwise.

Lack of the Sacred

Secularism also oftentimes creates *a longing for the sacred*. In a secular worldview, pragmatism reigns. Only that which can be objectively verified is true. There is no concept of sin, eternity, or the soul. There is no value for human life. Beauty loses meaning, since it is neither transcendent nor purposeful. Holiness has no place, and reverence for anything mystical is missing. There is simply no room for the sacred.

I was once leading a Bible study in a Sarajevo apartment building with a group of young Bosnian college students. They were, by all appearances, not practicing

Muslims. At one point, a Bible was set on the floor. These young, nominal Muslims gasped and immediately lifted the book off the floor. Despite their secular orientation, they immediately objected that it was a holy book and deserved to be treated with respect. It was sacred. Secularism had not erased this concept from their psyche in the way that it has for nonpracticing Christians in the West.

Similarly, of course, the Qur'an must be carefully handled. A mosque is a place of God's presence. There is reverence for the prophets and a caution in discussing them. A person with even minimal connections to Islam will often find the secular worldview to be profane. They will not be satisfied with the naturalistic worldview that is reductionist and amoral. The holes produced by secularism are evident to the nominal Muslim.

Finding Solace in an Islamic Identity

The shortest path to a nominal Muslim's heart might actually be through Mecca. The suggestion here is not that the person must embrace Islam on their way to understanding the gospel. Rather, there is an echo of an Islamic worldview that will resonate with them when they hear of Jesus and begin to learn more about him. A person whose secularism is challenged will often pivot to their Muslim cultural heritage and identification rather than see themselves as nonbelievers with no faith. It may lead them to lean into their Islamic background more heavily.

For this reason, it is important to be aware of how to best communicate the gospel to a Muslim, not simply a secular Muslim. One should have a clear understanding of Islamic beliefs about Muhammed, how Muslims view the Bible, how the Bible has come to us over the centuries, answers to challenges regarding the crucifixion of Jesus and a readiness to discuss the Trinity. These are foundational topics that many Muslims, secular or not, will want to discuss.

I noticed a pattern in my multiple conversations with secular Muslims in Bosnia. If interested in Jesus, a secular Muslim will ask many questions and seek to learn as much as possible. As Jesus' message begins to confront their worldview and any solace they derive from a "Muslim" identity, the person would go to the mosque and begin to ask the imam about these issues. Then, in subsequent conversation, the discussion would turn to standard Islamic arguments given by Muslims against Christianity. This is why, despite the appearance of secularity, the evangelist should be aware of these issues and ready to discuss them.[6]

Reaching Nominal Bosnian Muslims with the Gospel

Here are three principles to guide an approach to communicating about Jesus with nominal Bosnian Muslims, and which may apply to other Muslims as well.

---

[6] There is a potential problem, however, if one relies on argumentation. This will have a tendency to push people further from Christ rather than pull them into a relationship with Jesus.

Live in transparent Christian community

Jesus did not dispense a lot of methodology in his ministry. One thing he did say was, "A new commandment I give to you, that you love one another: just as I have loved you, you also are to love one another. By this all people will know that you are my disciples, if you have love for one another" (John 13:34–35 ESV). The way that others are to know that you are a disciple of Jesus is for them to observe the kingdom relationships between believers.

We have already mentioned that secularism challenges relationships in the family and community. Transparently living in relationship with other Christians while allowing Muslim friends into the inner circles of those relationships is a strong evangelistic tool. Often Christians live dual lives; they have Christian friends with whom they are intimate, and then they have those who are more the object or goal of their outreach. This keeps those on the outside from seeing the power of the Holy Spirit work in relationships.

Accept that conversion is a process

Western Christians, particularly in the last generation, were likely to see evangelism as a call to decision. For a secular Muslim, being challenged to make a decision without adequate time to understand and process the ramifications of those decisions may create a serious misunderstanding about the gospel.

A secular Muslim may have to first want to discuss secular objections to religion before discussing the specifics of either Christ or Islam. Do not assume, even from the most educated secularists, that they have any biblical literacy.

A French secular person once asked a friend who was talking about his faith, "Have you never heard of the Enlightenment and what it did to religious belief?"

My friend replied, "Of course I have, but have you been made aware of the Reformation?"

This sophisticated French intellectual had never learned about the Reformation, and this interaction opened a door for further interaction.

In the past few years, the chronological Bible story method has become widely used in outreach with Muslims. This is an excellent strategy to use with secular Muslims. Be careful, however, not to simply take the same material and approach that is being used broadly and attempt to apply it with secular Muslims. The repetitive nature of stories made for oral cultures will not always work in highly educated modern contexts. Carefully think through the Socratic discussion method and adjust it for the context in which you find yourself. The parables of Jesus make for good material to discuss in both a group setting and a one-on-one encounter.

Recognize that as a part of the process of evangelism you might be awakening latent Islamic influences. Don't fear this, but instead recognize it as a positive sign of spiritual seeking. If you attempt to "close the deal" before the Holy Spirit has worked in a person's heart you might inadvertently leave them at this point in their process.

Show honor to the person

A positive contribution that secularism has given to humanity is respect for each individual. This was a result of the Enlightenment's emphasis on individuality and is, for the most part, in alignment with Christianity's emphasis on the dignity of each person. It is, however, imbued with the guilt/shame paradigm in contemporary Western culture.

Though secular Muslims will have an expectation of respect in the Western sense, most also labor under an honor/shame paradigm.

Fikret was a young Bosnian college student. He didn't have an appreciation for Islam until soon after meeting new Christian friends at a local café. A group had formed with the intent of studying the teachings of Jesus. During the ensuing weeks they had discussed Jesus' parables, and Fikret was very interested in Jesus. One week Jesus' ancestry was mentioned, and a debate about Jews began. Fikret tried to explain the position that most Muslims hold regarding the Jewish occupation of Palestine. The Christian leader, in an effort to pursue a robust dialogue about the issue, made the counterpoint that the Jews had been there before the Muslims. A sharp and pointed argument began.

At one point the Christian leader said that Jesus was a Jew, and even the Qur'an speaks highly of Jesus. It was an unassailable point that Fikret could not dispute. He never returned to the discussion group because he had been shamed in the unplanned and unscripted group setting. Fikret felt that there was a lack of honor in the exchange; there was no way "out," and therefore he had lost face before others. While the point was correct and made with the goal of bringing truth to the discussion, it cut off the possibility of further relationship.

From the standpoint of an honor/shame culture, the Palestinian situation is intractable. It highlights decades of public shaming of Muslims by the Western powers. Fikret's story highlights the danger of having a Socratic dialogue (a Western way of discussing something) in an honor/shame context. While secular on the surface, Fikret's underlying worldview remains tied to his Islamic background.

Conclusion: Is Bosnia Unique?

A quick glance at history reveals that the experience of the Bosnian culture's rapid transformation is not unique. The Iranian revolution in the late 1970s is an obvious example. More recently, the changes in Turkey may yield a much more muscular Islamic presence in a country long touted as an example of a secular Islamic state. At this point in history, the notion that secularism will displace Islam as it has in Christian Europe is dubious at best.

It would be a mistake to conclude that the absence of outward religious piety among so-called "secular Muslims" always means they do not retain deeply embedded elements of an Islamic worldview. The predictions of the secularization theory have proven to be false in the West and much more so among Muslim people.

Christians who live and work among nominal Muslims such as those in Bosnia need to take their religious heritage seriously in order to communicate appropriately and effectively the life and message of Jesus. However, this understanding is only a starting point. Life-on-life exposure to the kingdom of God in Christian relationships is perhaps the most powerful tool in the Christian's arsenal. In making this observation, it is clear that what the New Testament apostles taught and practiced regarding the spread of the gospel message is as true today, among "secular" Muslims, as it was then among the Roman citizenry.

Reflection Questions

1. How would you describe "secularism" as being different from "nominalism"?

2. How do you think that nominal Muslims (those who are not showing outward expressions of their belief system) are similar to or different than nominal Christians?

3. In the New Testament, can you think of any mention of nominalism or people that held nominal religious views? (Cross-reference Luke 8:13, Luke 6:47–49, Matthew 25:1–13, 1 John 2:19, and 1 Corinthians 5:11 as possible examples.)

References

Beeson, Trevor. 1982. *Discretion and Valour: Religious Conditions in Russia and Eastern Europe*. Minneapolis: Augsburg Fortress Publishing.

Bhutia, Jigmey, and Tom Porter. "Around 2,000 Women Protest Hijab Ban." *International Business Times*, February 8, 2016. http://www.ibtimes.co.uk/around-2000-women-protest-hijab-ban-bosnia-1542501.

Bilefski, Dan. 2008. "Islamic Revival Tests Bosnia's Secular Cast." *New York Times*, December 26. http://www.nytimes.com/2008/12/27/world/europe/27islam.html?_r=0.

Casanova, Jose. 2006. "Rethinking Secularization: A Global Comparative Perspective." *Hedgehog Review* 8: 7–22.

Eberstadt, Nicholas. 2015. "The Global Flight from the Family." *The Wall Street Journal*, February 21. https://www.aei.org/publication/global-flight-family/.

Ibrahimpasic, Emira. 2012. "Women Living Islam in Post-War and Post-Socialist Bosnia and Herzegovina." PhD diss., University of New Mexico.

Inglehart, Ronald, and Pippa Norris. 2006. *Sacred and Secular: Religion and Politics Worldwide*. Cambridge: Cambridge University Press.

Jenkins, Philip. 2011. *The Next Christendom: The Coming of Global Christianity*. Oxford: Oxford University Press.

Pew Research Center. 2006. "Muslims in Europe: Economic Worries Top Concerns About Religious and Cultural Identity." *Pew Research Center*, July 6. http://www.pewforum.org/2011/06/22/global-survey-tensions/.

———. 2011. "Tensions with Secularism and Modernity." *Pew Research Center*, June 22. http://www.pewforum.org/2011/06/22/global-survey-tensions/.

———. 2015. "Wealthier Nations Less Religious; U.S. an Exception." *Pew Research Center*, March 12. http://www.pewresearch.org/fact-tank/2015/03/12/how-do-americans-stand-out-from-the-rest-of-the-world/ft_15-03-10_religiousgdpscatter/.

Stark, Rodney. 2015. *The Triumph of Faith: Why the World Is More Religious than Ever*. Wilmington, DE: ISI Books.

Sutton, Philip W., and Stephen Vertigans. 2005. *Resurgent Islam: A Sociological Approach*. Cambridge: Polity.

Wilson, Bryan. 1982. *Religion in Sociological Perspective*. Oxford: Oxford University Press.

Egalité, Fraternité, and Cous-cous: Ministry to Muslims in the Context of a Resurgent Islam and French *Laïcité*

The recent surge in Muslim violence and consequential rise in Islamophobia over the last decade or so in France has been sparked in part by conflict over the role of religion in the public sphere and a global resurgence of Islamic radicalism. Though this relatively recent state of affairs can be associated with the passing of legislation in 2010 banning such things as wearing the Muslim veil in public and various attacks by Islamists that have plagued the country in the years following, it must be remembered that France's history with Islam is long and has been fraught with conflict from the very beginning. These current conflicts do not hinge so much on the issue of political and military confrontation as much as on a conflict of ideals.[1] The Muslim worldview, which demands the legitimacy of public religious practice, is a direct affront to France's official position and commitment to a strict separation of church and state summed up under its unique understanding of *laïcité* (secularism).

Historical Conflicts with Islam

France's first real encounter with Muslims can be traced beyond the era of the Crusades (Morrison 1969, 5) to the famous Battle of Tours (732 AD). It is here that Charles Martel is credited with turning back the invasion of the Arab forces of the Abayyad Caliphate under the leadership of Abdul Rahman Al Ghafiqi. Though this battle put a stop to Islamic advance in France, Islam did not disappear from the European theater.

By the middle of the eleventh century, the relationship between Christian and Muslim entities had reached a tipping point. Fueled by the ambitions of the emir, the Seljuk Turks extended their reach over vast areas of Central Asia and provoked a growing anxiety over the possible collapse of the Byzantine Empire. Despite theological differences that divided the Eastern and Western branches of the church, in 1095 AD the Byzantine emperor made an appeal to Pope Urban II for help to fend off the Muslim forces threatening stability to a shrinking Christian presence in the East. In response to this appeal, Urban called for a holy crusade for the purpose of coming to the aid of Christian brothers and sisters living under the menacing advance of the Seljuk Muslim Turks.

It is not insignificant that this first of eight religio-military expeditions (which later became known as the "Crusades") originated in Clermont, France. For although the Crusades

> had their origins in every region of Europe, from Portugal all the way to Lithuania, they were principally and essentially a French enterprise. Thanks to this influence, France became the center of European politics: the most powerful and influential State on the continent. Yet France came out of it bloodied by the Crusades, having lost more human lives than all the other countries of the Christian West together. (Santosuosso 2004, 217)

Furthermore, the Crusades sought not to convert, but to eradicate heretics or to conquer holy places—in other words, to expel and win, but not to convince. Thus they further fueled antagonism and mistrust between Muslims and Christians (Roy 2010, 42–43).

Colonialism, Immigration, and Islam

France's current relationship with Muslims is largely the fruit of its colonial expansion dating from the early to mid-1800s, which brought the Maghrebi regions of northern Africa—in particular, Morocco, Tunisia, and Algeria—into the Francophone world. This colonial presence led to waves of immigration following each of the major wars

---

[1] While not the root cause, the impact of France's involvement in the Gulf wars and NATO conflicts in Iraq and Afghanistan is not irrelevant.

in the last 150 years, by which France initially replenished a gutted labor pool to fuel its recovery and later economic expansion.

Throughout the decades of the 1960s and 1970s, France struggled to manage the politics and logistics of immigration and its burgeoning immigrant population. Interestingly, it was not until the 1970s that the issues surrounding cultural and religious differences between persons of Maghrebi background and the French began to draw the attention of French lawmakers, political and social scientists, and the Roman Catholic Church. All this began to change, however, in 1976, when France adopted a new policy allowing certain immigrants to legally bring their families to live with them in France.[2] This policy of *regroupement familial* (family unification) allowed thousands of North African wives and children to join their laborer fathers, brothers, and uncles and take up residency in France.

Islam and the Second- and Third-generation Immigrant

By the 1980s, the resident population of people of Maghrebi[3] background had given birth to a sizeable second generation. These sons and daughters of immigrant laborers, or offspring of mixed marriages, found themselves confronted with a new and pressing problem—identity:

> "When I visit my family in Morocco, they refer to me as 'Whitey' or 'Frenchy' (a reference to my unconsciously adopted habits, accent, and outlook which I have taken on from my French home), and when I am in France they call me an Arab (meaning liar, criminal, and undesirable). I'm too French to fit in with my family of origin and too Arab to fit in with my French surroundings. I don't know who I am or where I fit."[4]

For many, the difference between the world at home, where traditional values were strictly maintained, and the public world, where liberal morals were encouraged and religious faith ridiculed, was too great and too complex to navigate. Added to this difficult context were the temptations and stresses of life often lived in run-down housing complexes marked by drugs and violence. Over the last several decades, an appeal to Islamic traditions was introduced into this volatile mix in an effort to restore an identity to a generation of Muslims torn between its Maghrebi background and its adopted secular-society home. In many of the large housing complexes across France, fundamentalist imams and self-appointed spiritual advisors have sought to reconnect the youth of the banlieux (suburbs) to their Islamic heritage through the

---

[2] Based on preconditions of having adequate lodging and financial resources.

[3] Charles and Lahouri 2003. Not all Muslims in France are of Maghrebi background. According to a report issued by the Ministère des Affaires Etrangères et Européennes, 2007, significant numbers of Muslims from Turkey, Ivory Coast, Cameroon, Lebanon, and the Middle East are also present and active in France. However, the vast majority of Muslims—more than 80 percent—are from the Maghrebi regions of North Africa.

[4] This quote is a compilation of comments, as opposed to a direct quote from one individual, heard and read from people of Maghrebi background living in France. It is in quotes as it represents the collective voice of the second-generation person of Maghrebi background living in France.

creation of neighborhood associations, organization of prayer rooms and mosques, and celebration of Islamic festivals (notably Ramadan and *Eïd al-Fitr* and *Eïd al-Adha*).

In addition to these efforts, the rise of religious behavior of Muslim immigrants in France can be partly attributed to the following:

- The fact that mosque construction has taken a front seat in the Muslim agenda in France beginning in the 1980s. In June 2010 the rector of the Grande Mosquée de Paris declared that the number of mosques in France must double from approximately two thousand in 2010 to some four thousand to accommodate the growing number of practicing Muslims (Chazan, 2015).

- In 2003 the *Conseil Français du Culte Musulman* (CFCM) was founded in an effort to have a unified body to represent the various groups of Muslims in France. The CFCM, representing over four million Muslims, seeks to address issues such as the construction of mosques, the training of imams, and the regulation of businesses related to halal products.

The increase in religious activity and identity among immigrants has been the subject of numerous studies.[5] For the largely Muslim immigrant population in France (and across Europe in general), this revival of interest and intentional religious identity has been marked by several publicly visible elements. First is the above-mentioned construction of new mosques and local prayer rooms. Second, more Muslim men and women are wearing Muslim apparel and other religious symbols in public. Third, a larger and more sophisticated commerce has developed built around Muslim products and services.[6] Finally, in order to assure the transmission of the faith to subsequent generations, the CFCM has encouraged the establishment of religious organizations such as youth clubs, associations, and Islamic schools, as well as the increased publication of Islamic materials (i.e., books and DVDs) for adults and children.

The Rise of Salafism

One of the growing expressions of Islamic faith currently is a fundamentalist movement known as Salafism,[7] which has as its aim to return to an understanding and practice of Islam that is derived directly from the "pious ancestors" of the faith (Adraoui 2014; Amghar 2008, 2011; Gouëset 2015). Salafism first emerged in the 1900s as an intellectual movement at the al-Azhar University in Egypt. It was later embraced and financed by Saudi Arabia, who exported the ideology in an effort to head off what they called a corruption of Islam through the modern influence of "other" (largely Western) societies and cultures (Stanley 2005). Salafist proponents increasingly claim to represent

---

[5] Including those by the Pew Research Foundation, The Center for Immigration at the University of Houston, and the European Values Systems Study Group.

[6] These range from housewares and halal foods to dating services, counseling practices, and travel companies specializing in the hajj.

[7] According to Amghar (2011), Salafism has risen dramatically in France over the last couple of decades. Estimates suggest that the movement counts nearly fifteen thousand adherents (a threefold increase since 2004) who frequent some one hundred mosques scattered across the country.

a "purified" minority within Islam that alone possesses the truth, which makes them far superior to any "others"—be they Jews, Christians, or even other Muslims.

Salafists, with their literalist interpretation of the Qur'an, have become a common spectacle in France and can be identified by their appearance: Men do not shave their beards and fit their pants into socks so they do not go lower than their ankles, and women are veiled and cover their bodies in abayas or hijabs.

It should be noted that most Salafists[8] in France consider themselves to be "pacifists" or "quietists" who reject the idea of armed jihad (Adraoui 2014, Gouëset 2015). "Nevertheless, their approach to the texts is extremely literal and functions according the principles of Sharia law. And though Salafism does not systematically lead to physical violence, it is necessary to remember that today's neo-Salafism can be a gateway" (Seniguer, quoted in Euro-Islam 2015). This is best exemplified by Mohamed Merah, who became interested in Salafism before he killed seven people in Toulouse in 2012, and again by those who carried out the attacks across Paris in November 2015 that left 130 dead and over 400 injured—attacks celebrated by Salafist leaders across the Muslim world (Middle East Media 2015).

The Toulouse incident was sandwiched between a January 2015 attack on the Charlie Hebdo offices in Paris, which left more than twelve dead—including eight journalists, singled out apparently for their cartoon depiction of Mohammad. In an attack attributed to an ISIS sympathizer, Mohamed Lahouaiej-Bouhlel, a delivery-type truck was driven through the crowds of locals and tourists celebrating Bastille Day, killing eighty-six and injuring hundreds more. This series of incidents, despite the claims of certain experts who argue that Salafism is a nonviolent ideology and that it should not be confused with jihadi terrorism (Gouëset 2015), has nevertheless fueled a growing distrust of Islam in general, renewed calls for increased national security, and fanned the rhetoric of conservative political positions against nonintegrationist practices (Poirette et Baudin 2016).

Islam and *Laïcité* in Conflict

Despite the fact that Muslims who actively practice Islam make up a relatively small minority of France's overall population,[9] this revival of Islamic identity and practice promotes values that are foreign to those of French culture. It is therefore particularly troublesome for those charged with political oversight of an increasingly multicultural, multiethnic, and religiously plural constituency.

---

[8] According to Adraoui (2014), Salafism can be divided into three separate and conflicting currents. The "Jihadists" intend to restore an Islamic state. The "Reformists" seek to enlarge their influence through engagement in state politics. Finally, the "Purists" avoid activism of any kind and focus on nonmilitant religiosity.

[9] Making use of the figures presented by the two studies mentioned later in this chapter, a population of 6 million Muslims (which maybe be generous) multiplied by the level of participation of 20 percent (which is the percentage said to attend the mosque at least twice per month) puts the number of "practicing" Muslims in France at 1.2 million among a total French population of nearly 70 million.

What troubles the French more than anything in this discussion of religious identity and activity is the pressure such religious display puts on the limits of *laïcité*. The framers and defenders of the law of 1905, which established the permanent break between the church and the state, attempted to make clear that the law was not intended to suffocate or eliminate religious identity or activity. Their prime objective was to remove state influence from the church, and vice versa, and to remove religious life from the public sphere so as to relegate it to the private one. In so doing they intended to level the playing field for faith expressions other than Catholic, by removing direct privileges and government control of religious affairs.

However, while French Catholicism allows for a divide between the sacred the secular, Islam does not (Fregosi 2008, 36). According to a 2008 study conducted by *l'Institut National d'Etudes Démographiques* (INED), for the great majority of French Catholics religious identity (private affiliation) requires no corresponding regular (public) religious activity to be associated with it.[10] How very different from an Islam in which the religious life is woven into the entire daily routine and involves such things as daily prayers (five times a day), dietary restrictions (no pork or alcohol), modest apparel (especially for women), and traditional gender roles in the home and workplace.

Ministry to Muslims in Response to Islamic Resurgence

The last several decades have seen an increase in mission activity, which focused on Muslims in general and people of Maghrebi background in particular—both in the Maghrebi countries of Algeria, Morocco, and Tunisia, as well as in France. Though there is room for additional study in regard to the effect of the civil war in Algeria (1991–2002) on religious sentiment toward Islam, both popular media and academic sources recount the increased incidence of conversion to Christianity among people of Maghrebi background following this period (Kefi 2005). Though a cause and effect relationship of increased mission activity to reported increased numbers of Muslim converts has not been established, it has resulted in the development of specialized mission-related resources (such as language-specific radio programs and printed materials) and a heightened mission interest in the people of Maghrebi background.

A Brief Overview of Protestant Mission Efforts

Early Protestant missionary efforts in the Maghrebi regions of North Africa in the mid to late 1800s found expression in the establishment of orphanages, schools, and medical clinics and assisted with community and agricultural development, with a particular focus on helping the poor. Despite their contributions to the welfare of the local populace, Protestant missionaries, in contrast to their Catholic counterparts, were often discouraged by French authorities. They feared the Protestant missiological approach

---

[10] More than 95 percent of French between the ages of 65–79 and 88 percent between the ages of 18–24 declare themselves to be Catholic, but less than 10 percent attend Mass at least twice a month.

(which was unencumbered with political ties) involved activities that could potentially upset local Muslims and, as a result, negatively weigh on Franco-Maghrebi relations.

Mission activity in the Maghrebi regions of North Africa continued throughout the nineteenth and twentieth century with little fanfare. A review of Protestant mission history in these regions would highlight women such as Lillias Trotter[11] and Daisy Marsh,[12] although the names of many others are forgotten beyond the memories of family and friends. Then, in the late 1970s and early 1980s, a new awareness of the Arab-Muslim world was spawned by the Middle East oil embargo of 1973–1974 (Trumbore 2002) and the Iranian revolution of 1979 (Smitha). This sparked an increased interest in mission efforts directed toward Muslims. A new crop of missionaries prepared and left for service in Muslim lands, including the Maghrebi regions of North Africa. A decade later, with renewed focus on people groups and their place in the "10/40 Window,"[13] another wave of missionaries went to Europe, but with a focus on immigrant populations of Hindus, Muslims, and East Asians.

Current Ministry Models

Ministry directed at Muslims in France is currently enjoying a renaissance of sorts fueled by contributions from several entities: North American missions, French missions, French evangelical Protestant churches, and Muslim-background believers themselves. Each of these sources of mission activity contributes uniquely to a growing pool of evangelical resources and an increasingly visible population of Christians of Maghrebi background.

North American missions

A shift in missions understanding, from geography to people groups, helped fuel an increase in mission efforts directed at Muslims in Europe. In response to this perceived new opportunity, in the 1980s and 1990s several non-French mission agencies established bases of operations in France for the purpose of conducting mission activity among people of Maghrebi background.

The arrival of American missionaries, in particular, brought a new focus on forming ethnic-specific churches among the emerging population of CMB (Christians of Maghrebi background) as an outgrowth of the homogeneous-unit principle of church planting developed by Donald McGavran (1955; McGavran and Wagner, 1990). However, there

---

[11] Blandenier (2003, 471–72). Lilias Trotter first went to Algeria as a self-funded missionary. In 1888 she founded the Algiers Mission Band, which became Arab World Missions in the 1960s. She died in 1928 in Algiers, Algeria.

[12] Banaat (2006, 1–2). Daisy Marsh, raised in Algeria by British missionary parents, studied nursing in London before returning to minister to Kabyle Berber peoples in Marseille, France, in 1972. Her knowledge of the Kabyle Berber language enabled her to prepare radio programs for the Kabyle Berbers of Algeria from 1973–90.

[13] Joshua Project n.d. The term "10/40 Window" was coined by Christian missionary strategist Luis Bush in 1990 to refer to regions of the eastern hemisphere located between 10 and 40 degrees north of the equator, a general area that in 1990 was purported to have the highest level of socioeconomic challenges and least access to the Christian message and Christian resources on the planet.

are only a few Maghrebi ethnic churches; most CMB attempt to integrate into the general population of the French evangelical Protestant church (FEPC).

Furthermore, due to cultural clashes in the early to mid 2000s that raised the profile of Muslim immigrant communities in Europe, a number of North American missions that had previously worked with non-Muslim European populations began adding expertise and allocating resources directed at Muslim immigrants.[14]

French missions

Though North American mission agencies number in the dozens, if not hundreds, agencies organized and directed by French evangelicals are few. Also, French missions, such as *Mission Evangélique parmi les Nord Africains* (MENA), generally pursue a mission strategy seeking the successful integration of Muslim converts into existing French evangelical churches. Besides identifying, preparing, and sending missionaries to the Muslim world, MENA works closely with French churches to equip and mobilize their members for ministry among Muslims locally. Their strategy includes cultivating both intercessory prayer and a practical love for Muslims that can move them toward an open hearing of the gospel message.

French Evangelical Protestant churches

Though the evangelical church in France remains relatively small, it is growing. In 1960, evangelicals in France were estimated to number 100,000 (Nicole 1962, 20; Fath 2005, 185), but by 2005 they had grown to approximately 350,000, according to Fath (ibid,, 214).[15] Mixed in with this changing religious demographic are the immigrants of the Maghreb. Government demographics indicate that virtually every reasonably sized city in France has a sizeable population of them. Over time, members of local churches come into contact with some of these immigrants quite naturally at work, school, or any number of public situations. Furthermore, if the local church is involved in social assistance in any form, it will invariably have contact with Muslim immigrants who have personal and social needs. One of the very encouraging results of this is that both popular media (Kéfi 2005; Fdesouche 2014; Lekdja 2001) and academic studies (Kronk 2016; Fath 2005; Reisacher 2001) provide evidence to suggest that immigrants of Maghrebi background are coming to faith in Christ at an increasing rate due to the increased contact between them and members of evangelical churches. Recent research indicates that Christians of Maghrebi background cite contact with a local French evangelical Protestant church (FEPC) and contact with a Christian friend or family member as the most significant catalysts to conversion (Kronk 2016, 173).

An example of how the gospel is at work among people of Maghrebi background people in France is clear from this testimony of a young man, Mohammad, from Paris.

---

[14] TEAM and Greater Europe Mission are good examples of this.
[15] Daniel Lieschti (2012, 1, 11) puts the number of evangelicals in France at 450,000.

When I was about eighteen years old I went through one of those "adolescent crises" surrounding my cultural identity. Though I had grown up in France and had a French education, I really didn't know if I was French, Arab, or Berber. I was unbalanced. At some point, I met a Catholic priest who was very involved in social causes who did lots of things with youth—like me. I began to hang out with him and the others in the "group," and I began to feel part of them, kind of like a new family. We were all kind of "hippies," and we had a certain friendship for each other. But I soon became involved with drugs and alcohol. I wasn't at all satisfied with my life and I had no interest in spiritual or religious things, neither the Christianity of this priest nor the Islam of my parents.

I started to read the Qur'an and get familiar with the doctrine of Islam. I tried to practice my faith. My objective was to somehow find peace for myself. I also took an interest in other religions—but they all said they were the "truth," and that bothered me. Nevertheless, this only motivated me more to find the "real" truth.

At some point in time, I finally cried out to God and said, "God, if you exist, show me the truth." I was living in Grenoble at the time, and one day as I was walking through one of the main plazas in the downtown area I saw a group of Christians singing and talking to people around them about Jesus. They really had this shining joy. After they sang they went over to the people who were listening to tell them about Jesus.

One day, not too long afterward, one of the guys I met from that singing group spoke to me about John 14:6, where Jesus says, "I am the way, the truth, and the life. No one comes to the Father but my me." There, all of a sudden, I saw a response to my prayer. Perhaps Jesus was truly the truth that I had been seeking.

Within days, I came across another group from a local church that was singing and talking to the people that gathered around them. One of the singers came over to me—he kind of looked like a person of Maghrebi background—to talk about Jesus. He invited me to a church conference dealing with cults and the gospel. The next day, I went to the church where the conference was being held and I heard people singing. It was like a wave of joy and light swept over me all at once. I was struck by the power of what I was hearing and feeling. The people in the church were singing as if the Lord was really right there with them. I was impressed. It was in that conference that I discovered the Bible, and it opened my eyes. And there again, I saw that God had answered my prayer. When the speaker asked if anyone wanted to accept Jesus, he asked that we raise our hand and stand up. And so I did. I stood up and I went to the front of the church, and I received an incredible joy.

Several weeks later, I was able to buy my own Bible and I began to read it. As I read the Old Testament, I was deeply touched by the stories, especially those in Genesis. I began to attend the church that hosted the conference. There, in that place, I was able to find my identity in Christ as part of the body of Christ. Nevertheless, the more time I spent in this church, the more I felt certain racism and a sense of inferiority as a Christian of Maghrebi background. The people in the church didn't understand my culture or the issues associated with my Muslim background. Within two years I left that church for another, smaller one, with the hopes of finding a true spiritual family.

The story of this young man highlights several common characteristics that emerge from the growing number of conversion stories of CMBs in France.

First, people of Maghrebi background have a powerful sense of confused identity. As young Mohammad noted above, though he had grown up in France and had received a French education, he still did not really know who he was. This sense of confused identity leads many, like Mohammad, to seek internal peace wherever they can find it—in religion, in politics, or in self-destructive behaviors.

Second, this search for identity leads many to seek answers to ultimate questions. Due to the pluralistic religious context of France, this quest can lead the seeker to explore his or her own religious roots in light of other religious options, such as Christianity.

Third, meaningful contact with a local church is often a critical component in the conversion process. In Mohammad's story, hearing Christians singing and seeing their joy had a significant impact on him.

Fourth, Mohammad's search was enhanced by the forging of a relationship with a Christian who spoke to him of Jesus and extended an invitation to him to another church event.

Fifth, because of the prominent role of the church in the conversion process, initial affiliation with a local church is a natural outcome of conversion. However, as Mohammad noted, sustained cultural differences and misunderstandings often result in the departure of the CMB for another church with the hope of finding a true spiritual family.

Christians of Maghrebi background

The future of sustained ministry to Muslims in France is in the hands of the growing number of Christians of Maghrebi background, many of whom have already become established in both local church and parachurch ministries in France and across the Maghrebi regions of North Africa. Through a combination of personal ministry and active ministry associations, CMBs now exercise an increasing influence on evangelism and discipleship patterns in the work among Maghrebi people, as well as on the place of the CMB in the church.

Conclusion

France's unique religious history with Muslims from North Africa has provided a rich and complex context for ministry to Muslims today. The increased numbers of immigrants from these regions into France, coupled with a heightened interest in—and multiplication of resources directed at—ministry to Muslims have contributed to a growing population and visibility of Muslim converts to faith in Christ.

Additionally, the current climate of religious pluralism and global instability seems to be contributing to a general receptivity on the part of Muslims to the gospel in France as well. For as noted by both popular media and academic research, increased incidence of Islamic-related or Islamic-inspired violence appears to result in an increase in receptivity and responsiveness to the gospel for at least two reasons.

First, religious violence (as experienced in the Algerian civil war) stirs emigration, in this case from Algeria to France. Those who did so, moved from a religiously monolithic context dominated by Islam to a religiously pluralistic context with increased access to Christianity. Second, religious violence is self-discrediting for some adherents who expect religion and religious faith to be primarily concerned with personal well-being. Militancy, for these, provokes a search for a new philosophical and/or religious identity. As a result, some eventually experience conversion to Christianity.

In addition to the external "push" of factors such as Islamic violence and the "pull" factors of a pluralistic religious economy, the presence of Christians of Meghrebi background and Muslim-friendly ministries such as Oasis, L'Ami and others provide opportunities for Muslims to explore the Christian faith from a perspective that minimizes cultural differences. Finally, increased contact with FEPCs and Christian friends and family members provide a relational context that serves as a bridge to the Christian faith. The challenge at this junction of mission history in France is not so much the establishment of a pertinent witness of the Christian faith but the successful discipleship and integration of the Muslim converts either into existing FEPCs or ethnic churches designed to reflect the cultural milieu of the person of Maghrebi background.

Reflection Questions

1. How does France's unique religious history affect current ministry models to Muslims today?

2. What cultural aspects of the Maghrebi immigrant must be considered as part of a coherent evangelism strategy?

3. What reasons can be given for encouraging integration of the CMB into a French evangelical Protestant church (FEPC)? Similarly, what reasons can be given for establishing CMB ethnic churches? Which strategy should be pursued in France, and why?

References

Adraoui, Mohamed-Ali. 2014. *Radical Milieus and Salafis Movements in France: Ideologies, Practices, Relationships with Society and Political Visions*. Badia Fiesolana, Italy: Max Weber Programme of the European University Institute.

Amghar, Samir. 2008. "Le salafisme en France: de la révolution islamique à la révolution conservatrice." *Critique internationale* 3 (40): 95–113.

———. 2011. *Le salafisme d'aujourd'hui. Mouvements sectaires en Occident*. Paris: Michalon.

Banaat, Abu. 2006. "Daisy Marsh: Missionary to the Kabyles, Effective Christian Kabyle Radio Ministry in the Light of Discriminatory Algerian Language Policies: 1973–1990." *St. Francis Magazine* 3 (2):1–6.

Blandenier, Jacques. 2003. L'Essor des Missions Protestantes. In *Précis d'Histoire des Missions, vol. 2: XIXe siècle et première moitié du XXe siècle*. St Légier, France: Editions Emmaüs.

Charles, Gilbert, and Besma Lahouri. 2003. "Les Vrais Chiffres." *L'Express*. December 4. Accessed December 8, 2010. http://www.lexpress.fr/actualite/societe/religion/les-vrais-chiffres_494290.html?p=2.

Chazan, David. 2015. "Demand for More Mosques in France Raises Tension." April 6. http://www.telegraph.co.uk/news/worldnews/europe/france/11518106/Demand-for-more-mosques-in-France-raises-tension.html.

Euro-Islam. 2015. "Salafism Gains Popularity Among French Muslims." *Euro-Islam*. April 26. http://www.euro-islam.info/2015/04/26/salafism-gains-popularity-among-french-muslims/.

Fath, Sebastien. 2005. *Du ghetto au réseau: Le protestantisme évangélique en France 1800–2005*. Genève: Editions Labor et Fidès.

Fdesouche. 2014. "La gendarmerie algérienne recense les chrétiens en Kabylie." Fdesouche India. August 17. http://www.fdesouche.com/497559-la-gendarmerie-algerienne-recense-les-chretiens-en-kabylie#.

Fregosi, Franck. 2008. *Penser l'islam dans la laïcité*. Paris: Fayard.

Gouëset, Catherine. 2015. "Pourquoi il ne faut pas confrondre djihadistes et salafistes." *L'Express*. November 11.

Joshua Project. n.d. *Joshua Project*. Accessed July 26, 2016. https://joshuaproject.net/resources/articles/10_40_window.

Kéfi, Ridha. 2005. "Ils ont choisie le Christianisme." *Jeune Afrique*. July 4.

Kronk, Rick. 2016. "Christians of Maghrebi Background in France and French Evangelical Protestant Churches: The Role of Social, Cultural and Religious Values on Conversion and Affiliation Processes." PhD diss., Evangelische Theologische Faculteit, Leuven.

Lekdja, Sadek. 2011. "Ces Kabyles qui préfèrent le Christianisme." *Radio France Internationale*. 7 mai.

Lieschti, Daniel. 2012. *Les Eglises protestantes évangéliques en France: Situation en 2012*. Paris: Conseil National des Evangéliques de France (CNEF).

McGavran, Donald. 1955. *Bridges of God: A Study in the Strategy of 1981 Missions*. New York: Friendship Press.

McGavran, Donald, and C. Peter Wagner. 1990. *Understanding Church Growth*. Grand Rapids: William B. Eerdmans Publishing Company.

Middle East Media Research Institute. 2015. "Des Cheiks salafists djihadistes justifient les attentats de novembre; l'Etat Islamique prêt à « déplacer la bataille vers vos propres pays.»" *Middle East Media Research Institute*. November 18. http://memri.fr/2015/11/18/des-cheikhs-salafistes-djihadistes-justifient-les-attentats-de-paris-letat-islamique-a-declare-quil-allait-bientot-deplacer-la-bataille-vers-vos-propres-pays/.

Morrison, Cécile. 1969. *Les Croisades*. Paris: Presses Universitaires de France.

Nicole, Jules-Marcel. 1962. "The French Speaking Areas." *Christianity Today*. July 1962, 20.

Poirette, Bernard et Clémence Baudin. 2016. Attentat à Nice : « Je propose qu'on déclare le salafisme hors-la-loi », lance Nathalie Kosciusko-Morizet. RTL, 19 juillet.

Reisacher, Evelyne Annick. 2001. "The Process of Attachment Between the Algerians and French within the Christian Community in France." PhD diss., Fuller Theological Seminary.

Roy, Olivier. 2010. *Holy Ignorance: When Religion and Culture Part Ways*. New York: Columbia University Press.

Santosuosso, Antonio. 2004. *Barbarians, Marauders and Infidels: The Ways of Medieval Warfare*. Boulder, CO: Westview Press.

Smitha, Frank E. n.d. "The Pahlavi Monarchy Falls." *Frank E. Smitha*. http://www.fsmitha.com/h2/ch29ir2.htm.

Stanley, Trevor. 2005. "Understanding the Origins of Wahabism and Salafism." July 15. https://jamestown.org/program/understanding-the-origins-of-wahhabism-and-salafism/.

Trumbore, Brian. 2002. "The Arab Oil Embargo of 1973–4." *Freedom Investments*. http://www.buyandhold.com/bh/en/education/history/2002/arab.html.

6

Yakup Korkmaz

Biblical Approaches to the *Nurcu Gülen* Movement in Turkey

In 2002 my wife and I moved to the country of Turkey to plant churches. In the fall of 2002 the *Adalet ve Kalkınma Partisi*, or AK party, also rose to power. In retrospect, it was this political change that began the re-Islamification of Turkey. Many have connected the AK party and its success with the man Fetullah Gülen and his movement,[1] for which the foundation was laid by Said Nursi. Before moving to Turkey, I was completely ignorant of Fetullah Gülen and Said Nursi, their brand of Islam, and the impact of the movement. I now realize that understanding this movement is key to reaching many Muslims not only in Turkey but in many other countries as well.

---

[1] Although they had a close relationship in the past, Turkish president Tayyıp Erdoğan and Fetullah Gülen have since split ways. However, Gülen, in a recent interview, stated that he does not support any particular party. On July 15, 2016, there was an attempted military coup in Turkey. The AK party has since accused Gülen and his followers of being behind the coup. Now the government considers Gülen's followers members of a terrorist organization. Thousands of Gülen's followers have been thrown into prison. While this does not directly impact the Nurcu, it does mean Gülenists will be scattered all over the world, seeking asylum, and will give rise to the opportunity to engage them with the gospel in their new host countries.

I first met devotees of Gülen in the beginning of our second year in Turkey. We developed a deep relationship as a family with them. I came to realize that these people were not only open to religious dialogue and listening to the gospel message, but that they had been overlooked by the evangelical missionary world that seeks to reach Muslims. I had not read anything about them in literature concerning approaches to Muslims, and I had not encountered anyone who had ministered among them. In fact, while taking Introduction to Islam as part of a master's program in Muslim studies, I discovered that my professor, though fluent in many languages and the author of several books, was ignorant of this Turkish brand of Islam.

I later realized that the majority of my training in Islamics was from an Arab perspective and that evangelistic approaches to Muslims was specifically geared toward Arab-background Muslims. There has been a gap in methodology and approaches geared to reaching groups like the *Nurcu* (pronounced *noorjoo*), which means "followers of the light," and those of the Gülen movement, known as *Fetullahçı*.[2]

Nurcu Muslims on the Margins of the Evangelical Radar

On June 4, 2011, Erick Stakelbeck from the Christian Broadcasting Network featured the Gülen movement and its intentions. CBN was the first in the evangelical Christian world to cover Fetullah Gülen and his movement. The thrust of Stakelbeck's article, which was titled "The Gülen Movement: A New Islamic World Order?" was to expose American Christians to this little-known man and movement. This new order, which scholar David Tittensor calls "Islam's Third way" (2014), is a Muslim missionary effort through global education, lifestyle evangelism, and social business.

On July 27, 2013, Jill Nelson authored an article in *World Magazine* about Fetullah Gülen called "Turkey's Inside Man." The article highlighted the political and religious turmoil in the country of Turkey and Gülen's influence in Turkish politics since 2002. According to this report, Gülen has two faces: One is deeply involved in Turkish politics and the Islamification of Turkey; the second propagates a more moderate Islam through education. The latter is the face that is well known in the West and presented in the United States. This is evident by its 146 charter schools and interfaith dialogues to influence and proselytize its Turkish brand of moderate Islam (CASILIPS 2017).

What exactly is the Gülen movement and who are the Nurcus? How are they different than Muslims found elsewhere? How can Nurcus be identified and effectively reached with the gospel?

---

[2] For the purpose of this chapter, I will be using the term Nurcu to denote both groups. The Nurcu and Fetullahçı are generally connected to the same movement with little distinction. However, technically the term Nurcu denotes a follower of Said Nursi, emphasizing the religious or pious aspect of the movement, while the term Fetullahçı is used derogatively to denote the followers of the political/power aspect of the Gülen movement.

To understand Turkish Islam, specifically the Gülen movement, one must first understand what sets its adherents apart from classical Islam or other forms of Islam that one might encounter in the Muslim world. In this next section I will summarize the political and religious beliefs of the Gülen movement and Said Nursi. I will also outline some tools to identify a Nurcu, as they generally blend in with society without clear identity markers. Lastly, at the end of this chapter I intend to present a clear biblical approach to reaching Nurcus for Jesus Christ, whether at home or abroad. My intention in this chapter is to be practical—not just academic—as I draw upon my fourteen years of interaction with Nurcu Muslims.

Traditional Islam versus the Gülen Movement

One spring several years ago I had the privilege of sharing my faith with hundreds of Kurds while traveling with a local friend who introduced me as the *papaz* (priest) wherever we went. From these contacts I became very close to one young man in particular. He has since moved to Istanbul to attend university and work. Because he was from a poorer family and an Arabic speaker, he was immediately approached by the Nurcu group. They offered him fully furnished free housing, a TV, a PlayStation, etc. They proposed that he serve as an *abi* (older brother) to the other young Nurcu recruits that he would room with. They saw him as a perfect candidate because of his command of the Arabic and Turkish languages. He could lead the prayers at the *Işık evi*[3] (lighthouse), the local gathering of young Nurcus, help them in their understanding of the Qur'an, and train them to live out the Sunna (the body of Islamic custom and practice based on Muhammad's words and deeds).

One evening my friend invited me to come and present Christianity to the young Nurcus at the Işık evi. Obviously this type of opportunity is just what a missionary to Muslims is looking for, so I jumped at the providence of God in this. I arrived that evening, after a five-hour bus ride. (Traffic in Istanbul can sometimes be overwhelming, even though we live in the same city!) I was ready to present Jesus to these first-time hearers. It was the first time for them to hear the gospel, meet a Christian, and see a Bible.

Unlike my encounters with Muslims in the past, I found a deep interest among my hearers, and they were not antagonistic. They listened for over two hours to how the Old Testament prophets proclaimed the Messiah and his work and how all these prophecies were fulfilled in Jesus. They had many good questions, and they allowed me to pray with them after our meeting adjourned. The ease with which I was able to share my faith in this meeting offers insight into the type of Islam represented by the Nurcu movement.

---

[3] *Işık evi* (pronounced *ughshook ehvee*) are the small groups (house mosques) that have been established around the world by the Nurcus.

If I had approached a Sufi gathering or presented at a normal local mosque in Turkey, I believe the response would have been much different. In the opportunities I have had to evangelize at Sunni mosques, the proclamation of the gospel usually turns into a debate. What is important to realize is that the reason for the more cordial response and openness to listen to the message of Christianity by Nurcus is related to their founder, Said Nursi. To be clear, there is not just one type of Islam, but many islams. Even to compare and contrast the Nurcu beliefs and practices to the teachings of classical Islam is difficult.

Said Nursi

The Nurcus' founder and interpreter of Islam is Said Nursi, also known by the honorific title *Bediüzzaman*, or "matchless one." Said Nursi (1873–1960)[4] was born in Bitlis, an eastern Kurdish province of Turkey. The title *Said* (pronounced *psy-eet*) means he was in the lineage of Muhammad, which gives him a sense of minor noblity among his fellow Muslims. Eventually his followers became known as Nurcu, from the Arabic word *nur* (pronounced *noor*), meaning "light," referring to the aura that shines from the face of a pious person. Said Nursi wrote a comprehensive commentary of the Qur'an and other works in Turkish.[5] This body of written works has been the catalyst for the global Gülen movement.

Because Said Nursi lived in a time of unprecedented scientific and technological discoveries, along with the demise of the Ottoman Empire and Islam, he, like other liberal Muslim writers of his day, sought to reconcile modernity with Islam. Although there is some overlap in the Nursi brand of Islam with other forms of liberal Islam, the teachings that make the *Nurcu* movement distinct from traditional Islam are the following:

- Said Nursi believed that there was no dichotomy between natural science and religion; this unity should be taught over and beyond the old traditional education system as taught in the madrassas. Scientific discoveries, in fact, prove there is a Creator and give a fuller understanding to the Qur'an (Yavuz 1999, 587).

- Democracy and Islam are not necessarily at odds with each other. Nursi believed that sharia law was not sacred but the opinion of jurists, and that they should be an elected assembly of the people (ibid., 591).

- There can be an individual interpretation of the Qur'an: religion can be lived and worked out individually.[6] Nursi's focus was on the individual Muslim consciousness that would transform society from within. The outcome would be the restoration of sharia law (ibid.).

---

[4] There is a discrepancy among scholars about the date of his birth.

[5] One can purchase the English volumes at www.sozler.com.tr and find them in English at www.nur.gen.tr. Said Nursi's works can also be found at www.nesil.com.tr and www.risaleinur.com.tr. These websites will aide those who wish to be familiar with the *Nurculuk*.

[6] See Alparslan Kuytul from the Furqan foundation and his critique of the teachings of Fetullah Gülen. Furkan Vakfi, April 11, 2014, https://youtu.be/Rov4ojBYaJk.

- Nursi was committed to a nonviolent approach to the spread of religion rather than to the jihad of the sword.[7] This nonviolent approach sets him apart from his contemporaries, such as Hassan al Banna and Sayyid Qtub, the founders of the Muslim Brotherhood, whose aim was to reestablish Islam in Egypt and abroad through any means necessary.
- Nursi believed that Muslims should be in dialogue with Christians and Jews. In the face of atheism and indifference toward religion, Muslims should unite with pious Jews and Christians for a greater cause and not concentrate on differences (Michel 1999, 326–27).

These last three points give Christians who desire to share the gospel with the Nurcu an advantage as compared to other Muslim contexts. This was exemplified in the illustration above. We will look back at how we can utilize these points for evangelization, but first we must briefly look at the Nurcu movement of today.

Fetullah Gülen[8]

While waiting at the American consulate in Istanbul a few years ago, I overheard an interview with a consulate worker and a Turkish man applying for his visa. The conversation went like this: "What is the purpose for applying for a visa to America?" the consulate worker asked. When the Turkish man replied, "I am going to take money to *Hocaefendi*," the consulate worker immediately approved his visa.

Fetullah Gülen, affectionately known as *Hocaefendi* ("master teacher"), resides in Saylorsburg, Pennsylvania, and is a disciple of Said Nursi. He is the head of the Nurcu movement, also known as the Gülen movement. Gülen, who was born in the eastern Turkish province of Erzurum in 1941, has carried on Said Nursi's ideas in his teaching and writing within his own organization. Gülen's movement is said to have successfully brought together Islam with modernity and science (Yavuz 1999, 593). The key difference between Nursi and Gülen is Gülen's emphasis on Turkish nationalism (ibid.), which is seen clearly in Gülen's various schools and charity organizations around the globe aimed at teaching Turkish culture and language and the Nurcu brand of Islam. Aside from the *Işık evleri* (house groups) and emphasis on religion, Gülen's movement is made up of a network of media, educational, charitable, economic, and political institutions worldwide.

In 2005, a Turkish television program conducted an exclusive interview with Fetullah Gülen during Ramadan. This is how he summarized his movement:

> Muslims are to go to the darkest places in the world, to open schools, preparatory schools and to bring students to these schools. They are to take Muhammad to these places in the world. We are to take the Qur'an to these. If we do this, the sunnah will not be absent from these areas and the Qur'an will no longer be absent.[9]

The overarching goal of the Gülen movement is to spread Islam—period.

---

[7] Michel (2003, 42–3). These ideas on jihad are also found in Nursi's Damascus Sermon.
[8] Not his real name. *Fetullah* means "God's conqueror"; *Gülen* means "The one who smiles."
[9] Accessed from https://youtu.be/9lNu4nGURJQ (link discontinued).

Apart from religious dialogue, which provides an open door for a Christian to share with a Nurcu, an important convergence with Christian missionary endeavors is Gülen's emphasis on education. He has opened hundreds of private K–12 schools, preparatory schools, charter schools, and universities around the world.[10] This is in keeping with Nursi's ideas that education reform was needed in Turkey, yet taking it much further. In many of these schools the medium for instruction is English, which offers the opportunity for many Christian educators and professors to apply to work at the various locations. Also, as many of my Christian Turkish and Kurdish friends have pointed out, Gülen studied Christian missions and realized that education along with charitable services are helpful in the propagation of religion. If imitation is the sincerest form of flattery, then this Islamic version of Protestant mission efforts should be taken as a compliment.

Nurcu Finder Tool Kit

This subhead may sound humorous, but I believe it is necessary for missionaries to be equipped with the right tools. Aside from the obvious, such as finding Gülen schools, charitable organizations, and businesses, a missionary may very well meet Nurcus on the street. With trained observation, it is often possible to have a good idea about a Muslim's political and religious views before you even strike up a conversation. Then, by asking the right questions, you can further understand their worldview and create a meaningful opportunity to proclaim the gospel.

In the Muslim world, appearance is very important: One's dress, facial hair or lack thereof, style of head covering, shoes, etc., distinguish one religious or political group from another. Therefore Muslims often notice these details in order to categorize an individual. Of course, Muslims do this immediately and naturally.

For example, if a man identifies with a Marxist group, he may have a long, unkempt beard and hair (in solidarity with Karl Marx) and wear dark, olive-green clothing. A woman would wear plain clothes and no makeup, keeping her hair straight and unadorned. To identify himself as a traditional Muslim, a man would have very short hair, covered by a small skull cap, and a long, kempt beard, trimmed near the face and long in the chin. He might wear baggy *shalvar* pants, along with a vest. The traditional Muslim woman would cover her entire body and wear a black head covering that almost covers her entire face.

Nurcu men typically wear a white button-down dress shirt tucked into khaki pants, their hair will be short but not as short as a traditional Muslim's, and they will generally be either clean-shaven or have a small and short mustache (in solidarity with Fetullah Gülen). With their dress pants, shirts, and shoes, we would call Nurcu men "clean-cut." Nurcu women have a very distinct look as well. They generally wear a

---

[10] For a comprehensive and updated list of Gülen charter schools located in the United States, refer to CASILIPS 2017.

tight head scarf covering all of their hair, and upon this they tuck into their coat another heard scarf that loosely covers their head yet still shows their face. They also may wear long trench-type coats. Like the men, they are also very well dressed. Turkey's first lady, Emine Erdoğan, personifies the image.

Once you are fairly certain you are talking with a Nurcu, feel free to let them know that you are aware of the works of Said Nursi, and ask if they identify with his teachings. Ask what they think about his views concerning religious dialogue. Perhaps even contrast this to the stereotypical depiction of Islam in the Western media. With this approach you might be able to ask, upon your first meeting, if you could learn more about their faith and at the same time present the Christian faith to them and their friends. They will probably welcome this opportunity, and you will have an open audience to share your faith. At the same time, be prepared to ask good questions and learn from them. If you tell them you have read any of Said Nursi's works, they will be very pleased, and this will also help you build rapport with your new friend and give you a platform to discuss Nursi's ideas and evaluate them using a biblical lens.

Differences in Sharing with a Nurcu

Of course, reaching Nurcu with the gospel is in many ways similar to reaching other Muslims, particularly well-educated ones. For example, hospitality is important because it builds the kind of trust that is needed to have the deep religious dialogue that Nurcus enjoy. Yet, in other important ways, engaging in gospel conversations with a Nurcu is much different than with most Muslims in Turkey. What sets adherents of the Followers of the Light movement apart from typical Turkish Muslims is that they are taught what they are to believe in community and are encouraged to study and read for themselves. Their emphasis on education[11] gives the missionary an advantage in discussing spiritual matters or really anything related to their religion, because you can assume they are more familiar with the Qur'an, Hadith, history, and even other religions than the average Muslim.

Unlike most other Muslims, Nurcus will not generally attack the foundations of the Christian faith during first encounters. In a conversation with most Muslims, the missionary will be immediately confronted with the following objections: The Bible has been changed or corrupted, the Trinity is tri-theism, God cannot have a son, and Jesus did not die on the Cross. Conversely, the Nurcu are not antagonistic. For example, a Nurcu with whom I was sharing the gospel once said to me, "I read Matthew chapter 5 as you requested; and I accept these rules, as every Muslim would, because they are coming from a divine source." Not exactly what I expected.

---

[11] This emphasis on education and their model of education is based on Christian foundations (whether or not they would acknowledge it). See the doctoral dissertation of Lisa Pursley (2013; 60–61, 67).

Now I would like to offer several points of specific advice that will greatly help when engaging Nurcu with the gospel.

First, as with all Muslims, the gospel witness needs to ask many questions. However, in the context of working with members of this movement, this is perhaps even more important because often times they will use words and ideas very differently than their meaning in classical Islam.

A second and related point is that those who wish to bear witness to followers of Fetullah Gülen must not only familiarize themselves with the Qur'an and Hadith but also with the writings and philosophy of Said Nursi. Understanding his thinking is an important gateway into understanding their worldview—thus how they will understand both the Qur'an *and* our witness of Christ.

Related to this second point is the way the movement uses specialized religious vocabulary, because the Nurcu have specific religious terms for each area of theology. Although the concepts behind the words are not significantly different than those in standard Sunni orthodoxy, the Nurcu terms for these are very different—terms that would not be known or understood by an average Turkish Muslim. The concepts behind these terms, however, would be familiar: God's will, general revelation, Muhammad's teachings, and the Qur'an. If you are familiar with the Nurcus' particularities, it will probably pique their interest for deeper theological conversations with you.

A third point has to do with the fact that the Nurcu movement is so strongly oriented toward the intellect and away from the emotional. For this reason, the gospel witness must learn the appropriate use of rhetoric and logic. Used in the right way, a well-thought-out apologetic can cause the Nurcu to research a topic and then later passionately continue in a discussion that might otherwise be a dead end with other Muslims. I recommend taking a presuppositional approach to apologetics with Nurcu, specifically employing the transcendental model.[12] It seems that few have attempted to adapt this model for witness with Muslims, but I have personally seen great success with it.

Although it seems counterintuitive in light of what I have just stated, we must not forget that Nurcu also have emotions. They are deeply devoted to Said Nursi and Fetullah Gülen, not just as teachers but as spiritual masters, in a way that is similar, yet different, to a South Asian Sufi who is devoted to his pir. Thus, although the Nurcu are trained to be better critical thinkers than the average Muslim, their devotion to their spiritual mentors is strong, and it is still very hard for an individual to break away and embrace Jesus Christ.

The fourth point relates to Nursi's and Gülen's obligation upon their followers to engage in religious dialogue (Yücel 2013, 199–200; 205). In fact, the Gülenists

---

[12] For an introduction to this method and how it is used among intellectuals such as atheists, see John M. Frame (2015). James J. Pursley (2016) presents a similar model with Muslims in his thesis.

have been criticized by other Muslims for being too open and too friendly to Jews and Christians (ibid., 204). This fourth point allows countless opportunities for the missionary to carry out ongoing personal dialogue with the Nurcu and even organize events where Christianity and the gospel message are presented without fear of debate and antagonism.

A final point touches on the important issue of missionary identity. This, of course, is a huge topic, and there is a wide spectrum of opinion in the mission world on this issue. But no matter what public identity you would choose, I recommend that gospel workers are clear about the evangelistic dimension of our faith. Nurcus will understand the responsibility we feel to share gospel truth with them since they often feel the same responsibility concerning Islam. Also, they are likely to feel betrayed if they realize this about you later in the relationship.

Conclusion

Blame for the attempted military coup in Turkey on July 15, 2016, was cast on the Gülenist movement. Nurcus have since tried to distance themselves from Gülen. Due to these events, and Gülen's alleged involvement in them, thousands of his followers have been targeted and imprisoned. Many have fled Turkey seeking asylum, and thousands working with the Gülen organization overseas are now exiled from their homeland, unable to return to Turkey.

The recent upheaval among the Nurcus and followers of Gülen calls for Christians to seek them out wisely and compassionately and present the only "kingdom that cannot be shaken" (Heb 12:8 NIV). Those who reside in the diaspora may now be apprehensive to discuss their connection with Gülen, and those who remain in Turkey are fearful. Nevertheless, the Nurcu continue to gather together and will continue to propagate their brand of Islam through dialogue.

The Nurcus' brand of Islam offers unique features that allow for unprecedented opportunities for the missionary seeking to present the Christian faith to them. Features that set them apart are 1) their focus on individual interpretation of the Qur'an; 2) a nonviolent approach to the propagation of their religion; 3) an emphasis on education and critical thinking; and lastly, 4) their compulsion to dialogue with Christians.

Sometime back I began a long interaction with a Nurcu medical doctor that continued for months via email. I reached out to him with a combination of the above points of approach, using different tracks at different times. It was a long give-and-take, asking each other many questions concerning Islam and Christianity. We thoroughly challenged one another on many points of theology and religious history. As a result of our relationship, he eventually felt comfortable enough to encourage his own son to learn about Christianity from me. This experience captures what a gospel-centered relationship with a Nurcu can look like. May they no longer be on the margins of the evangelical radar.

Reflection Questions

1. What factors set the *Nurcu* Gülen movement apart from other forms of Islam which could allow the missionary easier access and openness?

2. What specific teachings of Said Nursi, if any, could be used to find redemptive analogies?

3. What are some methods of reaching the Nurcu, and what questions would you ask your Muslim friend, and why?

References

CASILIPS (Citizens Against Special Interest Lobbying in Public Schools). 2017. "A Guide to the Gulen Movement's Activities in the US: Gulen Charter Schools in the United States." *CASILIPS*. Last modified April 17, 2017. http://turkishinvitations.weebly.com/list-of-us-schools.html.

Frame, John M. 2015. *Apologetics: A Justification of Christian Belief*. Edited by Joseph E. Torres. 2nd ed. Phillipsburg, NJ: Presbyterian and Reformed.

Michel, Thomas, S.J. 1999. "Muslim-Christian Dialogue and Cooperation in the Thought of Bediuzzaman Said Nursi." *The Muslim World* 89, (3–4) (July): 325–35.

———. 2003. *Reflections on Said Nursi's Views on Muslim-Christian Understanding*. Istanbul: Söz Bosim Yayın.

Nelson, Jill. 2013. "Turkey's Inside Man." *World Magazine*. July 27. https://world.wng.org/2013/07/turkeys_inside_man?.

Pursley, James J. 2016. "Addressing Muslim Objections Using the Presuppositional Model of Apologetics Can Be Defended on Historical, Biblical and Practical Grounds." Master's thesis, Reformed Theological Seminary.

Pursley, Lisa J. 2013. "International Teachers' Attitudes Towards Inclusion in Turkey." PhD diss., Regent University.

Stakelbeck, Erick. 2011. "The Gülen Movement: A New Islamic World Order?" *CBN News*. June 4. https://www.youtube.com/watch?v=lhqMQQrn3Q0.

Tittensor, David. 2014. *The House of Service: The Gülen Movement and Islam's Third Way*. New York: Oxford University Press.

Vahide, Şükran, and Ibrahim M. Abu-Rabi'. 2005. *Islam in Modern Turkey: An Intellectual Biography of Bediuzzaman Said Nursi*. Albany: State University of New York Press.

Yavuz, Hakan. 1999. "Towards an Islamic Liberalism." *The Middle East Journal* 53 (4) (Autumn): 584–605.

Yücel, Salih. 2013. "Muslim-Christian Dialogue: Nostra Aetate and Fetullah Gülen's Philosophy of Dialogue." *Australian eJournal of Theology* 20 (3) (December): 197–206. http://aejt.com.au/__data/assets/pdf_file/0008/603458/Yucel_Muslim-Christian_Dialogue_Dec13_Vol20.3.pdf.

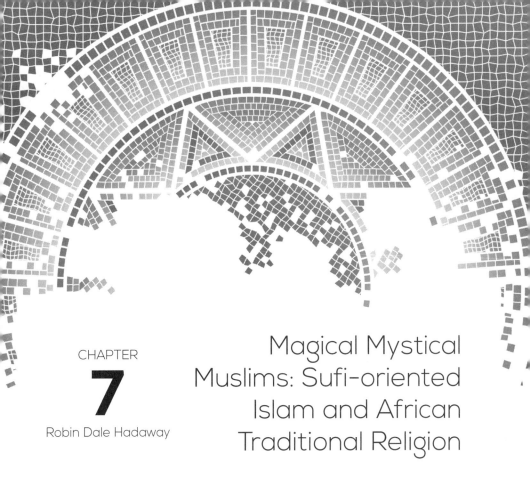

7

Robin Dale Hadaway

Magical Mystical Muslims: Sufi-oriented Islam and African Traditional Religion

When an anthropologist asked some Muslim tribesmen from northern Africa about the present attitude of his people toward the spirit world, they said, "We Bedawiet[1] believe that there are spirits everywhere, especially after dark. We never let our children out of sight" (Jacobsen 1998, 150).

Although most of the people groups in northern Africa claim adherence to orthodox Islam, beliefs in magic and mysticism persist and even dominate across the continent. One colonial official records an example of two spells practiced by Muslim peoples in an earlier day. On a recent trip to northern Africa, I confirmed the continuation of such practices.

---

[1] Beja (sometimes spelled *Bega* or *Bija*) is the Arabic term for the tribe and is the commonly acknowledged name for them. Ausenda (1987, 26) states, "These nomads were given, by Arabs and Abyssinians [Ethiopians], the common name of Beja." They call themselves the *Bedawiet* (Ornas and Dahl 1991, 1; Jacobsen 1998, 5). They should not be confused with the Bedouin tribes of North Africa and the Middle East who are not racially or linguistically similar to the Beja people.

Sorcery to cause dissension between a man and his wife: A man named Mohammad must catch a chameleon and a man named Ali cut off its head. This is dried and powdered, and mixed with donkey dung. The mixture is then deposited underneath the bed or sprinkled near the house of the couple whose future happiness is to be jeopardized.

A spell to kill one's enemy: A dung beetle is wrapped in a piece of cloth cut from the clothing of the person against whom the spell is directed and his name written thereon. It is then buried or burned and as it decays or is consumed the bewitched person falls ill and dies. (Clark 1938, 28; *emphasis mine*).

Folk Islam blends pure Islam with the early religious customs and habits of everyday people (Saal 1991, 51). Parshall (2006, 2) says that fully 70 percent of Muslims follow folk Islam. In Africa, there seem to be two principle types of folk Muslims: (1) African traditional religion (ATR) folk Muslims and (2) Sufi folk Muslims.[2] In northern Africa, both often coexist and intertwine simultaneously. In this part of the world there is often a blending of Sufism and ATR that is hard to separate.

While serving as a relief and development worker in northern Africa during the 1990s, I noticed that the vast majority of Muslims followed a folk variety of Islam rather than the orthodox version of the faith. Among the Beja tribe of southern Egypt, eastern Sudan, and northern Eritrea,[3] I observed that many aspects of Beja beliefs resembled the ATR of the Sukuma tribe of Tanzania, the site of my previous ministry during the 1980s. This chapter features the folk Islam of the Beja tribe of Sudan because they typify African Muslims who are heavily affected by a mixture of traditional African religion and Islamic Sufism.

ATR Folk Muslims

Observing the Beja, an Arab historian noted, "Behind the appearance of Islam they [Beja] hide corrupt practices" (Owen 1937, 196). Another researcher says, "Islam in the pre-colonial period was a corporate Islam to which all the subjects automatically belonged, despite the fact that many of the Sudanese were 'mixers,' retaining many non-Islamic customary practices" (Kapteijns 1989, 254). Like many other Muslims in northern Africa, during the colonial period the Beja continued their penchant for overlaying a veneer of Islam on traditional religious practices.

Islam sits lightly on their consciences: they are not completely irreligious but they are not devout. The prayers of the Hillmen [i.e., the Beja] are perfunctory and to a great extent not comprehended by the worshipper; Ramadan is little regarded ... the pilgrimage rarely made.[4] (Clark 1938, 5)

---

[2] Parshall (2006, 4) calls Sufism "a fairly well-defined influence within folk Islam."

[3] The Beja are a tribe of approximately 1.25 million persons, though estimates of the number vary widely. One expert projected their number to be about 2.5 million (Jenkins 1996, 2), while another researcher placed the population at 700,000 (Beja 1979, 282).

[4] The Red Sea port at Suakin (sixty kilometers south of Port Sudan) serves pilgrims and travelers embarking for Mecca through Jeddah by way of a ferry (Roden 1970, 18).

The folk Islam of the Beja appends other spiritual beings into the Muslim faith schema. These divinities answer to the name of "spirit humans"[5] and may alternately benefit or harm members of the tribe. Beja believe "spirit animals" and "spirit insects" accompany the "spirit humans" (Jacobsen 1998, 58). These beings populate a pantheon of lesser deities that are both feared and venerated. "The cultural world of the Beja is a world inhabited by a host of spirits. Although there are Muslim and good-intentioned spirits, most Hadendowa Beja are mainly concerned with the malevolent ones, as well as the capricious ones which occasionally create problems (1998, 34).

Werehyenas are beings who transform themselves back and forth between animals and humans. They frighten many Beja. Folklore claims they steal babies, drinking their blood (Ausenda 1987, 429; Jacobsen 1998, 36). Beja also believe in various kinds of ghosts (Jacobsen 1998, 254) and greatly fear the spirit world. Both urban and rural Beja daily converse about potential spirit attacks. They so dread the jinn[6] that they call these spiritual beings "ins," not desiring to risk offending them by even verbalizing their true names (Jacobsen 1998, 150–51). The Beja employ numerous folk Islamic practices to counter these threats.

In the Beja worldview, diseases consist of spirits possessing both personality and intentionality (Jacobsen 1998, 89, 106). The diviner or healer, often the same person, discovers the source and prescribes the cure for a host of spiritual and physical maladies caused by evil spirits (ibid., 152–54). As a result, divination rituals command great respect among many Muslim peoples in northern Africa who see no conflict between such ATR practices and Islamic rituals.

> Islam does not ask their adherents to abandon their accustomed confidence in their mystical forces. Far from it. In the voluminous Qur'anic storehouse of angels, jinns and devils, whose number is legion, many of these traditional powers find a hospitable home; and passages from the Qur'an are cited to justify their existence as real phenomena. (Lewis 1980, 60)

The Zar possession cult[7] comprises perhaps the most important and unusual extra-Qur'anic spiritual phenomenon existing in the Islamic world. Besides northern Africa, Zar spirit possession can be found in Central, South, and Southeast Asia. Possessing men, women, and children, Zar spirits are agents believed to cause sicknesses, paralysis, bleeding, swelling, irritability, and even marriage problems (Jacobsen 1998, 62, 155). Satisfying Zar spirits often requires a gold payment and offering blood sacrifices (Ausenda 1987, 433; Jacobsen 1998, 219, 235). In direct violation of

---

[5] T. A. Ibrahim, interview with the author, May 1, 2010, Pittsburgh, PA. Most Beja dismiss the notion of identifying the "spirit humans" as ancestors. I asked Ibrahim, an English-speaking Beja leader residing in the United States, about these spirit humans. He said they are not jinns, but "helpers of the jinns." These spirits could be classified as "familiar spirits."

[6] The jinns are the spirits in Islam. Usually evil, sometime capricious, dealing with the jinns is the subject of much of the attention in folk Islam.

[7] Jacobsen (1998, 62) says Zar possession is more common among the Beja than other Muslim groups in Sudan.

most representations of Islamic law, "A Zar ritual ideally involves even drinking of sacrificial blood by the sufferer" (Jacobsen 231).

In cases of severe possession, three-day parties[8] honoring the entity are often held. Celebrants perform a mock marriage whereby the spirit weds an individual, attaching the Zar to their host for a lifetime (ibid 156). At these festivals both the patient and those attending the ritual often fall into trances where they are beaten with whips by Zar doctors without feeling any pain. Zar possession ceremonies feature the striking of sacred drums and violent, trance-like dancing (ibid 71), not unlike the *ngoma* (drum and dance) ATR rituals of the Sukuma tribe of Tanzania.

The most common kinds of Zar spirits include an Ethiopian prostitute, a British colonial military officer, and a western Sudanese working woman (ibid., 236). Any of these three may possess either a man or a woman. The Beja differentiate between ordinary madness and Zar spirit possession (ibid., 244). They also distinguish between "Muslim spirits," such as jinns and devils, and "non-Muslim" Zar spirits. Understanding that Zar spirits are not part of the orthodox Muslim faith, one Beja stated, "Well, Zar ceremonies are not Islamic, but Zar spirits are present among us, so what can we do?" (ibid., 71). The tribe exhibits a certain pragmatism in regard to the supernatural and advises negotiating with the evil spirits when necessary (ibid., 262).

The Beja also enforce a number of cultural prohibitions. Some of their subtribes possess a fear of persons and foodstuffs originating outside the Beja lands (ibid., 261). Although Beja territory borders the Red Sea, the tribe has a taboo against eating fish ("Beja" 1979, 283). The Beja feel the same way about consuming chickens or eggs (Ausenda 1987, 340). Unlike the Arab and African tribes in other parts of Sudan, the Beja enforce a ban that prohibits their females from milking livestock (Ornas and Dahl 1991, 99). Only men are permitted to do this kind of labor (Ausenda 1987, 92). Camel-milk products protect consumers from illness, according to Beja theory (Jacobsen 1998, 26), but pregnant women should avoid crossing the trail of a camel so as not to incur the risk of a miscarriage (ibid., 257). Mother-in-law avoidance constitutes another taboo that endures as a strong cultural observance (Paul 1950, 239).

The Beja believe that certain magical practices bring good fortune and protect from evil influences. After speaking about an illness, many Beja spit on the ground, asking for God's protection from the evil forces (Jacobsen 1998, 109). Traditional Beja families hang a decorated straw mat or an embroidered blanket on the walls of their homes to repel the jinns from their dwellings at night (Ausenda 1987, 414–15). Some Beja burn medicine pills in the manner of incense, inhaling the smoke instead of ingesting the medicine orally (Jacobsen 1998, 82). Magical ornaments adorn marriage houses to convey fortuity and fertility to newlyweds (Clark 1938, 11).

---

[8] Zar sacrifices involve a great economic hardship. One Zar doctor's diagnosis required seven sheep (Jacobsen 1998, 211) while another Zar party necessitated the expenditure of the equivalent of half the cost of a Mercedes-Benz automobile (ibid., 238).

Most Beja children wear amulets to protect them from attack by spirits (Jacobsen 1998, 150–51). Parents place hyena-teeth necklaces around the necks of their children to guard them from danger (ibid., 174, 193).

Sufi Folk Muslims

In addition to the folk Islam that has so much in common with ATR, there is another kind of popular Islam that is very much part of life in northern Africa. Earlier historians once assumed that Muslim traders and intermarriage brought Islam to the region (Paul 1954, 64). Many historians now believe the Islamification of northern Africa occurred primarily through the Muslim missionary activity of a number of Sufi orders.

> The Islamization of the Beja in general and of Hadendowa in particular was stepped up by the effort of various missionaries, both from the Arabian peninsula and from the lower Nile [Egypt], who came to the region toward the end of the eighteenth century or the beginning of the nineteenth. Most of these missionaries belonged to Sufi tarikas, one of the many religious expressions that go under the all-embracing bracket of Islam. Sufi tarikas, or "ways," are sects which profess to achieve close-ness to God through the teaching of mystical thought and the performance of special ecstasy-inducing rituals. Perhaps for this reason, Sufi movements have had considerable success among Beja in general and Hadendowa in particular. (Ausenda 1987, 433–34)

Sufism represents a template upon Islam, as well as a division of the faith. Some Muslims see Sufism as heretical; others view it as an important part of Islam and the religion's most effervescent expression (Chittick 2000, 3; Ernst 1997, xi). Many Muslims see Sufi customs as primitive fantasy distorting true Islam (Ernest 1997, xvii). Ernest (xiii) estimates that about 50 percent of all Muslims currently practice a form of Sufism. One writer (Karrar 1992, 2) observes the manner in which Sufis self-identify in Sudan: "The Sufi orders in Sudan, as in the rest of the Muslim world, never constituted a world of their own. In the view of most Sufi shaykhs and followers, Sufism and sharia were entirely interlocking manifestations of faith." *Sufis*, often called the mystics of Islam, come from both the Sunni and Shi'ite portions of the faith (Marshall, Green, and Gilbert 2002, 28; Braswell 1996, 97; Sookhdeo 2007, 45). Conversely, two secular experts discount the term *mysticism* as inaccurate (Ernst 1997, xvii; Chittick 2000, 1).

According to Chittick (2000, 29), there are two principle kinds of Sufis: (1) the God-intoxicated or "drunken" and (2) the contemplative or ascetic. The former is linked with ecstatic conduct and are representative of Muslim mysticism. Ascetic Sufis are temperate by contrast and contemplate the inner life. These quieter Sufis emphasize the value of the deeper life and are also mystics. The former seems to be more prevalent in northern Africa.

Sufism probably developed partially in reaction to a perceived barrenness and stiffness in orthodox Islam. Parshall (2006, 12) claims that folk Islam cannot be understood apart from a knowledge of Sufism. In describing the Sufis, Ruthven states, "They inject a warmth into Islam which is lacking in the legalistic observance advocated by Sunni 'ulama'[9] or in the fanatical loyalty of the Shi'ites to the tragic memories of their Imams" (2006, 225).

Sufism developed early in Islam through teachers such as al-Muhasibi, AD 781–837, and his pupil and contemporary, Junaid. They attempted to combine asceticism and mysticism with a proper observance of the sharia (ibid., 227). This new spiritual path within Islam continues to enlarge through writers such as al Sarraj, who penned the first surviving Sufi writing in 988 (Parshall 2006, 15). Sufis hold that the path to God is not based on doctrine but on feeling, experience, and introspection (Braswell 1996, 97). Ruthven comments on this:

> Yet from the first there were Muslims whose psychic or spiritual needs were unsatisfied by mere obedience to the deity and the dutiful observance of his commandments. They sought a closer and more intimate relationship by means of ascetic practices, arduous spiritual exercises and complicated liturgies. They came to be known as Sufis, after the woolen garments (*suf* = wool) allegedly worn by the early exemplars of this movement, as well as by the followers of Jesus whom they particularly admired. (2006, 221–22)

Abu Hamid al-Ghazali, AD 1058–1111, is credited for giving Sufism respectability among other Muslims. As a Muslim scholar, Ghazali experienced a personal crisis that led him to try to reconcile mysticism with official Islam (Braswell 1996, 98). Ghazali believed both in the necessity of ritual and emotion (Ruthven 2006, 233). He held that religious certainty depends upon religious experience (Braswell 1196, 98). His unique synthesis won him the appellation of *mujaddid*, or renewer, of Islam (Esposito, Fasching, and Lewis 2009, 252). Although he never founded a Sufi brotherhood or order, Ruthven states,

> Ghazali's work served to reintegrate the whole legal superstructure with the psychic or spiritual infrastructure, re-injecting into the Qur'an and the Sunna, and into the edifice of law built upon them, the sanctity of the Prophet's mystic consciousness. For this he has been called the greatest Muslim after Muhammad. (2006, 35, *emphasis mine*)

As Sufism grew throughout the centuries, this expression of Islam became less orthodox in faith and practice (Braswell 1996, 97). For this reason, Sufism can be viewed as one of the major avenues of folk Islam. Sufi Islamic practices generally possess very much of a folk religious orientation (Parshall 2006, 4). Beja Sufism seems even more linked to traditional religion. Ausenda notes:

> … among the Hadendowa [Beja division], whereas there exist, as in other ethnic groups in the region, beliefs in Werehyenas.[10] This is seen to be a result of inter-gabila suspicion. At gabila[11] level, the main religious form probably was an *ancestor cult*, which has now developed into Muslim Sufi tarikas, of which seven are present among Gash Delta Hadendowa. (1987, 22, *emphasis mine*)

---

[9] Religious officials or scholars.

[10] The werehyena idea resembles the werewolf of Western folklore

[11] In Arabic, *gabil*, or *kabil*, is the simple word for "tribe."

Some Sufi practices in Sudan in general and among the Beja in particular resemble some of the ancestor-veneration customs of ATR (African traditional religion). Pilgrimages are encouraged to visit the shrine of a departed sheikh, usually on the Sufi saint's birthday or the Prophet's birthday, for those who cannot afford to go to Mecca. Ausenda (1987, 449) states, "The Sufi sheikh is the intermediary between his followers and God." The Hadendoa Beja also believe the souls of dead Sufi sheikhs have supernatural powers—a belief that orthodox Sunni Muslims consider blasphemous.

> According to the sheikh, the difference between the followers of Sufi tarikas and the "orthodox Jama'i Sunni" is that the latter say that these are two different kinds of religion. The one to be followed should be only the "open religion," which has its basis the Qur'an and the Prophet's deeds and utterances contained in the hadith (Ar.), the written tradition. According to the Gadri (a Sufi tariga), and to most Sufi, there is also a secret religion, known only to initiates. According to the secret religion, God talked directly to special people. The Sufi sheikhs say that when good people die, they become better than before. Their souls can do anything as if they were not dead. According to the Jama'i Sunni [i.e., orthodox Islam], this is not true. (Ausenda 1987, 436)

Of the seven Sufi orders that are said to exist, one originated from within the Hadendoa tribe. In 1951 Sheikh Ali Betai of Hamash Koreb, at the age of twenty-one, began an itinerant preaching ministry traveling by camel across eastern Sudan. The young mystic claimed to have seen the Prophet—who told him to present a simple message—in numerous dreams. Everyone desiring piety should repeat the shahada thirty times before dawn and after sunset, read the Qur'an, and recite "Thanks be to God" and "God be praised" thirteen times.

Despite this noncontroversial message, Sheikh Ali Betai was hounded by the British and Egyptian-Sudanese authorities and spent time in Sudanese prisons in Aroma, Kassala, Khartoum, and Wadi-Halfa. Nevertheless, the cleric built schools and mosques in Kassala, Halfa Jedida (New Halfa), Hamash Koreb, and Gedaref in the name of his Sufi sect. The popularity of his still unnamed tarika resulted in the expansion of Ali Betai's religious enterprise into Khartoum, Omdurman, and El Obeid.

The popular sheikh died in 1978, and his son, Suleiman Ali Betai,[12] took his place as leader of the tarika (Ausenda 1987, 444–46). Sufi Muslims dominate Sudan (Karrar 1992, 1) and northern Africa. Sufis emphasize the recitation of the names of God as the key to entering heaven (Ernst 1997, 85). Many of the religious healers and their ecstasy-producing rituals come from the seven Sufi orders extant in eastern Sudan (Ausenda 1987, 433–34).

---

[12] In 1991 my family and I (my wife and three children) met with Sheikh Suleiman Ali Betai and four of his followers in Kassala, Sudan.

ATR and Sufism: Magic Meets Mysticism

One of the ATR alterations to Islam involves Sufism and the spiritual activity of departed Sufi saints. Many of the Beja tribe believe the souls of deceased holy men remain in their tombs and are available to greet and assist supplicants during pilgrimages to their shrines, especially on the saint's birthday (Ausenda 1987, 437). Some researchers view Beja Sufism as "quite close to an ancestor cult since Sufi sheikhs may belong to the same gabila [kinship group] or one bound by stipulated kinship ties" (ibid., 448). Ausenda reports this example of Beja ATR-like practices:

> The Tijania [a Sufi order] is spreading to the Hadendowa through the activity of an Epshar sheikh. This member of a gabila [subtribe] belonging to the Bishariin, another Beja tribe, is making the tarika a vehicle for the *cult of his ancestors*. On the anniversary of the prophet's birth, on the twelfth day of the month of Rabia el Awel, all Beja followers of this tarika congregate at Telhadio' about fifteen kilometers east of the Gash [River] in the hills. The Epshar sheikh's *ancestors are buried there* and the ziara, the visit, to their tombs is performed the same way as are visits by other tarikas to their saints' tombs. (1987, 442–43, *emphasis mine*)

As a general rule, the Beja avoid discussing the deceased, especially children who have died (Jacobsen 1998, 337), although premature death occurs frequently in Beja society (ibid., 76). Then again, this is not unusual—the majority of Americans also speak about death reluctantly. The Beja bury their dead in rock mounds rather than in the traditional manner of Islam (Delany 1982, 59). Beja accept the Islamic concept of life after death (e.g., a paradise with sensual delights). Nevertheless, ATR and folk Islam convinces the Beja that the spirits of the departed remain either to help or hinder the living. Beja Sufi sheikhs reinforce these concepts that are outside the bounds of traditional Islam.

Beja sacred places consist of the shrines of their Sufi saints and, of course, their mosques. The Beja outwardly revere Islam's holy sites but rarely choose to travel the short distance across the Red Sea to participate in the pilgrimage to Mecca (Gamst 1984, 135).

The Beja recognize quite an array of religious personnel. The *basir* (plural, *busara*) is a diviner who possesses the ability to see the unseen world both physically and spiritually. Combining knowledge of anatomy, herbs, and folk techniques, busara discern illnesses and treat patients accordingly, primarily through homeopathic medicine. This specialist also counts bleeding, cutting, and branding as techniques at his or her disposal. The spiritual quality of *heequal* (blessedness, holiness, or luckiness) endows some of the busara with special powers, but most content themselves with a mostly homeopathic approach (Jacobsen 1998, 63–64).

The female cowrie-shell reader represents the primary fortune-telling caste among the Beja. Other Sudanese ethnic groups practice this kind of divination as well (Ausenda 1987, 419). The diviner predicts the future or diagnoses a disease by casting seven cowrie shells on the ground and reading a story through their random placement. The fortune-teller may prescribe a cure, but a *faki* (folk healer) or Zar doctor usually administers the treatment. The faki sometimes employs herbal remedies similar to the homoeopathic medicine of the basir. Usually the faki treats patients through the agency of the Qur'an. Treatments such as reading, wearing, eating, or drinking Qur'anic verses are examples of the blending of Islam and traditional religion. A common treatment consists of whispering certain Qur'anic verses over specific parts of the body or drinking the ashes of the holy book to cure specific maladies (Jacobsen 1998, 105, 154), all in the name of Sufism. In a surprising twist, one man was told by a diviner that his sickness was due to too much Qur'anic reading (ibid., 207)!

Most of these faki utilize "spirit helpers" (i.e., unknown spiritual beings) in their duties (Jacobsen 1998, 67–68). Serving their communities often in a dual role as Sufi sheikhs, fugara easily blend the medicinal and spiritual aspects of their healing arts (Ausenda 1987, 425). Traditional Beja folk Muslims believe the faki possess a hereditary baraka,[13] passed down from sheikh to sheikh (el Hassan 1980, 102). "The concept of baraka is indeed very central to religious beliefs of the Beja, and Trimingham rightly observed that Beja pay special attention to people said to have baraka" (Jacobsen 1998, 22). Many Beja hold that baraka can be essentially "stored up" from generation to generation through the holy lineage of Sufi sheikhs (ibid., 58). Such concepts demonstrate the blending of Sufism and ATR that often transpires in northern Africa.

Fugara discern the cause and prescribe treatment for most of the physical, emotional, and spiritual problems experienced by the Beja. Alternatively, possession by an unpredictable and troublesome Zar spirit requires a specialist. Should a faki (traditional healer) fail to effect a cure, the patient often resorts to visiting a Zar doctor. Not categorized as a Muslim healer, the Zar doctor is a medium, possessed by a powerful spirit himself (or herself), who successfully negotiates with the Zar spirit dwelling inside his patient (Jacobsen 1998, 156). Blood sacrifices form the foundation for effecting cures for Zar maladies (ibid., 231). Zar doctors often intertwine herbal, homeopathic, medical, and supernatural elements in treating spirit possession (ibid., 85). "A trial and error strategy may lead people in the same instance of sickness to seek a basir, then a medical doctor, then another basir, then a fagir [faki] and finally a Zar doctor" (ibid., 205).

Beja folk religion places a high value on sacrifice. At the one-year anniversary of the death of a prominent Sufi sheikh, Hadendowa Beja offer special sacrifices at the tomb. The new sheikh's followers pledge their fealty to the successor by ceremonially placing tree branches upon his head. The people also sacrifice a calf or sheep, allowing the blood to fall ritually upon the new sheikh's feet. The novice leader receives the

---

[13] Spiritual power and blessing. Ornas and Dahl (1991, 84) define *baraka* also as "divine grace."

best of the meat and distributes the remainder to the people (Ausenda 1987, 455). Many Beja sacrifice animals to prepare the soil spiritually prior to cultivation and planting. "Before the sowing of their rain crops a karama[14] sacrifice is made on the spot. A bull, a naga, a sheep or goat is slaughtered according to the extent of the area to be sown or the wealth of the cultivator" (Clark 1938, 20).

Beja fear the "evil eye," which represents the most prominent practice of witchcraft among them. Jacobsen (1998, 169–70) reports the Beja evil eye sometimes resembles the simple envy of Western societies. The Beja also believe witches and sorcerers move around in the evenings, eating the souls of their enemies (Nadel 1945, 84). The Beja practice the projection of evil thought, believing contagious magic[15] improves the power of their swords (Gamst 1984, 135).

Missiological Implications

Western missionaries are not generally trained to reach the kind of Muslims described in this chapter. Rather, most Christian workers receive instruction in refuting the history, practice, and claims of orthodox Islam. Such apologetics are very much beside the point when presenting the claims of Christ to Beja. As folk Muslims, they view the Qur'an as a charm or healing elixir, greatly different from those who see the holy book as the written guide for faith and practice. The missionary must find ways of communicating that the power of the gospel is more powerful than the magic of spirits, ancestors, or sheikhs. This is not an easy task.

I contend that apologetic, polemic, and dialogue methods possess limited value with the Beja because cognitive arguments fail to satisfy the questions posed by folk religion. I believe a successful approach to Muslims like the Beja will start with understanding their worldview, and Hiebert, Shaw, and Tienou (2000, 224–26) offer a threefold model that is very helpful as it opens the discussion about three primary religious value worldview axes: (1) guilt-innocence; (2) shame-honor; and (3) fear-power.[16] In particular, they point out that whereas most Westerners operate out of a developed concept of guilt and innocence, traditional societies revolve more around the fear of the supernatural and a desire for power over unknown spiritual entities and occurrences.

In his well-known book on this threefold worldview model, Muller says that most Muslims see the world through a shame-honor orientation rather than the guilt-innocence concept dominant in Western societies (2013). I contend that for folk Muslims influenced by ATR, like the Beja tribe of Sudan, the fear-power worldview prevails. Despite this, elements of the shame-honor worldview, as well as portions of the guilt-innocence value system, persist as secondary themes in their culture.

---

[14] *Karama* possesses several meanings in Arabic. Ideas include "nobility, generosity, high-mindedness, token of esteem, miracle (worked by a saint)" (Wehr 1976, 822). In folk Islam, *karama* often describes a sacrifice offered as a token of esteem to God in order to cause something positive to happen.

[15] With contagious magic, the object of the magic comes in contact with the agent of the magician to effect the cure or curse (Levi-Strauss 1985, 194–95).

[16] Although much more could and should be said about this threefold worldview orientation, that exceeds the scope of this chapter. Muller (2013) offers a thorough treatment of the subject in his volume *The Messenger, The Message and the Community*.

Thus gospel messengers to the Beja must understand all three, but focus their presentation on the area of fear-power.

Additionally, the Sufi folk Muslims among the Beja might require an even more nuanced approach; most evangelism methods fail to account for their desire for a deeper, more meaningful spiritual life. They would probably be more suited to understand issues of guilt and innocence, if the gospel were presented within a framework that emphasizes how the moral aspect of sin keeps us away from personal intimacy with God rather than the impersonal and transactional "legal" framework that is common with Western evangelicals.

And finally, it may help to consider the ATR and Sufi sides of the Beja worldview as two sides of the same coin. How might we speak to them together? Viewed from this angle, the missionary should find a way, in word and deed, to present Jesus as both one more powerful than their fears and one who beckons them to experience a real, yet mystical, union with him.

Conclusion

An old Beja proverb states, "You have to seek good things, but bad things come out of their own accord" (Jacobsen 1998, 35). The Beja view life as capricious, unpredictable, and inhabited by whimsical and sometimes malicious spirits (ibid., 34). Most of the nominally Muslim Beja, like many peoples in northern Africa, approach the supernatural through their unique blend of Islam and traditional religion.

Two main streams feed into folk Islam: (1) traditional religious practices (including ATR); and (2) Islamic influences, especially Sufism. While working with the Beja people of southern Egypt, northern Eritrea, and eastern Sudan, I noticed that their religion had much in common with the ATR practices I had observed among the Sukuma tribe of Tanzania. For this reason, I have presented the Beja ethnic group as a baseline and model for observing the blending of ATR and Sufism among folk Muslims. And even when they do practice Islamic orthodoxy, it is often deeply intersected with folk Islam.

These Sufi-influenced Muslims of the African traditional religious world may inhabit the fringes of Islam, but they are far more numerous than most Westerners realize.

Reflection Questions

1. Should a Christian worker ministering among the Beja in Sudan know how to cast out evil spirits and perform exorcisms? Why or why not?

2. How would you approach working with a Muslim tribe in Africa that was heavily influenced by ATR and Sufi Islam?

References

Ausenda, G. 1987. "Leisurely Nomads: The Hadendoa (Beja) of the Gash Delta and Their Transition to Sedentary Village Life (Sudan)." PhD diss., Columbia University.

"Beja." 1979. In *The Family of Man: The Peoples of Africa*, 281–83. Tarrytown, NY: Marshall Cavendish Publishers.

Braswell, George W., Jr. 1996. *Islam: Its Prophet, Peoples, Politics and Power*. Nashville: Broadman and Holman Publishers.

Chittick, W. C. 2000. *Sufism: A Short Introduction*. Oxford: One World Publications.

Clarke, W. T. 1938. "Manners, customs and beliefs of the northern Beja." *Sudan Notes and Records* 21:1–29.

Delany, F. 1982. "Graves in the Langeb-Baraka area." *Sudan Notes and Records* 33 (1): 58–59.

El Hassan, I. S. 1980. "On ideology: the case of religion in Northern Sudan." PhD diss., University of Connecticut.

Ernst, C. W. 1997. *The Shambhala Guide to Sufism*. Boston: Shambhala Publications.

Esposito, J. L., D. J. Fasching, and T. Lewis, eds. 2009. *World Religions Today*. 3rd ed. New York: Oxford University Press.

Gamst, F. C. 1984. "Beja." In *Muslim Peoples*, 130–36. Vol. 1. Westport, CT: Greenwood Press.

Hiebert, Paul, Daniel Shaw, and Tite Tienou. 2000. *Understanding Folk Religion: A Christian Response to Popular Beliefs and Practices*. Grand Rapids: Baker.

Jacobsen, F. F. 1998. *Theories of Sickness and Misfortune among the Hadendoa Beja of the Sudan*. London and New York: Kegan Paul International.

Jenkins, Orville Boyd. 1984. *The Path of Love: Jesus in Mystical Islam*. Nairobi: Communication Press.

———. 1996. "Beja People Summary." Unpublished working paper (February). Nairobi: Interfaith Research Centre.

Kapteijns, L. 1989. "The Historiography of the Northern Sudan from 1500 to the Establishment of British Colonial Rule: A Critical Overview." *The International Journal of African Historical Studies* 22 (2): 251–66.

Karrar, A. S. 1992. *The Sufi Brotherhoods in the Sudan*. London: C. Hurst & Co., Ltd.

Levi-Strauss, C. 1985. "The sorcerer and his magic." In *Magic, Witchcraft, and Religion*, edited by A. C. Lehmann and J. E. Myers, 192–202. Mountain View, CA: Mayfield Publishing Company.

Lewis, I. M. 1980. *Islam in Tropical Africa*. 2nd ed. London: Hutchinson University Library for Africa.

Marshall, P., R. Green, and L. Gilbert. 2002. *Islam at the Crossroads*. Grand Rapids: Baker.

Muller, Roland. 2013. *The Messenger, the Message and the Community*. 3rd ed. Surrey, BC: CanBooks.

Nadel, S. F. 1945. "Notes on Beni-Amer society." *Sudan Notes and Records* 26: 53–94.

Ornas, A. H. A., and G. Dahl. 1991. *Responsible Man: The Atmaan Beja of Northeastern Sudan*. Stockholm: Rekalam and Katalogtryck.

Owen, T. R. H. 1937. "The Hadendowa." *Sudan Notes and Records* 20 (2): 181–208.

Parshall, Phil. 2006. *Bridges to Islam: A Christian Perspective on Folk Islam*. Grand Rapids: Baker.

Paul, A. 1950. "Notes on the Beni-Amer." *Sudan Notes and Records* 31: 223–45.

———. 1954. *A History of the Beja Tribes of the Sudan*. London: Frank Cass and Company Ltd.

Roden, D. 1970. "The twentieth century decline of Suakin." *Sudan Notes and Records* 51: 1–22.

Ruthven, Malaise. 2006. *Islam in the World*. New York: Oxford University Press.

Saal, W. J. 1991. *Reaching Muslims for Christ*. Chicago: Moody Press.

Sookhdeo, P. 2007. *Global Jihad*. McLean, VA: Isaac Publishing.

Wehr, H. *Arabic-English Dictionary: A Dictionary of Modern Written Arabic*. 3rd ed. Edited by J. M. Cowan. Ithica, NY: Spoken Language Services.

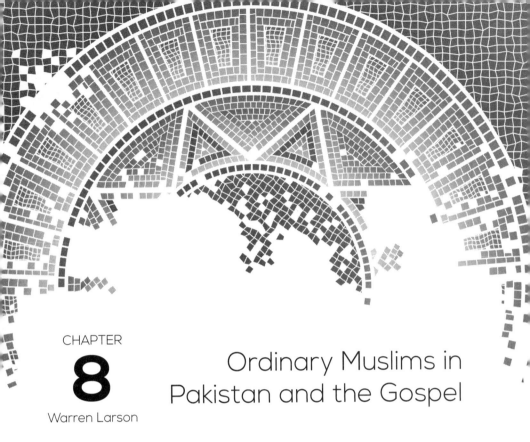

CHAPTER

8

Warren Larson

Ordinary Muslims in Pakistan and the Gospel

Islam, for many Pakistanis, is like Multan, in the central part of the country. This city is home to 165 *pirs* (saints) (Chaudhry 2002, 91–96)[1] and reflects the entire nation. Pir places are visible from one end of the country to the other. Multan is an ancient city and reportedly the place where Alexander the Great (fourth century BC) invaded India (ibid., 17–18).[2] Folk practices are also very old and existed long before the birth of Islam in AD 680. One section (Cantonment)[3] is newer, cleaner, and more organized, and the streets are straight. Approaching from the outside, this is what first meets the eye, but one must keep going to "experience" the old city. Here streets are crooked, bazaars are crowded, and customers dicker for better prices. Orthodox (traditional) Islam is like the Cantonment in that dogmas, plus denials, are clear. In contrast, folk practices

---

[1] Locals say Multan is best known for *gard* (dust), *garmi* (heat), and *ghor* (shrines).
[2] It is reported he suffered severe injuries in the battle but recovered from his wounds.
[3] Paul Hiebert (1985) is to be credited with the analogy that folk practices are like an ancient city.

are mystical and hard to define, but very real (Musk 1989).[4] That said, the line of separation between folk and traditional Islam is often thin. "People of the shrine" are usually also "people of the mosque."

Before living in Pakistan, I knew little about Muslims, and it took years to understand folk practices. This is what I learned over time: Women are the best patrons—lighting candles and tying bits of clothing or hair on the tomb.[5] Seeking to bear a son, in need of healing for a sick child, or desperate for help in an abusive relationship, they make their requests and vow to give something back when the need is met. Shrine activity, however, is only the tip of the iceberg. Life for many is a daily struggle involving the evil eye (Dundes 1992),[6] jinn, amulets, charms, incantations, demons, angels, plus a whole lot of fear. Above all, there is a felt need for baraka[7] (spiritual power, clout, and good luck) (von Denfer 1976, 167–86).

This chapter begins by looking at historical, political, and religious elements that contributed to the birth and development of Pakistan. Despite a strong puritanical movement (*Pakistan* means "Land of the Pure"), folk practices are widespread and here to stay (Marsden 2013, xii–xv).[8] The purpose is to explain how to be "gospel relevant" (Hiebert 1985, 15) in Pakistan by taking ordinary Muslims seriously. My sense is that what is true of Pakistan is mostly true of Muslims in South Asia and beyond.

The Background: A Country at War with Itself

Islam officially came to the subcontinent in the eighth century (Geijbels 1976, 147),[9] and Sufi[10] influence can be traced back to the eleventh century (Chaudhry 2013, 30). Pakistan was part of British India until 1947, but at partition up to fifteen million people were uprooted in what was the most massive and violent transfer of humanity in history. Most Hindus fled what would be Pakistan, while Muslims poured in. Estimates are that one million were slaughtered by frenzied mobs (Collins and Lapierre 1976).

Almost immediately the country went to war with India over Kashmir, and hostilities continue to this day. In 1971 the country broke apart, and East Pakistan became Bangladesh (again a million lives lost). Leaders attempted to bolster identity by reminders of the India threat, and many have appealed to Islam as the rallying point, but the nation remains sharply divided (Sayeed 1995).[11]

---

[4] This is an excellent resource for Christian workers. Bill Musk was the first to speak of folk Muslims as "ordinary" (meaning most).

[5] Saints can be dead or alive. Some shrines are simple, attended by locals; others are ornate mausoleums, and pilgrims come from great distances.

[6] The widespread belief that envy, or any kind of ill will, can cause physical harm to others and their possessions.

[7] "Holders of baraka" include Muhammad, the Qur'an, tombs, saints, other special people, and various objects.

[8] Marsden stayed with a traditional Deoband family whose views about jinn were basically folk Islam.

[9] The Arab conquest took place in AD 711 under the direction of Muhammad bin Qasim

[10] Sufism is the "inner path" that seeks to know God directly. Its teaching and methods are achieved by giving the Qur'an and Islamic revelation mystical and spiritual interpretations.

[11] Based on my study of Wahabbis, the Muslim Brotherhood, and Maududi, I believe such an emphasis will backfire in Pakistan and throughout the Middle East.

This country is unique in that it was the first in modern history to make religion the raison d'être, even though this is not what Muhammad Ali Jinnah (its founder) had in mind.

> There can be no doubt that Jinnah was a secularist and against theocracy. In his speech to the Constituent Assembly on 11th of August 1947, he had given a picture of Pakistan which was nothing short of a secular state in which Muslims and non-Muslims could live together and be its citizens, with equal rights of citizenship, and that religion would be a private affair of the individual, having nothing to do with the administration of the State. (Munir 1979, xv; quoted in Larson 1998, 79)

However, since hard-liners insist that Jinnah favored a partisan Muslim state, there has been endless wrangling about ideology and identity. Whereas India came up with a constitution in a year, it took Pakistan nine years to do the same, with numerous amendments. One statement, in particular, is troubling and open to interpretation. Article 198 says, "No law shall be passed that is repugnant to Islam." Given the fact that there may be as many as forty thousand madrassas (Qur'anic schools) (Weaver 2002, 9), Islamists such as Maulana Maududi have succeeded in making the nation more religious, although many Muslims resent having it forced down their throats (Larson 1998).[12] Minorities are increasingly under pressure.

Ever since 1973, when Islam became the state religion, Islamists have attempted to "protect Islam." As a result, Christians have been hit hard (Presler 2015, 72–77)[13] under the blasphemy law ("the hanging sword"), and Ahmadis even more so (Anonymous PhD Candidate 2015, 14–27).[14] The constitution promises religious freedom for all in order that everyone can "profess, practice and propagate" his religion (Article 20a), but goes on to say, "All existing laws shall be brought into conformity with the injunctions of Islam as laid down in the Quran and Sunnah. … No law shall be enacted which is repugnant to such injunctions" (Article 227) (Presler 2015, 72–77).

The irony is that despite these rigid rules that have been put in place through an Islamist movement, Pakistan's culture and society have deep roots in Hinduism, and possibly Buddhism. Such influences were present when the nation was born, and distinguishing between cultural and religious practices is difficult. Mosques, madrassas, and *mazars* (shrines) have stood side by side for centuries, and folk Muslims sincerely believe they are devout followers of Islam (Schimmel 2003, 106).[15]

---

[12] My research suggests that Islamism in Pakistan is driving some Muslims to seriously consider Christianity.

[13] He says ongoing mob violence and court cases undermine confidence and create uncertainty because believers "internalize the blame." Eighty percent of Christians have menial jobs.

[14] Even the governor of the Punjab, Salman Taseer, was gunned down in 2011 for opposing them [these laws? Either these laws or Islamists].

[15] Schimmel (2003) is careful to give her article a title that is not judgmental as to who is orthodox and who is not.

The Spirit World of Muslims

Several years ago, Muslim friends of ours experienced a terrible tragedy. The husband, a strong, healthy police officer, suddenly got sick and died. His widow informed my wife it was no accident: A disgruntled relative had put a curse on her, but something went wrong and it struck her husband. Left with ten children to care for, educate, and marry off, the burden was almost more than she could bear. Such a reaction to tragedy is common, but the question is, *where* do these ideas come from?

A Foundation for Folk Beliefs

Earl Grant's reply is that this kind of thinking is deeply rooted in the religion itself. "Folk," or "popular," Islam, he says, is not just another subsystem; it is an animistic substrate that underlies most of what Muslims believe and do. It existed long before Islam emerged in the seventh century and has profoundly shaped every aspect of their lives (1988, 22–25). In support of his conclusions, consider the following.

First, the sacred sources of Islam (the Qur'an and Hadith) portray an animistic worldview (al-Ashqar 1988). The word *jinn* appears thirty-two times in the Qur'an; half of those incidents are paired with humans, and often their activity is associated with women (Jolin 2001, 73–85; also Ashour 1993).[16] The Hadith, too, is replete with references to jinn (Lewis 1985, 38).[17] They have rebelled against God[18] and cause all kinds of problems, such as epidemics, mayhem, and fits. In short, they do what humans do—eat, drink, marry, mate, and bear children; although, it is generally understood they do not have their own body (Attallah n.d.).[19]

Second, popular views of Muhammad provide a paradigm for pir prasti (saint worship) (Siddiqi 1998),[20] and veneration of the Prophet is not without Qur'anic support: He is a "beautiful model" (33:21) and to be obeyed as if Allah himself were speaking (33:33). Islamicist Wilfred Cantwell Smith is quoted with this statement: "Muslims will allow attacks on Allah … but to disparage Muhammad will provoke from even most 'liberal' sections of the community a fanaticism of blazing vehemence" (Schimmel 1985, 4, 238).[21] There is also some indication that the Arabian prophet resorted to magic. Muhammad Dashti, the late Iranian journalist, demonstrates that

---

[16] Jolin … refers to a Moroccan proverb that says "Women are the friends of the devil."

[17] Lewis quotes *Mishkat* vol. 2, 95–952 [That's a wide range!] to the effect that Muhammad sought refuge from the evil eye, as well as jinn, and says this worldview is "taken for granted" as part of the religious belief system.

[18] See Surah 72:1–15. Jinn cause problems (72:53), so avoid complimenting another lest it bring attention to the jinn. Practitioners, when called upon, often recite Surah 36 (*Ya Sin*), known as "The Heart of the Qur'an."

[19] A reference in the Hadith (Khan 1981, 1:583) is that Muhammad said jinn eat bone and animal dung. And since Satan spends the night in your nose, it must be vigorously blown in the morning (ibid., 4:156). Numerous Qur'anic references show the prevalence of jinn in pre-Islamic Arabia (6:100, 6:128, 37:158, 34:41, 122:6, 7:184, and 72:6).

[20] Such a book title, *Ninety-Nine Names of the Prophet Muhammad*, seems to go beyond veneration.

[21] Interestingly, Muhammad Iqbal, the "Father of Pakistan," was lavish in his praise of Muhammad but against "pirism."

Surahs 113 and 114 were revealed when a curse was put on him. Those two chapters are still used today to counteract curses (Dashti 1994, 159–60).

These observations are nothing new, as Samuel Zwemer pointed out nearly one hundred years ago:

> In no monotheistic religion are magic and sorcery so firmly entrenched as they are in Islam; for in the case of this religion they are based on the teaching of the Koran and the practice of the Prophet. ... The book itself, as we have seen has magical power. The superstitions that obtained in Arabia before Islam have been perpetuated by it. No orthodox Moslems doubts that men are able to call forth the power of demons and Jinn by means of magic (sihr). Everywhere there are professional means of magic, wizards and witches. ... The sorcerer who desires to exercise his magic art begins by sacrificing a black cock. He then reads his spell, ties his knots, or flings his magical readings into the wells. All this was done in the same fashion today as was customary before Mohammed. To such practices the last two chapters of the Koran refer. (Zwemer 1920, 162–65)

My purpose here is not to unfairly critique the Qur'an or deny positive features of Muhammad (such as his giving women more rights), but to recognize the foundation for folk practices. Workers must be aware of how much the Prophet is loved and be respectful in what they say about him. Above all, they must know how to present Jesus with love and understanding.

Glimpses of syncretism

One indication of syncretism in Pakistan is easily missed: the unforgettable display of richly adorned trucks. They are in multiple colors, displaying gorgeous scenes of nature, animals, and images of influential people in history. Although this is art, what many do not realize is that behind these paintings is an animistic worldview. Along with glamorous images, vehicles often display the hand of Fatima (Muhammad's daughter) to ward off curses, names of God, or verses from the Qur'an. Without insurance, and where automobile accidents are extremely common, drivers resort to folk practices for safety on the roads (Elias 2011, 29).

Another sign of syncretism that can also be overlooked is the Badshahi Mosque ("King Mosque"), the fifth largest mosque in the world. Although it was built in AD 1673 by Emperor Aurangzeb, who was a strict Muslim and against any form of folk practice, on the compound today are signs of folk and traditional Islam rolled into one. Outwardly it is the face of orthodoxy, a place of formal prayers five times a day; but off to the side of the huge prayer room is a winding staircase. On the second level, behind plates of glass, are twenty-seven artifacts of Muhammad—including his underwear! All are thought to procure much-needed baraka. The significance of such artifacts goes back hundreds of years. For instance, various caliphs wore the *burdah* (cloak of the Prophet) for power, influence, and good fortune. Allegedly, Umayyad Caliph Mu'awiyah's dying instructions were that Muhammad's nail trimmings be sprinkled on his eyes and mouth, in hopes God would have mercy on him (Margoliouth 2007, 20–27).

Saints and shrines

Right next door to this historic mosque is one of the most striking and decorative shrines in the land: the famous Ali al-Hujwiri site, better known as Data Ganj Baksh (Bestower of Treasure), patron saint of Lahore (Geijbels 1982, 23). Muslims flock to this place in search of blessing and success. Above the entrance to the mausoleum a sign says, "He who calls at your shrine never returns disappointed" (Osborne 1983, 49). A friend told me that while studying for his MA in English he came every week, and credits the saint for a passing grade.

Such places are thought to possess a sanctity and a flow of spirituality because the saint is believed to be a conduit for Allah's blessing. Devotees come with personal problems, such as health, infertility, or in search of baraka, and attach a symbol of their problem to the tomb (Chaudhry 1994, 85–98). After paying homage to the saint, they say a *dua* (prayer), and each request is transmitted to God. One village woman explained her visit this way, "You see, Sir, I am an ordinary woman. I approach Allah through the saint, whenever there are difficulties in my life. The saint is more powerful than I and so far all my requests have been fulfilled" (Geijbels 1978, 176–86).

Pirs may be called *baba*, *shah*, or *Hazrat* (all terms of respect). One of my sources discusses the activities of twenty-five prominent saints in the Punjab, categorized under their respective Sufi orders (Ali 1994). Another lists seventy-six in the Sind, and northern Pakistan is also home to a proliferation of pirs (Binder 2014). By the eighteenth century it is said you couldn't travel more than a few miles without seeing pirs throughout the entire Indian subcontinent, and during the British Raj they helped settle tribal disputes and kept things running smoothly (Ansari 1992, 22). Under the Pakistani government, shrines were brought under the *Auqaf* (religious) department, contributing to their power and political influence (ibid., 152–53).[22] In short, these sites became symbols of Muslim culture, and even of Islam itself.

Lest anyone think only poor people visit pirs, consider Lal Shahnaz Qalander (Red Eagle Mendicant) in Sehwan Sharif, two hundred miles north of Karachi. It draws pilgrims from all over the country and some from abroad. The saint was born in AD 1177, and the *urs* ("wedding feast," or death of the pir when he met his Lord) begins June 18 (Osborne 1983, 146). Horns blow and emotions are high as people look on with breathless anticipation. Numerous events take place: dancing, music, *mehandi* (henna treatments as is done at weddings), and many pilgrims linger for a feast of chicken curry, prepared in the massive kitchen (Schmidle 2009, 37–47). This is the patron saint of the Bhutto family, especially Zulfikar, prime minister in the early 1970s,[23] and his daughter Benazir. As related in her autobiography, while facing

---

[22] Pir Pagaro sided with the Muslim League (party) and wielded significant political power. It is said that he controlled twenty members of the Sind Assembly in 1955.

[23] After being ousted in a military coup, he was hanged by General Zia-ul-Haqq in 1979, despite calls for clemency by world leaders.

personal loss and political opposition, she clung to folk beliefs, despite being educated in the West (Harvard and Oxford) and twice elected leader (Bhutto 1988, 124, 138).[24] When interviewed by Mary Anne Weaver, she was wearing a little gold charm around her neck, with a verse from the Qur'an (Weaver 2002, 176).

I personally learned a lot about pirs from observing shrine activities at a place called Saky Sarvar, near the border of Baluchistan and close to our home. Prior to partition, pilgrims came from great distances, but after 1947 the crowds became smaller. It was a "religious fair," but there were additional attractions; prostitutes were on hand, bussed in from a distant city, to capitalize on the opportunity for extra income. Some men, dressed as women, danced provocatively on elevated platforms.[25] And there was the "well of death," where a motorcycle would begin at the bottom and wind its way to the top, while the wooden structure rocked precariously. Normally there was nothing in this barren, rocky place; yet during the three-day *urs*, locals flocked to the little white shrine on a hill.

A Muslim woman well known to our family gave birth to a son after her visit. She was given water to drink and vowed that if she had a son she would come back with a gift in hand. A verse from the Qur'an was written on a piece of paper and hung around her neck. One year later she had a baby boy and named him *Pir Baksh* ("given by the pir"). It should come as no surprise that many men in Pakistan bear the same name.

Doing daily battle

Ordinary Muslims constantly seek protection from forces perceived to be against them. To avoid the jinn, they may sleep with the light on, and then vigorously blow their nose in the morning—as noted, Muhammad said Satan spends the night in the upper part of your nose! They also refrain from whistling, as this could draw their attention. Since calamity is caused by malevolent beings, Muslims spend much time, energy, and money trying to ensure safety. Infants are particularly vulnerable, so may be kept hidden for forty days, and black soot is painted under their eyes. Mothers say a beautiful baby is ugly, and a precocious child is dumb, in order to confuse harmful spirits. Unmarried girls may also be at risk. The mother of a beautiful daughter worries that the mother of one somewhat less attractive might inflict harm through envy. Amulets with special Qur'anic verses are sewed into leather pouches[26] and hung on ankles, arms, and necks, or written on walls and vehicles.

Angels are also called upon for help, as are prophets, like Solomon, who had power over the jinn (Surah 2:102). The hand of Fatima is engraved in necklaces to

---

[24] Reportedly, thousands now flock to the site of her father's grave, and allegedly miracles are taking place, such as a barren woman giving birth to a son.

[25] Due to Islamization, begun in the late 1970s under General Zia, such activities may have now been stopped by government orders, or at least restricted.

[26] The greatest charm is the Qur'an. It protects buildings, buses, and babies; it is kissed, wrapped in a cloth, recited at birth/death, walked under for protection, used for divining/healing, and must never be questioned or critiqued.

guard against the evil eye and may be sketched on door knobs. Marshes, latrines, and garbage dumps (thought to be inhabited by jinn) are dangerous, so when visiting such a place the word *bismilla* ("in the name of God") is repeated for protection. *Mashallah* ("whatever God wills") is often written on the foundation of a new house to shield it from the eye of envy. And Islamic traditions say that when a man has sexual relations with his wife, he should ask Allah for protection from Satan; otherwise any child born of the union could be a devil (Khan 1981, 1:143).

Ministry in Context

Everything discussed up to this point leads us to ask how Christian workers should live and minister among folk Muslims (Stacey 1984).[27]

Understanding the "power"

Perhaps the best place to begin is with our own understanding: "If there is any one theme that dominates the Muslim it is the reality of power" (Grant 1988, 25). Detmar Scheunemann takes it one step further:

> Working for many years in a Muslim country, I have come to the conclusion that the power of Islam does not lie in its dogma and practices, nor in the antithesis of the Trinity, against the Lordship of Christ and his redeeming death, but in the occult practices of its leader, thus holding sway over their people. (Scheunemann 1975, 885)

As a new worker, I was not equipped in this area, and many others have expressed a similar lack (Stacey 1989, ix).[28] The quest for power is particularly pertinent for ministry among Muslim women. "To have a relevant witness, then, coherentism suggests a Christian must explore the local worldview and present the gospel with as much reference to the entire belief system as possible in order for it to be understood and accepted" (Strong and Page 2006, 34). One worker in South Asia suggests that our failure to understand the need of Muslim women for power and blessing may be the reason why little has been accomplished. We have thought that if men, who seem to control things, could be won, then the family would follow (Wray 2006, 146). This is not to suggest that women are greedier for power. Many have been marginalized, and they need to be given a voice. However, they also need to hear that complete deliverance from fear can only come through Christ, not through charms and other folk practices.

---

[27] This little book was very helpful during our early years in Pakistan in regard to knowing how to recognize and respond to demonic activity.

[28] She concluded that Western theological training had not prepared her to work with Muslims. For the first eight years she was unaware of Muslim involvement with demonism and the occult. Similarly, after observing shrine activities outside Islamabad, J. Dudley Woodberry (1990, 313–31) concluded that his studies at Harvard, under the direction of Sir Hamilton Gibb, had neglected this aspect of Islam. He knew about truth issues, but here power was much more important.

Thinking about suffering

The point is not to reiterate why God had to suffer. Kenneth Cragg has done an excellent job in explaining why Muslims tend to reject the Cross (Cragg 1956, 294–303).[29] The need is to convince Muslims of the value of suffering and to prepare converts for persecution. For this we must meditate deeply on God's suffering (Hill 2015), but we must also be able to demonstrate that suffering is not always a bad thing. There is a purpose, even if we do not have the answer. To get this across, it is often best to share about our own suffering, and how God has used it to shape and even bless us.

Obviously, discernment is crucial in understanding root causes as to why Muslims so desperately want to take charge of their difficult situation. In folk Islam, misfortune never happens by chance. And when misfortune inevitably does happen, the question in not so much "Why?" but "Who did it?" There is a sense of desperation that something must be done to alleviate the pain, and by utilizing an "expert" one can always place a counter curse. Undoubtedly this approach helps people take control and identify the "culprit," but it seldom brings healing. Instead it throws the door open to suspicion and can ruin relationships (Howell 2012, 130).

Alan Howell (2012) points out that God took suffering and turned it into something beautiful. Even though Satan has a hand in human suffering, Jesus defeated Satan on the Cross, and the day will come when Satan will be cast into hell. "Turning it beautiful" (ibid., 129) means to live and teach how suffering builds character; increases intimacy with the Lord; and, when handled right, glorifies God. "Count it all joy, my brothers, when you meet with trials of various kinds, for you know that the testing of your faith produces steadfastness" (James 1:2–3 ESV). Other relevant verses encourage us to cling to the goodness of God and what he has prepared for those who love him (2 Sam 12:13–23; Luke 13:10–17; John 9:1–7; 10:10; 11:25–26; 1 Cor 2:9; 15:54–55; 1 Thess 4:13–14) and that "He will wipe away every tear" (Rev 21:3–4 ESV).

Seeking to be a blessing

Although it is often hard to evaluate the effect of treatment for physical, psychological, and spiritual illness meted out at the shrine, one thing is certain: Often the poor have nowhere else to go for help in the midst of their despair. In contexts like Pakistan, where insanity is frequently diagnosed as possession by evil spirits and where exorcism can be very painful to the patient, there is tremendous hope for medical missions along with the gospel. The fact that Jesus is alive and that he is with us at all times through the indwelling Spirit will strike a responsive chord in many a Muslim heart. Stressing the work of Christ as mediator between God and humanity is extremely fitting in such settings. It is no wonder that the favorite verse of Muslims who took our Bible correspondence courses in Pakistan was "Come to me, all you who are weary and

---

[29] Cragg says that "the God of the Muslim cross" cannot suffer because his honor is at stake. Muslims reject the Cross, not from history but because it is unthinkable that God should suffer, or that he should allow his beloved prophet to suffer in such a shameful way.

burdened, and I will give you rest, … I am gentle and humble in heart, and you will find rest for your souls" (Matt 11:28–30 NIV).

Given the fact that many have been "taken in" by unscrupulous pirs, there is often suspicion among common folk that a lot of pirs are immoral, greedy, and charlatans. Frequently they amass a fortune by taking advantage of the poor. Christian workers therefore must not only stress the perfection of Jesus but demonstrate personal holiness. And, as pointed out, they must also overcome their own fears: "When MBBs (Muslim-background believers) were asked what they had learned from expatriate workers, many replied, 'They teach us to be afraid.' God does not call us to teach or model a spirit of fear to new believers" (Stricker 2006, 213). We need to apply Scripture to ourselves and with believing Muslim friends: "They will have no fear of bad news; their hearts are steadfast, trusting in the Lord" (Ps 112:7 NIV). We can comfort, encourage, and guide by sharing biblical passages that give assurance of God's presence at all times and in all circumstances (Ps 32:8; Prov 3:5–6, Rom 8).

In many ways, traditional and folk Muslims are quite similar. For example, both have the idea that God predetermines everything by his white-hot power. Islamic theologians have debated predestination, but as the following verses show, the Qur'an allows little room for human choice. For example, "No soul can believe except by the will of Allah" (10:100); "Ye will not except Allah wills" (76:29–31a). There are at least twenty-one statements that suggest God lets stray whom he will and guides whom he will. Basically, if God guides you, that is great; if not, you are doomed. In contrast, Jesus' followers have hope and assurance. The Hebrew word *barak* (blessing) literally means "to bend the knee," but it is not simply a matter of submission as slaves. We are his beloved children, and so the true meaning of blessing is joy and trust, unmarred by fear and care. Since we are his children, we can praise him at all times because he is looking out for us.

In conclusion, although Pakistanis believe that the overall will and control of Allah is final, and that one must trust in his sovereign will in the face of disease and death, the fact is they spend vast amounts of energy and money trying to fight it. Shrine activity is how Muslims put a human face on religion in trying to meet felt needs, and a thorough understanding of felt needs will open many doors for the spread of the gospel. If Allah is not delighted by obedience and is not displeased by sins, nor hostile to the arrogant, they must look for a way to meet felt needs. If Allah's hand is not close to protect and his eyes are indifferent to hostile forces, then charms, spells, curses, and incantations may be used to gain peace for the soul and health for the body. Illness does not just happen, say Pakistani Muslims; it befalls victims because of hostile forces like the evil eye and other menacing realities.

Ordinary Muslims need physical, emotional, and spiritual healing; and a Christian worker must work not only in a scientific way but in a spiritual manner. The gospel alone brings deliverance. And since veneration of pirs in Pakistan is done in an attempt to fulfill a deeply felt need (it leaves the heart empty), the cross cultural worker must make much of Jesus as the only one who has the power to save people from Satan, fear of evil spirits, and terror of the grave. Muslims feel a great need to know God personally, and the good news is that through Christ, they can.

Reflection Questions

1. Seeing how many Muslims live for the shrine (help, healing, guidance, solace), how should you minister in such situations?

2. How can you use your personal testimony about God, including your own suffering, in Christian witness?

References

Adeney, Miriam. 2000. "Why Muslim Women Come to Christ." In *Longing to Call Them Sisters*, edited by Fran Love and Jeleta Echeart. Pasadena, CA: William Carey Library.

Al-Ashqar, Umar Sulaiman. 1988. *The World of the Jinn and Devils*. Translated by Jamaal al-Din M. Zarabozo. Boulder, CO: Basheer Company.

Ali, Abdulla Yusaf. 1996. *The Meaning of the Holy Qur'an*. Beltsville, MD: Amana Publications.

Ali, Syed Ishfaq. 1994. *The Saints of the Punjab*. Rawalpindi, Pakistan: Pap Board.

Anonymous PhD Candidate. 2015. "A Comparison, contrast and critique of Ahmadi and Christian socio-political responses to Pakistan's blasphemy laws with special reference to the Christian Church in Pakistan." PhD diss., Australian Theological College.

Ansari, Sarah F. D. 1992. *Sufi Saints and State Power: The Pirs of Sind*, 1943–1947. Cambridge: Cambridge University Press.

Ashour, Mustafa. 1993. *The Jinn in the Qur'an and the Sunna*. London: Dar Al Taqwa Ltd.

Bhutto, Benazir. 1988. *Benazir Bhutto Daughter of the East: An Autobiography*. London: Hamish Hamilton Ltd.

Binder, Reinhold. 2014. "The Practice of Folk Islam in Pakistan with Emphasis and Special Consideration of the Hazara Division." Unpublished paper, Columbia International University.

Chaudhry, Hafeez-ur-Rehman. 1994. "Traditional and State Organization of the Shrine of Bari Imam." *Al-Mushir* 36 (3): 85–98.

———. 2013. *Saints and Shrines in Pakistan: Anthropological Perspective*. National Institute of Historical and Cultural Research, Centre of Excellence, Quaid-i-Azam University. Islamabad, Pakistan: Publisher Muhammad Munir Khawar.

Chaudhry, Nazir Ahmed. 2002. *Multan Glimpses*. Lahore, Pakistan: Sang-e-Meel Publishers.

Collins, Larry, and Dominique Lapierre. 1976. *Freedom at Midnight*. New York: Avon Books.

Cragg, Kenneth. 1956. *The Call of the Minaret*. New York: Oxford University Press.

Dashti, Ali. 1994. *Twenty-three Years: A Study of the Prophetic Career of Mohammad*. Costa Mesa, CA: Mazda Publishers.

Dundes, Alan, ed. 1992. *The Evil Eye: A Casebook*. Madison, WI: The University of Wisconsin Press.

Elias, Jamal J. 2011. *On Wings of Diesel: Trucks, Identity and Culture in Pakistan*. Oxford: Oneworld Publications.

Geijbels, M. 1976. "Islam in Pakistan." *Al-Mushir* 18 (5).

———. 1978. "Aspects of the Veneration of Saints in Islam with Special Reference to Pakistan." *The Muslim World*: 176–86.

———. 1982. *Muslim Festivals and Ceremonies in Pakistan*. Rawalpindi, Pakistan: Christian Study Centre.

Grant, Earl E. 1988. "Folk Islam: The Animist Substrata." *Theology, News and Notes* (December): 22–25.

Hiebert, Paul G. 1985. *Anthropological Insights for Missionaries*. Grand Rapids: Baker.

Hill, Wesley. 2015. "The God Who Cannot Suffer Suffered: How the Paradox Comforts Us in Our Own Pain." *Christianity Today*. May 15. http://www.christianitytoday.com/ct/2015.

Howell, Alan. 2012. "Turning It Beautiful: Divination, Discernment and a Theology of Suffering." *IJFM* 29 (3):129–37.

Jolin, Paula. 2001. "The Jinn in the Qur'an and in Popular Islam." *Institute of Islamic Studies*, McGill University: 73–85.

Khan, Muhammad Muhsin. 1981. *The Translation of the Meanings of Sahih Al-Bukhari*. Arabic-English. 9 vols. Beirut: Dar Al Arabia.

Larson, Warren. 1998. *Islamic Ideology and Fundamentalism in Pakistan: Climate for Conversion to Christianity?* Cleveland: University Publishers of America.

Lewis, P. 1985. *Pirs, Shrines and Pakistani Islam*. Rawalpindi, Pakistan: Christian Study Centre.

Margoliouth, David, S. 2007. "The Relics of the Prophet Mohammed." *The Muslim World* 27 (1): 20–27.

Marsden, Magnus. 2013. *Islam and Society in Pakistan: Anthropological Perspective*. Oxford: Oxford University Press.

Munir, Muhammad. 1979. *From Jinnah to Zia*. Lahore, Pakistan: Vanguard Books.

Musk, Bill. 1989. *The Unseen Face of Islam: Sharing the Gospel with Ordinary Muslims*. East Sussex, UK: MARC.

Osborne, Christine. 1983. *An Insight and Guide to Pakistan*. New York: Longman Group Ltd.

Presler, Titus. 2015. "A Toll on the Soul: Costs of Persecution among Pakistani Christians." *International Bulletin of Missionary Research* 39 (2): 72–77.

Sayeed, S. M. A. 1995. *The Myth of Authenticity: A Study on Islamic Fundamentalism*. Karachi, Pakistan: Royal Book Company.

Scheunemann, Detmar. 1975. "Evangelization Among Occultists and Spiritists." In *Let the Earth Hear His Voice*. Minneapolis: Worldwide Publications.

Schimidle, Nicholas. 2009. "Faith Ecstasy." *Smithsonian* 30 (4): 37–47.

Schimmel, Annemarie. 1985. *And Muhammad Is His Messenger: The Veneration of the Prophet in Islamic Society*. Chapel Hill, NC: The University of North Carolina Press.

———. 2003. *Islam in the Indian Subcontinent*. Lahore, Pakistan: Sang-e-Meel Publications.

Siddiqi, Muhammad Iqbal. 1998. *Ninety-Nine Names of the Prophet Muhammad*. Lahore, Pakistan: Kazi Publications.

Stacey, Vivienne. 1989. "The Practice of Exorcism and Healing." In *Muslims and Christians on the Emmaus Road*, edited by J. Dudley Woodberry. Monrovia, CA: MARC.

Stricker, Beth. 2006. "Communicating Christ in the Context of Persecution." In *A Worldview Approach to Ministry Among Muslim Women*, edited by Cynthia Strong and Meg Page. Pasadena, CA: William Carey Library.

von Denfer, Dietrich. 1976. "Baraka as Basic Concept of Muslim Popular Belief." *Islamic Studies* 15 (3): 167–86.

Weaver, Mary Anne. 2002. *Pakistan in the Shadow of Jihad and Afghanistan*. New York: Farrar, Straus and Giroux.

Woodberry, J. Dudley. 1990. "The Relevance of Power Ministries for Folk Muslims." In *Wrestling with Dark Angels*, edited by C. Peter Wagner and F. Douglas Pennoyer. Ventura, CA: Regal Books.

Wray, Yvette. 2006. "A Life of Ironies: Reaching South Asian Educated Urban Muslim Women." In *A Worldview Approach to Ministry Among Muslim Women*, edited by Cynthia Strong and Meg Page. Pasadena, CA: William Carey Library.

Zwemer, Samuel M. 1920. *The Influence of Animism on Islam: An Account of Popular Superstitions*. New York: The Macmillan Company.

———. 1973. *The Glory of the Cross*. Bombay: Gospel Literature Service.

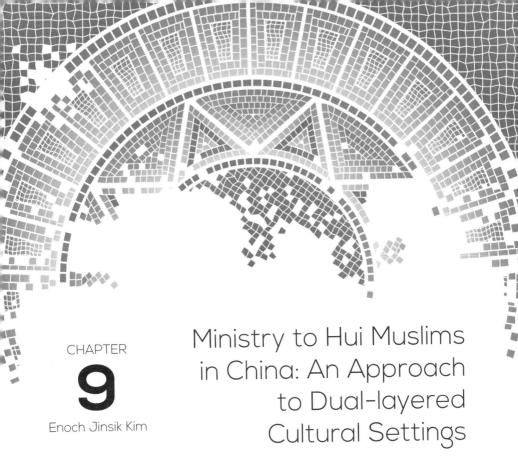

9

Enoch Jinsik Kim

Ministry to Hui Muslims in China: An Approach to Dual-layered Cultural Settings

My family and I lived in China for sixteen years, serving as missionaries to share the gospel with the Hui, one of about a dozen Muslim ethnic minorities in the country. With a population of 13.4 million, they are the largest Muslim ethnic group in China (Joshua Project 2017). Despite various evangelistic efforts over the past few decades, very few Hui have responded to the gospel.

This chapter presents a case study in reaching the Hui. However, the concepts presented are representative of the ministry context for reaching millions of people in other Muslim minorities in China. Of course, I am aware that among the various Chinese Muslim ethnic groups, each has formed distinct cultural identities, given their unique historical backgrounds. Therefore, I do not believe they necessarily share the specific cultural themes of power and pride, which I have summarized as the theme of the Hui. However, since all Chinese Muslim communities are currently experiencing complex social changes due to rapid modernization, the concept of the two-layered cultural settings I describe through this case study provides what I believe to be a solid starting place for effective evangelistic ministry.

There following four main concepts support the ministry strategy discussed in this chapter: 1) What are the traditional cultural themes of the subject ethnic group? 2) What is the new face of modern Muslims in the city? 3) How can the double-layer cultural structure of modern Chinese Muslims be identified? 4) How is the good news relevant to the subject ethnic group?

Background of the Hui

The Hui are one of fifty-six ethnic groups officially recognized in China. They are the largest Muslim group, followed by the sometimes better-known Uyghur people. The history of the Hui in China reaches almost back to the time of Muhammad, more than 1,300 years ago. During this time they engaged in a variety of social and vocational roles, including those of merchants, nomads, and soldiers, among others.[1] Traditionally, the Hui have lived in the northwestern region of China, but over time many have migrated so that now they are found in all the major cities across China.

The Hui's ethnic roots originate from Central Asia and Middle Eastern regions, including Persia, Pakistan, Turkey, and Mongolia. Thus the culture of the Hui is a fusion of the Mongolians, Tibetans, Han Chinese, and other peoples in northwestern China. Similar to most other Muslim ethnic groups in China, the Hui generally separate themselves from the Chinese majority (the Han) and establish communities around centrally located mosques (Ekvall 1939, 19). These Islamic communities, which are essentially Chinese Islamic enclaves, are neighborhoods where a sense of belonging is fostered among residents and the resources needed for daily life are readily available. These resources include useful information and social networks, as well as ethnic restaurants and markets offering halal foods. The neighborhoods of Sunni Muslims are referred to as *gedimu*, which is simply the Chinese transliteration of the Arabic *al qadim*, meaning "ancient or old." There is much diversity within the Hui, since many Islamic religious sects have found a place among them through history.

Because the Hui are a distinct culture and the practice of their religion affords limited common ground with the majority Han, they have historically perceived the central government's policies as a means of cultural assimilation through coercion. To protect their freedom to practice their religion, the Hui and other Muslims occasionally rebel in armed clashes with the government.[2] A recent conflict involving the Hui occurred in 1975 during the Cultural Revolution. These disturbances in the Yunnan province prompted Red Army troops to forcibly shutdown all Hui religious activities for a time (Dillon 1999, 164).

---

[1] Broomhall (1966, 64–68); Andrew (1921, 14); Lawton (1985, 4); Gao (1997, 35–42); Leslie (1986, 129–30); Andrew and China Inland Mission (1921).
[2] Leslie (1986, 129–30); Lipman and Violence (1990, 71–73).

Their Traditional Face

Paul Hiebert referred to critical contextualization as a method to communicate the gospel using a culturally sensitive approach (1987, 109–11; 1999, 381–82). The approach involves four guidelines: 1) an exegesis of culture, 2) an exegesis of Scripture, 3) a critical evaluation of past customs in light of new biblical understandings, and then 4) the development of new contextual practices. I use this specific method to study cultural themes within Chinese Muslim ethnic groups (Kim 2013, 189–95).

The cultural themes which are thus found can serve as important raw information. This information can be used to understand cultural signs and symbols that determine why groups prefer to act in the ways they do. It also can be an important stepping-stone in helping Christians present a culturally appropriate message to them (ibid., 193–94).

In order to identify core Hui cultural themes, I analyzed six significant social structures, symbols, and signs. The following traditional community resources fell into categories relevant for such an analysis: the *qingzhen* (or ethnic community),[3] the *qingzhen* (or ethnic restaurant), and the mosque. Likewise, core cultural themes can be found by analyzing traditional social activities/ceremonies, including rites of passage,[4] endogamy,[5] and those attitudes which give the community a collective sense of superiority.[6]

Results from analyses of these familiar elements in Hui daily life consistently pointed to two cultural themes: power and pride (ibid., 192–93). These likely developed as a way to address their basic physical and social needs and have shaped survival strategies for living under China's Han majority (ibid.). These twin themes of power and pride have been expressed in both healthy and unhealthy ways.

Their New Face

Hui power and pride are engaged mostly through traditional cultural elements. However, because they are facing the challenge of rapid urbanization, like all Chinese,[7] attempting to define Hui culture only through these traditional cultural themes is inappropriate. Given that, like most people living in urban areas, they attend public schools, earn a living in diverse workplaces, and sometimes reside in mixed ethnic communities, the Hui also must acquire the knowledge needed to live peacefully and comfortably among others. In other words, the Hui today interact with other ethnicities in a manner unlike their ancestors, who generally lived in isolation. Now, because of broad exposure to others, the Hui need to understand their diverse ethnic neighbors in order to maintain profitable vocations and businesses (Hoffman 2001, 44–49).

---

[3] Gladney (1987); Andrew and China Inland (1921, 37–40).
[4] Kim (2009, 167–68); Gladney (1998, 142–43); Hai (1992, 57).
[5] Gladney (1998, 249); Kraft (1996, chap. 21); Shaw (1988, 97–102). Endogamy refers to the custom of marrying only within the limits of a local community, clan, or tribe.
[6] Dillon (1999, 47–49); Gladney (1987, 516); Geertz (1968, 79).
[7] Zho (2000, 10); DFID 2004; The Library of Congress (n.d.).

Moreover, Lu has noted that the influence of new nontraditional values and ideas communicated through various media sources (2001, 18, 102), or even through government modernization policies, are impacting individual perspectives and the group's worldview. This evolution in values, ideas, and opinions can be more easily understood if we observe the *YEU-Hui*, or young urban educated Hui (Kim 2011, 355–56).

The YEU-Hui generation is defined as a group that was born after the Cultural Revolution (1965–76) and has experienced major social changes throughout the 1970s until the present time. They have been influenced by traditional family value systems, but likewise have experienced massive social change and broad outside influences through advanced education and social networking (Lu 2001, 11).

A larger proportion of YEU-Hui has advanced further through the Chinese education system than previous generations. The Hui traditionally preferred to send their children to ethnic schools, mainly inside of their mosques, for study (Andrew and China Inland 1921, 33–34). However, as they are increasingly exposed to contemporary social rigors of urbanization, the number of them enrolling in formal or public schools is growing. Consequently, the Hui have become part of a phenomenon called the *minkaohan*—that is, people who are identified as a minority group yet enter the mainstream educational system by taking entrance exams in the majority language of the Han Chinese.

Chen points out that these younger, educated Hui prefer living in cities, despite the difficulties inherent in urban life (2001, 5–7). Among urban dwellers, the post-Mao era generations of YEU-Hui share a strong familiarity with a mainstream influenced by ever-changing styles and perspectives introduced under China's revolutionary free-market economy (Zhang 2001, 206). The challenges introduced by the new economy to modernize China have also created a complex sociocultural environment for the Hui. Gillette brings to our attention the fact that the elements of society impacting the Hui revolve around increased social interactions with other ethnic groups, the new consumerism,[8] pervasive media influences, a propensity for individualism (2000, 12). These younger, more educated Hui have been the early adaptors (Rogers 2003, 287–92) and are influencing the rest of their ethnic group because of their ability to navigate successfully through the majority society while maintaining traditional cultural values (Kim 2009, 83–84).

Two-layered Cultural Settings

In 2009 I conducted a study among 232 people living or working in Xian City, China. The goal of the study was to compare young, educated urban Han with their Hui compatriots in order to pinpoint common social grounds between both groups. From that research I realized that the two groups exhibit similar patterns in their consumption of media content and platform selections. For example, both Han and Hui participants indicated that they enjoy DVDs or digital streaming movies, then music, and finally television dramas—in that order (Kim 2009, 365).

---

[8] Chen (2001, 5–12); Davis (2000, 1–2); Whyte (1995, 7–39).

Such patterns of media consumption coupled with living side by side in urban environments help to influence evolving values and preferences of Chinese Muslims. This is even clearer from common themes found across their survey answers regarding favorites. The two groups expressed very similar preferences for hobbies, new experiences, and values (ibid., 363). Likewise, concerns and needs felt by both the Han and the Hui young people centered around money/finances, love, marriage/family, jobs, social interactions, acceptance by others, and so on (ibid.).

While some answers in the survey affirmed traditional culture, others pointed toward cultural preferences and behaviors shared by different ethnic groups. This presents us with a two-layered structure of culture—that is, a surface layer forged by urbanization and a core of traditional life. This means any common ground is likely an external layer of culture, yet one that can serve as a kind of bridge of understanding to facilitate interaction between ethnic groups. Figure 1 below shows the conceptualized two-layered cultural model.

I found that individuals who identify as Hui but have been living in a city for more than ten years, or exposed to the city through work or school for more than fifteen years, become very open to outside cultures. These individuals are much more willing to broaden their communication channels than their cultural peers or relatives who are only familiar with the traditional Hui culture and lifestyle (ibid., 367). For this reason, it is most appropriate to view changes in the culture of Chinese Muslims as a two-layered process. The core layer is their background, which has been historically formed, and the second is that which has been influenced by modern urbanization.

Figure 1 conceptualizes the cultural setting of an urban Hui. The inner circle represents cultural elements formed by the tradition. The outer layer is mainly formed through living experiences that have triggered a need to adapt to change.

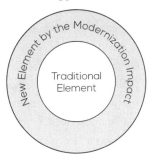

FIGURE 1: TWO-LAYERED CULTURAL SETTINGS MODEL

The outer layer represents a collection of skills and perspectives that facilitate successful interactions with other ethnic groups on a common ground where cross-cultural openness is possible. People represented by this model share many similar preferences because of this common external cultural layer. They have expanded socially beyond their original culture. Yet original elements remain rooted at the core of each individual's cultural frame. Because of these core cultural elements, people find they are not completely satisfied when only engaging in new cultural experiences. That is to say, their interactions and communications with different ethnic groups, facilitated by the external layer, do not completely satisfy an individual's holistic needs.

Emotional satisfaction is greater when an individual can interact with members of one's cultural group of origin. Therefore, as long as one's home culture is consistently shared and passed along generation after generation, at least trace elements of the core culture will continue to hold a root deeply within members who identify with that culture. Although ethnic group members may leave home, where their original cultural is most strongly shared, when opportunity arises these individuals will seek unity and cultural renewal by gathering together wherever they might have migrated. This is particularly true when individuals seek to regain their cultural identity or save their group of origin from political threats or suppression. Therefore, when returning to one's roots proves emotionally beneficial on an individual or group level, the motive to share cultural elements can be a way to bring revival.

Missiological Implications

This two-layered cultural settings model provides several implications for mission.

Mission at the midpoint: Not one-directional

In many theories regarding cross-cultural communication,[9] it seems generally accepted that those who share the gospel must do so from an incarnational posture.[10] In other words, missionaries or evangelists must be willing to sacrifice their own cultural identity in order to be effective communicators. Those theories project the premise that the hearer of the message does not have to make any cultural alterations to hear the gospel. Because the local culture has developed over time and is deeply rooted, Hiebert theorized that in order to share the message of the Bible effectively, those who serve cross-culturally need to learn relevant cultural patterns—culture and language—consistent with them (1985).

Yet the problem with these theories is that they ignore the fact that cultures are constantly evolving. In the case at hand, traditional Chinese Muslim groups face changes introduced by both urbanization and colonialization at the hands of centuries-old Chinese society. For this reason alone, the traditional evangelistic premise that local people will not change must be questioned. Chinese Muslims who have enjoyed their lives in *menhuan* (Sufi enclaves) and *gedimu* (ethnic enclaves) are now forced to understand a common community code, which allows them to work in and live at culturally diverse social junctures, such as urban Chinese neighborhoods, the office/factory, and marketplaces—even school.

---

[9] Kraft (1979, 148; 1991, 15); Box (1992, 141); Kincaid and Schramm (1975, 106); Burgoon and Ruffner (1978, 84).

[10] Conn (1984, 232); Kraft (1973, 212); Kraft and Gilliland (1989, 3, 12, 13, 135).

The shared common ground is each and every social juncture located somewhere between the cultures of Muslims and non-Muslims, like the Han or expatriates. It is in these social settings where transformation creates fertile common ground for interactions between Muslims and Christians to take place. Therefore, rather than relying exclusively on a one-way incarnational posture, an expanded middle zone where common grounds form can be the new place that allows for the communication of the gospel.

Communicating the Gospel using two-layered cultural settings

What should be an effective strategy for communicating the gospel to Chinese Muslims in this kind of two-layered cultural setting? This question is not only relevant for outreach to the Hui but also shows promise regarding outreach to many other Chinese Muslims. Of course, coming up with the best way to approach outreach could be stressful when dealing with multiple cultural elements, but using this model can simplify the matter by leading us to focus on two specific aspects of outreach as we think about mission strategy.

The external cultural layer equips Chinese Muslims to develop similar interests and behaviors that allow them to transcend ethnic and religious differences. Therefore, when communicating the gospel, mission and discipleship strategies used with other groups can be modified to be used fully or in part among Muslims as well. At least in cities (although perhaps not in isolated traditional communities or villages), sharing basic information regarding discipleship and evangelism can be more useful if language is not a barrier. Nowadays it can be useful to build on cultural cues held in common with other ethnicities, rather than focusing on differences.

In China, more than a few resources and teaching methods for Bible study originally designed for the majority are also used among YEU-Hui. This means that Christians have more opportunities to expand successful evangelism and discipleship strategies built on cultural common ground.

Nevertheless, there are unique traditional values and patterns that are relevant to a group functioning under a bicultural scheme that do not translate across cultures. Consequently, there will be limitations in crossover strategies, particularly when dealing with aspects of the gospel that require a deeper level of understanding to bring about changes to a group's value system. From that standpoint, methods of alternate worship styles and communication strategies should be enlisted to touch these deeper levels of culture. Socially appropriate approaches must speak to those cultural beliefs anchored by symbols, worldviews, relationships, and familiar social structures fostered by themes inherent in Chinese Islamic culture.[11]

---

[11] Kim (2013, 94–95). Based upon their cultural theme—power and pride—I have suggested "Biblical Concepts and Themes" and "Six Biblical Messages to the Hui" in order to find more fundamental and biblical answers than what the Hui have developed.

Beyond the Hui and Chinese Muslim, but for the two-layered generation

The external layer of the cultural setting among Chinese Muslims is growing thicker due to many influences arising from modernization. Consequently, many different ethnicities—including Muslims and non-Muslims—have begun to share information and values with each other. Social environments color the lifestyles of different ethnic groups to shape similarities in preferences experientially.

The outer layer of the two-layered structure has a common code that enhances the ability to interact and therefore gather information. This is the common code that enhances understanding among many groups beyond common cultures. Communication is a process that can occur only when two sides share common ground—that is, an external social layer that provides a platform where ideas, emotions, and values can be shared. This means that the external layer serves as a kind of bridge of understanding to facilitate interaction with other ethnic groups. For this reason, Muslims who develop a thick outer layer (or more bridges of understanding) are able to engage in more activities with various groups.

In light of this observation, the gospel could be understood and shared across common grounds when social junctures are enlarged. Figure 2 is a conceptual diagram of social connections experienced by a YEU-Hui who intersects with a number of other Chinese ethnic groups at the external layer. In this regard, imagine if there were an influential Christian among these four people, using the bridge of the external layer to create understanding of the gospel effectively (Smith 1992).

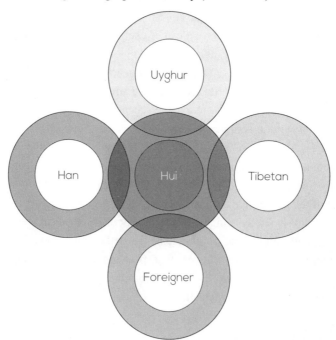

FIGURE 2: OUTER LAYERS AS BRIDGES

Jesus Understands Their World

The complexities of life for urban Hui can only be partially addressed by the resources of traditional culture. But Bosch reminds us that the gospel answers not only these questions but those raised by all cultures (2001, 426). We need to help Hui see that Jesus understands their predicament because he lived in a world very similar to theirs. Like most of them, he was raised in a small town and lived among a bitterly oppressed and marginalized people (Hertig 1995; Karris 1990; Matt 4:25; 5:3; 10:1–4; 11:19; John 15:4–5). Chinese Muslims experience insecurity, but seek to break free under their own efforts through power and pride. However, if Jesus' message of freedom and salvation is to impact the Hui, those who serve them must be able to explain that Jesus is the only source of true power to overcome such oppression.

Moreover, we must help ethnic minorities discover real pride through a redeemed identity that dismisses a collective sense of inferiority to the mainstream. The gospel can give the genuine *qingzhen* (purity and truth) that Hui traditionally claim as their ethnic identity (Matt 4:15–16; John 14:6). The fact that Jesus has dealt with their sin and shame (Bailey 1973) on the Cross is the answer that will bring them real purity and truth—the answer for which the Hui have been waiting over a thousand years. Someone must explain to the YEU-Hui that the gospel contains the answer for how the gospel functions on the outer layers of culture and how to experience peace across culturally common grounds.

It is interesting that the issues arising at the outer layer of shared culture also can be identified with the traditional themes of power and pride. In other words, seeking power and pride is a universal quest for overcoming insecurity. This new face of the Hui's traditional theme also needs to find its answer in Christ.

I believe this article, written by an admitted outsider who for many years shared in the daily lives of Chinese Muslims and their evolving culture, is just one step toward discovering common ground. This is a stepping-stone toward learning new ways to share the gospel. It may be too early to conclude that this newly conceptualized framework regarding cultural themes will be effective. Nevertheless, I pray that this proposal to bridge cultural divides will continue to be refined, especially by those Chinese who were once Muslim but have experienced transformation through faith in the Lord.

Reflection Questions

1. Does the increase of Muslims with a double-layered cultural identity present an opportunity or a challenge for evangelism?

2. With increasing opportunities to encounter many different cultures in urban areas, Muslims today can observe Christian lifestyles more easily than could previous generations. What should such a phenomenon suggest to Christians in terms of integrating both word and deed into their missional lifestyles?

References

Andrew, G. Findlay. 1921. *The Crescent in North-West China*. London: The China Inland Mission.

Bailey, Kenneth E. 1973. *The Cross and the Prodigal: Luke 15 through the Eyes of Middle Eastern Peasants*. St Louis: Concordia Publishing House.

Bosch, David Jacobus. 2001. *Transforming Mission: Paradigm Shifts in Theology of Mission*. American Society of Missiology Series. Maryknoll, NY: Orbis Books.

Box, Harry. 1992. "Communicating Christianity to Oral, Event-Oriented People." D. Miss. diss., Fuller Theological Seminary.

Broomhall, Marshall. 1966. *Islam in China: A Neglected Problem*. New York: Paragon Book Reprint Corp.

Burgoon, Michael, and Michael Ruffner. 1978. *Human Communication*. New York: Holt, Rinehart and Winston.

Chen, Nancy N. et al, 2001. *China Urban: Ethnographies of Contemporary Culture*. Durham, NC: Duke University Press.

Conn, Harvie M. 1984. *Eternal World and Changing Worlds: Theology, Anthropology, and Mission in Trialogue*. Phillipsburg, NJ: P&R Publishing.

Davis, Deborah. 2000. "The Consumer Revolution in Urban China." *Studies on China* 22. Berkeley, CA: University of California Press.

DFID (Department for International Development). 2004. "China Urban Poverty Study." http://www.dfid.gov.uk/countries/asia/China/urban-poverty-study-english.pdf.

Dillon, Michael. 1996. *China's Muslims. Images of Asia*. Hong Kong, New York: Oxford University Press.

———. 1999. *China's Muslim Hui Community: Migration, Settlement and Sects*. London: Curzon Press.

Ekvall, Robert B. 1939. *Cultural Relations on the Kansu-Tibetan Border*. Chicago: University of Chicago Press.

Gao, Zhanfu. 1997. "民族教育于甘肃少數民族地區的補貧問題 (Minzu Jiaoyu Yu Gansu Xiaoshu Minzu Diqu De Fupin Wonti)." The Journal of Gansu Mizu Yanjiu (甘肃少數民族研究) 1: 35–42.

Geertz, Clifford. 1968. *Islam Observed: Religious Development in Morocco and Indonesia*. The Terry Lectures. New Haven, CT: Yale University Press.

Gillette, Maris Boyd. 2000. *Between Mecca and Beijing: Modernization and Consumption among Urban Chinese Muslims*. Stanford, CA: Stanford University Press.

Gladney, Dru C. 1987. *Qingzhen: A Study of Ethnoreligious Identity among Hui Muslim Communities in China*. Seattle: Unversity of Washington Press.

———. 1998. Ethnic *Identity in China: The Making of a Muslim Minority Nationality*. Case Studies in Cultural Anthropology. Orlando, FL: Harcourt Brace.

Hai, Xuewang. 1992. "Tradition and Rule of Linxia Baifang (Linxia Baifang Huizu Fungsu Guilue)." *The Journal of Gansu Minzu Yanjiu* 2 (3): 57.

Hertig, Paul. 1995. "The Messiah at the Margins: A Missiology of Transformation Based on the Galilee Theme in Matthew." PhD diss., Fuller Theological Seminary.

Hiebert, Paul G. 1985. *Anthropological Insights for Missionaries*. Grand Rapids: Baker.

———. 1987. "Critical Contextualization." *International Bulletin of Missionary Research* 11 (2): 104–12.

———. 1999. "Cultural Differences and the Communication of the Gospel." In *Perspectives on the World Christian Movement: A Reader*, edited by Ralph D. Winter and Steven C. Hawthorne, 373–83. Pasadena, CA: William Carey Library.

Hoffman, Lisa. 2001. "Guiding College Graduates to Work: Social Constructions of Labor Markets in Dalian." In *China Urban: Ethnographies of Contemporary Culture*. Durham, NC: Duke University Press.

Joshua Project. 2017. "Hui, Muslim Chinese." *Joshua Project*, Frontier Ventures. https://joshuaproject.net/people_groups/12140.

Karris, Robert J. 1990. *Jesus and the Marginalized in John's Gospel. Zacchaeus Studies: New Testament*. Collegeville, MN: Liturgical Press.

Kim, Enoch J. 2009. "Receptor-Oriented Communication for Hui Muslims in China: With Special Reference to Church Planting." PhD diss., Fuller Theological Seminary.

———. 2011. "A New Entrance Gate in Urban Minorities: Chinese Muslim Minority, the Hui People Case." *Missiology: An International Review* 39 (3): 353–71.

———. 2013. "Power and Pride: A Critical Contextual Approach to Hui Muslims in China." *International Journal of Frontier Missiology* 30 (1): 189–95.

Kincaid, D. Lawrence, and Wilbur Schramm. 1975. *Fundamental Human Communication*. Honolulu: East-West Center, East-West Communication Institute.

Kraft, Charles H. 1973. "The Incarnation, Cross-Cultural Communication, and Communication Theory." *EMQ* (Fall): 277–84.

———. 1979. *Christianity in Culture: A Study in Dynamic Biblical Theologizing in Cross-Cultural Perspective*. Maryknoll, NY: Orbis Books.

———. 1991. *Communication Theory for Christian Witness*. Maryknoll, NY: Orbis Books.

———. 1996. *Anthropology for Christian Witness*. Maryknoll, NY: Orbis Books.

Kraft, Charles H., and Dean S. Gilliland. 1989. "Contextualizing Communication." In *The World among Us: Contextualizing Theology for Mission Today*. Dallas: Word Publishing.

Lawton, John. 1985. "Muslims in *China: An Introduction*." ARAMCO WORLD 36 (4).

Leslie, Donald. 1986. *Islam in Traditional China: A Short History to 1800*. Canberra, Australia: Canberra College of Advanced Education.

The Library of Congress. n.d. "Library of Congress Country Studies. China. Urban." http://lcweb2.loc.gov/cgi-bin/query/r?frd/cstdy:@field(DOCID+cn0058.

Lipman, Jonathan N., and Stevan Harrel. 1990. "Ethnic Violence in Modern China: Hans and Huis in Gansu, 1781–1929." In *Violence in China: Essays in Culture and Counterculture*, edited by Jonathan N. Lipman and Stevan Harrel, 71–73. Albany, NY: State University of New York Press.

Lu, Hsiao-peng. 2001. China, *Transnational Visuality, Global Postmodernity*. Stanford, CA: Stanford University Press.

Rogers, Everett M. 2003. *Diffusion of Innovations*. 5th ed. New York: Free Press.

Shaw, R. Daniel. 1988. *Transculturation: The Cultural Factor in Translation and Other Communication Tasks*. Pasadena, CA: William Carey Library.

Smith, Donald K. 1992. *Creating Understanding: A Handbook for Christian Communication across Cultural Landscapes*. Grand Rapids: Zondervan.

Whyte, Martin King. 1995. "City Versus Countryside in China's Development." The Fifty-Sixth George Ernest Morrison Lecture in Ethnology. Canberra, Australia: Australian National University.

Zhang, Li. 2001. "Contesting Crime, Order, and Migrant Spaces in Beijing." In China *Urban: Ethnographies of Contemporary Culture*. Durham, NC: Duke University Press.

Zho, Muzhi. 2000. Urbanization: Theme of China's Modernization (*城市化：中国现代化的主旋律*). Hunan People's Publishing House.

CHAPTER

10

Michael A. Kilgore

Context as Flypaper: The Island of Java in Indonesia

In the mid-1980s I attended a training for Christians who wanted to serve Muslims. The expert at the podium gave a broad-stroke picture of Islam in the world. To impress upon us the priority of reaching Muslims, he declared that the global Muslim population reached seven hundred million by 1984. He then asked each of us to indicate where we are interested in serving. When I said Indonesia, he muttered, "Well, if you look at their practices, they're not even real Muslims over there. Why aren't you going where there are real Muslims?"

After the session, I cornered him to ask, "If Indonesian Muslims are not real Muslims, then where do you get your global total of over seven hundred million?" He struggled to answer. But his claim about Indonesia long haunted me. Was I really going to a place where no one is truly Muslim?

After living for some time on Java, delving into their local communities and seeing a lot of customs that do not fit my previous impression of Islam, I *really* began to wonder. But then, after reading a broad range of books on folk Islam,

I discovered that writers as far back as Samuel Zwemer in 1920 mentioned most of the deviant customs I have seen in Java as practiced across wide swaths of the Muslim world—even as far away as Morocco (2009).

So, do Indonesian Muslims embrace beliefs and practices that violate textbook Islam? Definitely. But what does that say about whether or not they are "real" Muslims? As we'll discuss in this chapter, they feel every bit as Muslim as those in the Arab world.

Java

This chapter will focus on Java because of its overwhelming importance within the context of Indonesia, and even in the larger Muslim world. Java is approximately the size of Louisiana, but with a population exceeding 140 million. On a clear day you can fly from Jakarta to Surabaya in just ninety minutes, but in that time you have flown over one out of twelve Muslims on the face of the earth!

This impressive population on Java is comprised of three major people groups. The Javanese—the largest ethnic group in Southeast Asia—dominate the province of Central Java. They are also the power brokers across the entire archipelago. Javanese culture is like flypaper—everything that ever passed near it stuck, adding layer upon layer of belief and practice, sometimes seemingly in conflict with one another, in a cultural multilayered cake. They share Java with the Sundanese to their west and the Madurese to their east.

In ancient times, all three of these mega people groups followed a spirit termed *Hyang* and were involved with a form of ancestor worship that is now termed *Kejawen*, or *kebatinan* (inner mysticism). This early religion focused on localized spirits associated with unusual geographic features, such as an abnormally large banyan tree or the hazardous surf of the southern seacoast.

As Asian maritime trading moved into high gear, Hinduism came to Java beginning in the first century AD, becoming dominant in the seventh and eighth centuries. Buddhism came quickly on its heels, arriving around the second century and competing with Hinduism for centuries. Kalasan (Buddhist) and Prambanan (Hindu) temples near Yogyakarta show that some Javanese kingdoms allowed the two faiths to coexist and flourish during the same time frame—a precedent for Indonesian religious tolerance (Guillot 1985).

Even to this day, many key Indonesian religious terms have Kejawen and Sanskrit roots. Indonesian Muslims use sembhyang for their five daily *salat* prayers, though it originally meant reverence to the Hyang. But by the sixteenth century Islam had begun to be the prominent religion. Muslim traders from Gujarat and Yemen used their business connections to build ties with royal courts, eventually marrying princesses and then influencing kings to convert to Islam. These early pioneering Islamic messengers used creative means, including adaptations of the Hindu shadow-puppet epics, to propagate Islam. They also displayed elements of Sufi practice, which resonated in the hearts of Java's mystics.

This all occurred shortly before the Dutch came to exploit resources in what would become the Dutch East Indies. The Dutch told their European constituency that their primary purpose was to evangelize their East Indies subjects—yet this was an endeavor they persistently obstructed. Then, immediately after the Japanese occupation of World War II, Indonesia declared independence and became a secular democracy with the world's largest Muslim population (Herwanto 2002).

One of the first major movements to Christ in the modern history of Islam occurred among the Javanese after 1870. It was led by Shadrach, a former roaming mystic who took on the name *Kiai* (a title for a Muslim holy man). He used heavily contextual methods to win thousands of Javanese to faith. He and his disciples even won servants in the inner circle of the powerful sultan of Yogyakarta. Thankfully this sultan was confident enough of his own position that he allowed them to remain in his service. Many Javanese began to view the gospel as a valid option.

Again, after the Communist coup of 1965 and the horrendous carnage that ensued when Muslims performed widespread purges on anyone they could construe as a Communist, millions of Javanese got fed up with the brutality they associated with Islam and responded by choosing Christ (Garrison 2014; Willis 1977).

Islam in Java

To generalize about the faith of eighty-five million people is hazardous, because it is vitally important to understand how each of the Indonesian Muslim groups relate Islam to their own customary law, or *adat*. Adat—sometimes translated "local ancestral traditions"—accommodates spirit offerings, fetishes, life-cycle rituals, and visiting ancestors' and saints' graves to receive baraka—blessing or spiritual enablement.

In the middle of the twentieth century, anthropologist Clifford Geertz (1960) attempted to summarize three primary types of Javanese. *Abangan* are those who generally live in villages and retain much of their ancestors' *adat* with a thin but strongly adhering veneer of Islam. *Priyayi* are closely associated with the sultanates and retain many Hindu influences that added prestige to ancient royal courts. *Santri* are the more Arabized Javanese who have been schooled in *pondok pesantren* (disciples' hut)—a local variation on the classic Islamic madrassa. The people of Java are overwhelmingly *abangan* and *santri*, with the *abangan* outnumbering the *santri*.

Another helpful lens through which to view the Javanese, and indeed the majority of Indonesian Muslims, is through their organizational affiliations.[1] The Nahdlatul Ulama (NU) is the largest Muslim organization in the country, with about thirty million members. They passionately advocate for preserving traditional Javanese *abangan* beliefs and practices. The NU is opposed by the Muhammadiyah movement, which is nearly as large.

---

[1] These are similar in function to Christian denominations in the West.

A central practice defended by NU and *abangan* Javanese is the *selamatan* (mystic feast). This is regularly celebrated on auspicious occasions connected to cycles and passages of life, moving houses, or initiating any new business or educational endeavor. Neighbors come to the host's house and sit on the floor in a room filled with dishes of food. The host declares the purpose of the meal, generally seeking *baraka* (spiritual power) for some new initiative, or to protect from feared harm, or often to ask that the soul of a recently departed loved one be received at Allah's side. An imam then leads prayers in Arabic, with all the male guests intoning "Amin," while women look on from the kitchen door. Finally it is time to eat, but the food in the dishes is not touched. Its aroma is food for the spirits in the room. The host family quickly distributes multiple boxes of food to each male guest, at which each man quickly begins to quietly partake of his portion without conversing. After a couple of minutes, and before the food is even nearly consumed, one by one the guests arise and quietly depart, taking the remainder of their food, along with their extra boxes home for their families to enjoy.

Javanese hold strong convictions that these *selamatan* meals are vital for maintaining peace and balance in their villages, "so that nothing happens."

Members of the second largest organization in Indonesia, the Muhammadiyah movement, mock the *selamatan* custom. They embrace a reform movement that is against such local traditions—embracing the tensions of trying to be modernist-scientific while also leading Muslims "back to the Qur'an."

One field practitioner who coaches the local leaders of a fast-multiplying movement to Christ among Indonesian Muslims recognizes at least two types of Indonesian Muslims who "turn their noses up at folk Islam characteristics, yet ironically still practice folk Islam but to a lesser degree than the traditionalists."[2]

The Three Major Cultural Contexts of Java

The Javanese

Depending on how ethnicity is counted, the Javanese make up somewhere between 40 and 50 percent of Indonesia's total population. They set the tone and pace for nearly every factor that defines Indonesia.

The Javanese are a people who, right down to the village level, pride themselves in maintaining a highly refined culture. Honoring one another—especially those deemed to be in power—is extremely important to the Javanese. Guests from outside will be deeply impressed by Javanese polite manners. Yet the high value put on publicly honoring one another comes at a price. If a Javanese is upset with you it will not be evident, as they conceal their true feelings in multiple layers of culturally compulsory respectfulness. Thus when true heart feelings are tense, the Javanese find it very difficult to express their displeasure truthfully.

---

[2] Anonymous; email message to author, May 14, 2015.

This difficulty is multiplied when communicating with someone perceived to be of higher rank. Javanese are very sensitive to hierarchy. A national value—especially felt among the Javanese—says *"Asal Bapak Senang"*: "Whatever it takes to keep the boss happy."

I was amazed at how important these values are to the Javanese when I heard a believer comment on Jesus' peacemaking teachings in Matthew 18. After reading Jesus' clear instructions to go personally to an offending party and tell them directly what they have done wrong, a local believer ended the discussion by turning to Westerners in the group and commenting, "I don't know if it works for you Westerners, but I'm absolutely sure that God never intended for us to ever do this. It's just not something we could ever consider doing."

Upon embedding oneself in their society, many newcomers, including myself, have felt overwhelmed by Javanese friendliness and openness. Only after a protracted time does it become evident that, although receiving you with open arms, the Javanese also have a way of subtly holding you at an arm's length so that you really cannot know what they are really thinking.

As an American, I had to learn a lot about mutually respecting people—for which I continue to be thankful. But I found that some of the Javanese who heaped the most public respect on me were, at the same time, expressing their dislike of me behind my back, while others who seemed moderately respectful turned out to speak very highly of me when I was not around.

The Javanese express their refined culture in many and varied ways. Here I will mention just two.

The Javanese are the masters of shadow-puppet theater, or *wayang*—a genre that is also found elsewhere but is unquestionably taken to its highest level in Java. A *dalang* puppeteer brings a large wooden trunk full of dozens of thin rawhide puppets, their bodies and arms controlled by buffalo horn sticks. His assistants install a large white cloth screen in front of him and a bright light just behind him. A full Javanese *gamelan* orchestra sets up behind the dalang as he arranges sound-effect noisemakers controlled by his feet.

Around nine in the evening the *dalang* starts his epic story, manipulating puppets so that they throw their shadow on the screen for the masses on the other side to see. The *gamelan* orchestra players, led by a conductor, intuitively crescendo together at just the right moments. The puppets come on the screen in varied shapes and sizes. Javanese who have watched much *wayang* can immediately discern dozens of character features of a puppet even before it acts or speaks, each with their own personality and social rank. The story—full of drama and battles—ends just before dawn.

Many have noted that until the *wayang* puppet shows began to be seriously supplanted by television and YouTube, the Javanese learned nearly everything they knew about spiritual realities and human nature from them. There are good reasons that German anthropologist Niels Mulder has deemed wayang as "the Bible of Java" (Mulder 1975, 7).

Wayang may have lost influence in Java in the past few decades. No one should assume, however, that this open-air folk theater will die completely or quickly. I once heard a commentator state that every Javanese man prefers one particular *wayang* character over all the others, and that he consciously shapes his attitude every day to conform to what that *wayang* figure would do. My reaction to that comment was skeptical. Could this really still be the case in this modern age? When this claim was mentioned to a Javanese who had earned his doctorate at a seminary in the United States, he replied, "I don't think believers in Jesus should get that enthusiastic about the *wayang* characters. But to be honest, yeah, the one I prefer to imitate is …"

The second vital feature is Javanese language. It is expressed in seven different levels, each with distinct vocabulary. Before you can say a single sentence in Javanese, you must first determine not only whether the person you are addressing is higher or lower than you are in the social hierarchy but how much higher or how much lower. Fortunately, for Javanese living outside the immediate context of the sultans' palaces today, only three of the seven levels are still used broadly, with one holding dominance. Yet it remains that social hierarchy and the perceived need to clearly demonstrate respect for superiors is so engrained in the Javanese soul that one cannot even speak without first recognizing relative social positions. In short, Javanese culture does not value egalitarianism to the extent that Western cultures do (Taylor 1975).

These prominent features of Javanese customs and mores are mentioned in order to demonstrate that in this context *adat* is of more importance than textbook Islam. When you talk with Javanese Muslims about the distinctions between their adat and classical Islam, everyone immediately knows what you are talking about.

Considering the importance of *adat*, it is not surprising that in recent decades fruitful evangelism among the Javanese has at times employed the following local cultural elements:

- Adapted *selamatan* ritual meals—but where local leaders made it explicitly clear that the purpose of this *selamatan* is not to seek salvation but to celebrate salvation and benefits already granted through Jesus Christ.
- Stages of spiritual growth as disciples of Jesus Christ framed in redefined terms that are already familiar to Sufi-inspired Javanese *abangan* Muslims.
- Gamelan orchestra set up by a river and enthusiastically exploding into crescendo as each new believer emerges from the waters of baptism.
- *Wayang Wahyu* (Divine Revelation) shadow-puppet shows that chronologically relate the Bible's redemption story. This has worked best when a local team of evangelists intentionally collects the names and addresses of attendees

(sometimes via cards filled out to win door prizes) for later follow-up. In one case a performance led to the nearly immediate successful planting of a village church. On other occasions, a mayor of a major city and a governor of thirty-two million Javanese gladly witnessed these presentations of the gospel.

Clearly the Javanese have a rich culture preserved from pre-Islamic eras, and much in their culture has proven to be useful as communication tools for conveying the gospel.

The Sundanese

Apart from the relatively small work of the Reformed Church, gospel fruit among the Sundanese has come much slower than among the Javanese. And this despite the fact that many feel the Sundanese share the same spectrum of types of Muslims as the Javanese. Cultural anthropologist Linda Lentz writes, "Karl Jackson [1980] … found that a similar range in variation of beliefs and practices existed for the Sundanese as did for Javanese Muslims. In fact, only a bare majority of those surveyed were orthodox (or *santri*) Muslims" (2011, 63).

Perhaps more important is why *santris* make up only a bare majority of Sundanese. Lentz goes on to say, "While the religious leaders were more santri, the wives of the community leaders along with the elite women were notably more syncretic or *abangan*. This is in line with the findings of this study that women tend to preserve and pass on traditional practices" (ibid., 64).

Since the Sundanese share the traditionalist-modernist divide that is characteristic of the Javanese, we consider the best direction of ministry to be one that focuses on "Muslims," not "Islam." This is an absolutely critical distinction. If we shape our ministry approach around classical Islam, we will not touch the day-to-day lives of the vast majority of Muslims in this context. This simply is not their worldview.

It may indeed seem strange that tens of millions of people who regard themselves as good Muslims regularly engage in practices that don't match up with orthodox Islamic teaching and practice (however broadly that is defined). But in the eyes of local Sundanese, "*Adat* holds the secret to a meaningful life. What is important is that it came from the ancestors and the way things have been done in the past, and many Sundanese do not even know the meaning behind most of the rituals, nor is that important to them" (ibid., 66).

Also, it is quite interesting that these local traditions are never fully absorbed into the Sundanese understanding of Islam; while practiced together, the two are seen as distinct. One Sundanese explained that rather than mixed, they were *padukan* (a composite), where "the items being blended are still identifiable as separate items" (ibid., 75). At the same time, those who do practice *adat* traditions don't see any significant conflict between them and Islam. For them, although still distinct, the two can be made into a valid composite with their practice of Islam.

One longtime worker among the Sundanese, Matt Kirkas, emphasizes that although the Sundanese hold the five pillars in common with classical Islam, the fear of spirits is really the biggest item for them. An example is their belief in the spirits of a Hindu king's soldiers who, according to tradition, became tiger spirits when surrounded by an Islamic army. "All around West Java you will find statues of tigers, and people will have pictures of tigers in their homes for protection."[3] Islam is not addressing their primary heart concern of fear. Therefore, their outward Islamic practices do not mean what they at first may seem to mean. Although the Sundanese perform the five pillars, all the while they are trying to manage the relationship to the spirit world through other means.

One might ask, rightly so, which parts of this fused composite are more influential in Sundanese thinking. Going back to anthropologist Lentz, she says that the Sundanese she observed "desired to be good Muslims and tried to incorporate Islamic elements into the lifecycle rituals, but again, *these elements were being assimilated into Traditionalism not the other way around* [local Sundanese]. Traditionalism continues to be the foundation" (2011, *emphasis mine.*)

It is essential to understand that Sundanese traditionalism is the root and that Islamic elements were grafted onto it. This warns us of the distinct hazard, both among the Javanese and the Sundanese, that the gospel of Jesus Christ, when encountered, may be similarly assimilated into traditionalism, with local traditions as the foundation rather than the other way around. On the other hand, as the colonial era experience shows, any communication of the gospel that unnecessarily calls on them to reject their cultural customs will yield unnecessary resistance.

Kirkas shares that one reason the gospel never had as significant a breakthrough in West Java as it did in the rest of Java during the Dutch colonial days was that

> Dutch missionaries told people that they could not be circumcised if they wanted to be Christian because that was an Islamic practice. But in fact, it pre-dates Islam as it is a part of the Sundanese Tali Paranti cultural tradition. This led to the Sundanese rejecting the gospel in order to remain Sundanese. This rejection had nothing to do with wanting to remain Muslim.[4]

Kirkas also wisely observes that since much of this is based on fear of spirits, discipleship should look at the underlying spiritual questions being asked and how they are answered in this practice. Otherwise new believers will simply replace the crown of Islam with Christianity but still not reflect a biblical worldview.

This observation gets at the crux of a most vital point. *Kejawen* is a local form of animism—practiced by over one hundred million Javanese and Sundanese. Animists seek to influence malevolent and dangerous spirits or gods by performing ritualistic formulas. When people recognize that their formulas aren't working, they often seek new and improved ones. Many times, animistic Indonesian Muslims have joined

---

[3] Matt Kirkas (pseudonym), email message to author, May 15, 2015.
[4] Ibid.

churches and declared themselves Christians merely believing that baptism and the weekly performance of liturgical rituals offer superior formulas for controlling God and getting what they want out of him. Sadly, many churchgoers have merely swapped one animistic formula for what, in their minds, is merely another.

When we focus on cultivating faithful churchgoers (often an Achilles heel of ministries that prioritize church planting) while neglecting deep, personal disciple-making, we often end up leading people into decisions that are not nearly radical enough.

By contrast, I have seen new believers who—due to where they live—never have an opportunity to attend anything that looks remotely like a church service, but who have been profoundly impacted by their mentors to put Jesus Christ as the foundation of their worldview and thinking. Field-workers who focus on deep, personal disciple-making call their friends to this far more radical path and end up with Jesus Christ properly viewed as the cornerstone of their lives, as well as of the cosmos.

The Madurese

If the Javanese are refined and honoring, hiding their real thoughts behind multiple layers of polite respect, their immediate neighbors to the east, the Madurese, are the direct contrast—like the Scots of Southeast Asia. Bold, blunt, and brash, it never takes long to determine what your Madurese friend really thinks. If he dislikes you, he will find it impossible to hide the fact for more than a few seconds. If, however, he likes you, that too will be made abundantly clear and will almost always reflect a sincere commitment to loyal friendship. For better or for worse, you pretty much always know where you stand with a Madurese.

The Madurese are different than the Javanese and Sundanese in striking ways. Whereas the Javanese have seen huge breakthroughs for the gospel among several segments of their population in the late 1800s and then again since the anti-Communist purges of the 1960s, and the Sundanese have seen at least one above-ground denomination started since the colonial days, the Madurese have until very recently never moved in significant numbers to the gospel. Only one above-ground church was ever established among them—over one hundred years ago.

The pillar of Madurese society is the *pondok pesantren*, the Qur'anic preacher's school. The majority of Madurese gain their main exposure to education in a *pondok*, as they are called for short. This means that the *santri* (orthodox Islamic) element is far stronger here. Each *pondok* is led by a charismatic *ustad* called a *kiai*. If an *ustad* is a scholar of the Qur'an, the *kiai* has huge added value over and above this—supernatural knowledge and the power to work miracles.

At these schools every student spends years reciting long passages of the Qur'an and studying the *kitab kuning*, or yellow scripts (ancient Arab religious texts). One result is that Madurese *pondok* graduates often speak to one another in an archaic dialect of Arabic.

I once helped linguists assemble a team of Madurese to test a draft of the Madurese Bible. After a few hours the leading language consultant concluded that one Madurese we had sent had no business being there. He was clearly illiterate. However, he then noticed that from time to time this "illiterate" man would peek at a small book hidden in his bag under the table, then would be able to give quite informed answers. Finally, the language expert caught him in the act and insisted on seeing what he was peeking at. It was a transliteration of Madurese in Arabic script.

The man admitted, "I can't hardly read anything in Roman script, but I do just fine with this."

Though these linguists had worked for decades in Indonesia, they had never seen anything like this.

"Are there other people where you come from who read this script but can't read Roman script?" the consultant asked.

"Oh, on Madura island most people were schooled in *pondok pesantren* and so read Madurese in Arab rather than Roman script," came the reply.

The linguists realized that day that they needed to review their work in every Indonesian Muslim people group to see whether they had been producing their translations in the most accessible script. They had never before realized that some of these ethnic groups had so bonded with Arab culture that, while literate, they had somehow managed to remain illiterate in the Roman script used in the national language, Bahasa Indonesia, and in most Bibles.

Not only is Madura strongly affected by Arabic language, the Madurese tend to follow Arab customs much more closely than their Javanese and Sundanese neighbors. When I was working with a language helper to distill terms for family relatives, I caught my helper at one point and said, "That word can't mean 'son-in-law'! You just used it a few minutes ago for some other relative."

My helper denied any such thing and insisted that he had given me the correct word for son-in-law. Finally, I backed up my recording and made him listen to himself producing the same word sometime earlier for "nephew."

"Well, that's right too!" he insisted.

Then it struck me. Because Madurese fathers so closely follow the Arab consanguinity custom of marrying off their daughters to the girl's first cousin (Sailer 2013), the Madurese only use one term for both "nephew" and "son-in-law." If your nephew is not yet your son-in-law, he soon will be! Arab influence among the Madurese is strong.

At the same time, the Madurese are Nahdlatul Ulama (NU) oriented, still holding rituals to pray for their recent dead and enthusiastically participating in pilgrimages to seek baraka power at saints' graves and other power points. However, they haven't preserved nearly as much else of their pre-Islamic culture as have the Javanese and Sundanese. I first realized this while I was studying Madurese with my elderly language helper—who prided himself in being able to answer any question about Madurese culture that I could possibly conceive of asking.

I asked him, "How do you say 'hello' in Madurese."

"Assalamalaikum!" he replied.

"No, that's Arabic. I already know that. What I mean is, How do you say it in Madurese?"

"Assalamalaikum!" came his impatient repeat reply.

This line of questioning actually went on for another few minutes without me learning anything new until I asked, "What I mean is, How did Madurese say 'hello' before Islam came?"

My language helper's mouth dropped open in the stunned realization that he was ignorant of something basic in his own language. After long moments trying to dig something out of his deep memory, he reluctantly admitted, "I don't know … which means, probably no one knows. It's long forgotten!"

Nevertheless, there are a few very distinctive Madurese customs and mores. Two that most commonly come to mind are *kerapan sape* (bull races) and carok.

While "bull races" is fairly self-explanatory, *carok* is not. It is the custom that when confronted with intolerable shame, a man will use a curved sickle to disembowel the offending person. Sometimes *carok* is done with stealth, sneaking up on one's opponent from behind in a public market, reaching around their stomach, and giving the deadly slice. More courageous Madurese, of which there are many, will instead challenge their enemy to a public duel where both men go at it head-on until one is dead.

A key issue for believers seeking to reach Madurese is the question, What features of Madurese culture do we focus on in order to incarnate the gospel into the Madurese community?

As stated above, we are aware of several beautiful adaptations of Javanese culture that powerfully communicate the gospel. Among both the Javanese and Sundanese, colleagues have effectively used gospel-infused adaptations of the *selamatan* ritual meal—explicitly reinterpreted. While pursuing these approaches some colleagues have urged that we draw the line by only adapting local cultural elements rather than ever trying to adapt anything that is associated with Islam. But if this advice is followed among the Madurese, what is one to adapt? Bull races? *Carok*?

The Madurese present a more intense kind of intercultural communication challenge. When a culture so strongly discards most of their own traditions in a clear choice to replace them with their best perception of Arabized Islam, what is left to work with? Workers among the Madurese will find very little to work with if they refuse to even try to reinterpret the Islamic elements of their culture. Indeed, you cannot even speak their language unless you embrace Arab-Islamic cultural forms and dare to struggle through how to use them in manners that are faithful to the gospel.

One Indonesian believer from another region who has become effective in drawing Madurese to Isa Al Masih came to faith himself when he was an influential kiai. He testifies how his faith developed as he began to see *his* Nabi Mohammad and the revered Qur'an as a huge billboard pointing one way back to Nabi Isa Al Masih and the former holy books (the Bible). The way he sees it, if you get to Mohammad and the Qur'an and you pay attention to what they say, they tell you that you "missed your exit" and that you need to go back to find what you are looking for in *Nabi Isa Al Masih Junungan kita yang Illahi* (the prophet Jesus the Messiah, our divine Lord) and in the Injil (New Testament).

Another hopeful example of communicating the gospel effectively with Madurese has to do with universal Muslim festivals. I have encouraged several believers to consider using the Madurese celebrations of *Eid al-Adha* (or *Eid Korban*) to slaughter a goat while declaring the true meaning of Abraham's sacrifice. One year I found a local worker who showed uncommon passion for experimenting in intercultural communication. After I suggested the idea, he called a few days later and excitedly informed me that he had found the perfect goat to use on the upcoming holiday. The price he quoted was over two times the normal market rate. When I asked why, he informed me that he had found a huge, snow-white, spotless goat.

After buying the goat he marched it into the middle of a Madurese market, where he boldly and publicly declared that the sacrifice that God provided as a substitute for Abraham's son that day was a clear picture of how God intended to deal with man's sin problem. He proclaimed that the prophet Isa Al Masih is the Lamb of God who takes away the sins of the world, and that just as the lamb on the first *Eid al-Adha* died in the place of Abraham's son, so Jesus died in our place. As Abraham's son gladly received this substitutionary sacrifice provided by God, in the same way—if we desire to be spiritual children of Abraham—we must gladly welcome Jesus Christ, the Lamb of God, as our substitutionary sacrifice.

This one event became highly instructive in our experience among the Madurese and will help the reader grapple with the landmines and opportunities found in reaching an Islam-enthusiastic group like this.

On another occasion, some Javanese Christians had been holding Bible studies in their home that faced a kampong full of Madurese. Increasingly, they received threats—neighbors throwing bricks at their fragile tile roof and making frightening shouts as they sang praise songs together. Finally, they decided to stop meeting. But then a Muslim-background believer (MBB) asked them to continue it for at least one more meeting and to let him lead it. Instead of a motorcycle with a couple of Bible school students in white shirts arriving, the neighbors witnessed a couple of men arrive in dress normally worn by Muslim imams. Instead of the cheery smiles, they maintained serious demeanors.

When the participants had gathered, sitting around on the floor instead of on chairs, the MBB told them, "We're going to have a Bible study tonight and music, but we're going to do it differently from how you've done it before." He then read them a short paragraph from the New Testament in Arabic several times over. Then he coached them in memorizing it. Next he taught and led them in chanting it, quite loudly once they got the hang of it. Following that he took several minutes to explain to them in Indonesian the meaning of the passage and how it could apply to their daily lives. Finally, he had them stand, and with hands held upward to the ceiling before them, he led them in prayer—some in Arabic and some in Indonesian—offered in the name of Isa Al Masih.

After the leader and guests left, some of the same neighbors who had previously thrown bricks came over and gushed, "Wow, that sounded awesome! Why didn't you tell us you have music like that? Why didn't you do that all the time?"

Sadly, from the best we could find out, this Bible study group—favoring their worship preferences over their calling to reach their neighbors—never invited the MBB leader back and chose, rather, to close down their study in that community permanently.

Conclusion

Indonesian Muslims are not monolithic. Even just on the island of Java the three main groups—Javanese, Sundanese, and Madurese—have missiologically significant differences between them. This serves as a reminder that we must give particular attention to each context, sometimes right down to the neighborhood and clan, to assure that we communicate the gospel of Jesus Christ in ways that are clear and compelling. It also highlights the caution needed when teams working with one stripe of Indonesians want to critique the work of colleagues working with other types of Indonesian Muslims. And ultimately, fruitful workers, in the future, will need to skillfully blend traditional cultural themes with trendy modern relational and technological styles to faithfully communicate biblical grace and truth.

Reflection Questions

1. If you were seeking to make disciples among the Javanese or Sundanese, would you seek to adapt only cultural elements that existed in these cultures before Islam's arrival, or would you also choose to experiment with some of the more Arab-flavored, Islamic forms as well? What criteria would you employ?

2. In the Madurese context, how would you feel about employing, adapting, and reinterpreting clearly Islamic cultural elements? Why?

3. What takeaways do you gain from the story of the MBB leading a Bible study in a resistant neighborhood? What had the neighbors actually been objecting to? If the Bible study were at your house, what would you do next?

References

Garrison, David. 2014. *A Wind in the House of Islam: How God Is Drawing Muslims around the World to Faith in Jesus Christ*. Monument, CO: WIGTake Resources.

Geertz, Clifford. 1960. *The Religion of Java*. Chicago: University of Chicago Press.

Guillot, C. 1985. *Kiai Sadrach: Riwayat Kristenisasi di Jawa* [Kiai Sadrach: The History of Christianization in Java]. Original title *L'Affaire Sadrach, Un Esai de Christianisation a Jawa au XIXe Siecle*. Jakarta: Penerbit PT Grafiti Pers.

Herwanto, Lydia. 2002. *Pikiran dan Aksi Kiai Sadrach: Gerakan Jemaat Kristen Jawa Merdeka* [The Thought and Action of Kiai Sadrach: The Movement of the Free Javanese Christian Church]. Jogjakarta, Indonesia: Mata Bangsa.

Jackson, Karl D. 1980. *Traditional Authority, Islam, and Rebellion*. Berkeley, CA: University of California Press.

Lentz, Linda. 2011. "Sundanese Lifecycle Rituals and the Status of Women in Indonesia." PhD diss., University of Wales.

Mulder, Neils. 1975. *Mysticism and everyday life in contemporary Java: a cultural analysis of Javanese worldview and ethic as embodied in kebatinan and everyday experience*. Singapore: Singapore University Press.

Sailer, Steve. 2013. "Cousin Marriage Conundrum: The Ancient Practice Discourages Democratic Nation-Building." *The Unz Review*. January 13. Accessed July 31, 2015. http://www.unz.com/article/cousin-marriage-conundrum/ Accessed July 2, 2018. https://www.unz.com/isteve/cousin-marriage-conundrum/.

Taylor, David Bentley. 1975. *Java-Saga: The Weathercock's Reward, Christian Progress in Java*. Littleton, CO: OMF Books.

Willis, Avery T. 1977. *Indonesian Revival: Why Two Million Came to Christ*. Pasadena, CA: William Carey Publishers.

Zwemer, Samuel M. 2009. *The Influence of Animism on Islam: An Account of Popular Superstitions*. First published 1920. Reprint, Ithaca, NY: Cornell University Press.

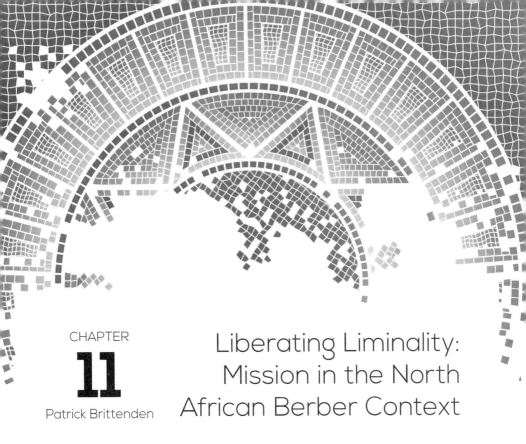

11

Patrick Brittenden

Liberating Liminality: Mission in the North African Berber Context

"A Muslim is what Islam tells them to be and Islam is what a Muslim tells you it is."
Bishop Kenneth Cragg (1913–2012)

Since I first heard them in the early 1990s, the simplicity, wisdom, and circular logic of the late bishop's words have remained for me the best adage to deal with the ambiguity in the particular-yet-universal character of Islam.[1] Nowhere is this adage truer than in the North African Berber context.[2]

North African Muslims confidently state that Islam in this region is predominantly orthodox, Sunni, and follows the Maliki judicial school. They claim that Islam alone has been able to unite Berber North Africa and keep it from tribal factionalism. Additionally, they insist that Islam alone has given birth to the great

---

[1] I was an undergraduate student of Arabic and Middle Eastern and Islamic studies at a conference for Christian students of Islam. Bishop Cragg was the guest speaker. To this day, I have not seen these exact words in print in any of Cragg's extensive works.

[2] McDougall (2006, 186). The term *Berber*, while possessing a pejorative connotation in orientalist (colonial) ethnography and historiography, akin to *Barbarians*, has nonetheless been self-appropriated by Berbers in Algeria and throughout the Maghreb. The term *Amazigh* is preferred by many academics.

Berber-Islamic dynasties, such as the Marinids of the thirteen to fifteenth centuries who produced some of the finest innovative minds of the Middle Ages, such as the great historian and philosopher Ibn Khaldun (1332–1406). In this sense, North African Islam, rooted in the orthodox judicial schools, has contributed to, and is firmly rooted in, a universal Islam.

However, other Muslims will confidently state that the Islam of North Africa has for centuries remained—at least until the 1930s—peacefully unaffected by the great theological disputes (such as the Wahhabi movement) of the "Eastern" Muslim world. There also exists a prevalent folk spirituality, with its cult of the saints, imaginative biographies, and baraka that are mediated through both the *marabouts* (spiritual mediators) and the *shurfa* (the supposed descendants of the prophet Muhammed) (Julien 1970, 337). Through this lens, North African Islam has a very distinctive particularity.

Still other "Muslims" in North Africa, such as the Algerian poet Kateb Yacine (1929–89), dispute the very idea that the Berbers of North Africa are in any way authentically Muslim at all. He argued that it is the Arabs—the *real* minority in North Africa—who have dominated the Berbers through "their religion" (Ouerdan 1990, 13). This perspective has been associated with intellectuals, writers, and activists in the Berber movement for some time,[3] but has not until recently been visible in broader social communities. The growing churches of North Africa are such visible communities (in Algeria more so than in Morocco or Tunisia) and are provoking essential questions about the presence of Islam as a fundamental plank of national identity in the context of North Africa.

For the cross-cultural worker committed to faithful and fruitful mission in this context, the task of accurately understanding the "true" nature of Islam can seem more than a little difficult. Cragg's wise adage reminds us that an appropriate missiology will need to take note of both the particularity of North African expressions of Islam *and* the influence of orthodox Islam on this particularity.

With this missiological challenge in mind, I propose to guide us on a brief tour of the development of Islam in Berber North Africa. Like a good tour guide, I will point out key features along our route. We will not be able to stop everywhere, but my task will be to remove some of the unfamiliarity most feel as they look out the window through which we observe this part of the Muslim world. I will endeavor to point out the paradox of particularity and universality in Berber expressions of Islam in North Africa.

However, the purpose of this tour is not only to "look out" at the landscape of Berber culture and Islam, but also to "look in" at our own story—that is, both the story

---

[3] McDougall (2006, 184–216). Though its roots predate independence, the origins of the Berber movement can most clearly be traced back to the 1960s and 1970s postindependence generation of Berbers who began to research and work on Amazigh identity. While this movement is trans-Maghrebian, it is most clearly identified with Algerian and Moroccan intellectual and writers.

of the church's mission in North Africa today and the story of the early church and its failings in this region. In part, it was these "failures" that set the scene for the growth of Islam across the region, so understanding this may provide a key to the church's mission in North Africa today.

The potential for greater ministry fruitfulness in this context therefore requires us to examine themes in the history and anthropology of Berbers as they have interacted with Islam, Christianity, and other universalizing forces. Looking out at the particular-yet-universal paradox of the North African Berber will need to be matched by looking in at the particular-yet-universal paradox of Christian identity and discipleship in this context. Both of these contexts are hybrid, or liminal.[4]

With an invitation to both look out and look in, our tour will end with us exploring the power of what I am calling "liberating liminality." This paradigm in the North African Berber context embraces the hybridity of both local Berber Muslim and Christian identities as a context for faithful and fruitful ministry and mission.

In the first phase of our tour, *Islamic expansion*, I will point out some key features in the historical expansion of Islam in this context. The second phase, *Berber resistance*, will explore the motif of a far-reaching anthropology of resistance among Berbers. The third phase, a *particular-yet-universal orientation*, will point out the tension (sometimes creative, sometimes destructive) between the "particular" and the "universal" in Berber history. In the final and longest phase, I will suggest how a lens of *liberating liminality* might enable cross-cultural workers to perform God's mission more faithfully and fruitfully in and beyond North Africa.

1. The First Phase: Islamic Expansion

Despite popular misconceptions, the emergence of Islam in North Africa was not primarily a triumph of the Arabs. The Arab-Islamic domination of "the Maghreb" (North Africa) did not last more than fifty years. Islam drew to itself almost all the Berber inhabitants of the region to the extent that even those least acquainted with orthodox practices were ready to lay down their lives in defense of their basic beliefs (Julien 1970, 338). In the mountainous regions of North Africa, however, Islam's influence was visible mostly as a unifying ideology, and it did not transform the manners and customs of the Berbers, who broadly remained faithful to their past.

Although Berber attempts to conform to Islamic norms were often in conflict with their ethnic identity, they tended not to openly contest the Arab-Islamic image imposed on them. Instead, resistance was expressed in the writing of their own history of conversion to Islam. The most influential of these is Ibn Khaldun's *Muqaddimah*, which highlights the significance of the Berbers' Islamic dynasties at the core of a political

---

[4] The term *liminality* describes an existence between realities or in transition between one identity and another. In anthropology, a liminal person is someone who exists in between two or more worlds, standing at a threshold between a previous identity, time, or community and a new reality. The central theme of this book is the exploration of precisely such "liminal" forms of Islam.

history of North Africa (Shatzmiller 2000, 14–16). In general, Berber resistance to Islam was subtle and much less militant than it had been under Roman rule.

What resulted was the eventual growth of prominent Berber-Islamic states in the region, the three most influential of these being the Almoravids, the Almohads, and the Marinids of the eleventh to fifteenth centuries. These dynasties ruled from modern-day Morocco across large swaths of North Africa. The last of these, the Marinids, represented a heterogeneous Berber society that valued individual thought and expression and offered sanctuary to innovative thinkers. The result was a Berber state inspired by Islamic norms and run by experienced Muslims (Shatzmiller 2000, 14).

As we pull our gaze away from looking out at the expansion of Islam in North Africa, we need to—but often do not—stop and look in at our own story and ask an obvious question: What happened to the vibrant early church of North Africa? Although the early stages of the Arab Muslim conquest encountered fierce resistance from Berbers, what church historians refer to as "African Christianity" did not offer vigorous opposition to Islam. Sadly, indigenous Christian communities in North Africa disappeared by the end of the twelfth century. Rather, it was Judaism that resisted Islam more robustly, with Jewish communities surviving—albeit in very small numbers—in an unbroken fashion to this very day.

Although it may be uncomfortable to us, any gospel engagement with Berber Muslim people today must reckon with the disappearance of the North African church. Kenneth Cragg has argued that the very inception of Islam was a "failure" of the Christian Church … a failure to demonstrate the Gospel in love, purity and fervour" (Cragg 1956, 245). As bold as this claim appears, the evidence from the rapid growth of Islam in North Africa appears to support it.

The Byzantine conquest of the former Roman provinces of North Africa in AD 533 resulted in the cultural and theological impoverishment of Roman Africa. Rather than contributing to the flourishing of the world Christian movement, the Byzantines brought slippery and divisive religious disputes, which the later Arab-Islamic invasion served only to aggravate (Sahas 1972, 16). One glaring example is the bitter struggle over Monophysite Christology related to the Council of Chalcedon in AD 451. Despite the influence of great North African church fathers such as Augustine, these disputes left the Berber church doctrinally and morally weakened.

It seems that the vibrant and influential church of early North Africa, in recession for at least two centuries prior to the arrival of Islam, was unable to resist the expansion of this new "Ishmaelite Heresy" (Sahas 1972).[5] The success of Islam in North Africa, therefore, was in part related to the failures of the church. If we do not learn the lessons from this failure, our evangelistic and church-planting efforts are likely repeat the same failures.

---

[5] This is the term used by seventh- and eighth-century Arab Christian apologist John of Damascus (Sahas 1972).

2. The Second Phase: Berber Resistance

As we look back out at the expansion of Islam in North Africa, we see that the thirteenth to fifteenth centuries were somewhat of a high point for Berber Islam. From that time onward, the outside influences of Arab domination and the resurgence of Europe began to push Berbers back in upon themselves. This shift to an inward focus points to a long-standing feature of "resistance" in Berber self-identity. This resistance, sometimes called "African particularism," is characterized by an allergic reaction to external authority that is clearly visible in early and later periods of Berber history (Shatzmiller 2000, 133). Scholars have used both the terms "resistance" and "African particularism" to define the relationship of Berber North Africa with a variety of occupying civilizations—whether Roman, Christian, Vandal, Byzantine, Islamic, Turkish, or French.

As we look both out at the expansion of Islam and in at the growth of the church in North Africa, we can see this resistance behind two puritanical movements that flourished among the Berbers, one in the Roman-Christian era and the second in the era of Islamic expansion. The first, Donatism, named after the Berber Christian bishop Donatist Magnus, flourished in fourth- and fifth-century North Africa. It was fundamentally about the need for Christian clergy to be morally pure when administering the sacraments in order for them to be effective. Though Donatism began with a theological dispute about the merits of accepting or rejecting the consecration of bishops who had recanted their faith during the Diocletian persecutions in AD 303–11, it soon became a movement of social and political discontent. In this sense, it was a movement of resistance and protest against the hegemony of Rome.

The second movement, Kharijism, was a sectarian, nonconformist doctrine that spread rapidly in Berber North Africa. Under the last of the Umayyad caliphs this puritanical movement had sent emissaries into North Africa to spread their egalitarian message (Shatzmiller 2000, 20). Kharijite nonconformism was naturally suited to the revolutionary temperament of the Berbers. This is observable especially in its opposition to Sunni orthodoxy, which was portrayed as a "tangible representation of Arab despotism and bureaucracy" (Julien 1970, 20). Hence it was also a movement of resistance and protest, but this time against the hegemony of Eastern Sunni orthodoxy.

The similarities between Donatism and Kharijism are strong. Both movements were episodes of a kind of class struggle, both were the seedbeds of asceticism and egalitarianism, both were linked with hatred of the ruling masters, and both were schisms of a revolutionary nature (Julien 1970, 20). Viewed in this way, they are part of an ongoing Berber culture of resistance and autonomy (Shatzmiller 2000, 12).

Algerian novelist Kateb Yacine argued that resistance to the power of the "state" (whether Roman-Christian, Arab-Islamic, or indeed French-colonial), is *the* defining feature of Berber North African history. In his view, the names of the players, religions, and cultures have changed, but the game is always the same (Ouerdan 1990, 13–15)—namely, resistance to foreign rule.

As we look out over the landscape of Berber history and anthropology, we can clearly see this suspicion of the "authorities" or the "state." One particular example is the resistance to imposed histories, or more specifically, the accusation of the "theft" or "falsification" of Berber history.[6] Resistance to history produced by foreign states (whatever their color or creed) in centers of the world detached from the local context is also linked with resistance to ethnographies of Berber identity created by "outsiders."

This is the accusation that activists in the Berber movement level at both French-colonial and Arab-Islamic ethnographers. The modern architects of independent Algeria worked hard to "name" Algeria as irreducibly Arab and Islamic. Conversely, colonial ethnography identified Berber Algerians (specifically the Kabyles) as somehow linked to Latin cultures and therefore more European. In this myth, Kabyles were portrayed as "noble savages," with a greater natural susceptibility than Arabs to being "educated" by the French *mission civilisatrice* and, significantly, more susceptible to being converted to Christianity (Guemriche 2011, 127). In seeking to counter this colonial ethnography and to argue for the inseparability of Berber and Arab under the banner of Islam, the twentieth-century Salafists were successful in reimagining a mythical national history in which Islam and the Arabic language were *the* defining features of an authentic independent Algeria. In this context, "Islam" became the rallying cry for the nationalist cause.

Looking back "in" at our story today, we can see that the progress of the Christian gospel and the rapid growth of the church in Algeria is occurring in just such a context of resistance, where Berber and national identities are being redefined. It is emphatically *not* the cause of this rapid church-growth movement, but it *is* nonetheless an important feature to recognize. It is also consistent with the kind of liberation that the gospel brings when "the whole Church believes, obeys and shares the whole gospel and goes to the whole world to make disciples of all nations."[7]

Recognizing this history of resistance to the power of universalizing ideologies (whatever the flavor) is therefore a key dimension to sensitive cross-cultural ministry in this context. The evangelist or the church planter will need to recognize both this feature of resistance and the quest for identity behind it. Fruitful evangelism and continued church growth into the second and third generation of believers from a Muslim background (MBBs), which is far from guaranteed, will need to reckon with the particularity of Berber resistance. However, as we look back out we will also begin to see that the resistance theme is linked with a kind of ambiguity in the particular-yet-universal orientation of Berber Muslims.

---

[6] Judith Scheele writes, "Access to ownership of historical sources . . . which is always described in terms of the written word (the ominous and omnipresent 'papers') necessitates and generates social and political influence" (2009, 74).

[7] The Cape Town Commitment of the Lausanne Movement. See https://www.lausanne.org.

3. The Third Phase: A Particular-yet-Universal Orientation

Both the particularity of Berber language and culture and the universal orientation of the Arabic language played a part in the success of the Berber Islamic dynasties. Historically, Islam was a tool of various Berber Islamic dynasties for consensus-building and unifying tribal bodies through setting universal religious goals. Islamic institutions, staffed with trained Berber speakers, supported the growth and expansion of the state. The use of both Arabic and Berber facilitated this process— Arabic as the universal language of the Muslim world and Berber as the particular language of the local context.

Despite cradling education, philosophy, and the ancient sciences, however, these Berber-Islamic dynasties were also deeply mystical religious societies. The changes in society—especially the rise of an individualized mystical religiosity from the fifteenth century onward—accelerated and heightened antagonism toward a monolithic universalizing Islamic state (Shatzmiller 2000, 14). The great theological disputes of the Muslim world were viewed with suspicion. Dissatisfied Berbers saw this as unavoidably linked to a kind of Eastern Arab-Islamic domination.

What seems to have developed across North Africa, beginning in the late fifteenth century, is therefore a popular mysticism with a clear anthropomorphic dimension. This is sometimes called "folk Islam."[8] The cult of the saints spread rapidly and was (and still is) witnessed in daily visits to the venerated tombs, annual feasts that commemorate the saints' death, and hagiographies that attest to the *baraka* (blessing or divine charisma) of the one whom the shrine honors—whether *marabout* (holy man) or *wali* (friend or saint of God) or *shurfa* (the Prophet's descendants). This movement of the heart flourished in the countryside and the mountains. Folk religious practice was, and still is, in the souls of Berbers.

These mystical movements seem to be addressing a particular-yet-universal paradox: the particularistic need to engage with the day-to-day spiritual and temporal needs of ordinary Berbers and the universal need to be accepted as authentically belonging to the worldwide Muslim ummah. The legitimacy of both the marabout and the shurfa to exercise influence and wield power was based on both these elements—namely, their ability to mediate divine charisma within the particularities of Berber daily life and their capacity to establish an ancestral line that leads back to the Prophet's family.

Behind this particular-universal tension is a question of orientation: Are Berbers primarily East- or West-facing? There are the Berberists in Algeria whose struggle for the inclusion of Kabyle as an "official" Algerian language has opened them to accusations of being part of the *Hizb Fransa* (party of France); they intended to lead Algeria back to France or in a more generally Western direction. In direct opposition stand the Salafist architects of modern Algeria's attempt to redefine Berbers in a

---

[8] See Musk (2003).

mashriqi East-facing orientation, with a synthesis of Berber authenticity and Arab identity (McDougall 2006, 189–216).

As we look back in at the growth of the church in North Africa today, we can see that this tension between the particularity of Berber identity and the universality of an Islamic identity is the margin in which the church is asserting itself. This question of orientation is highly pertinent for all cross-cultural workers and those supporting the church's growth in North Africa. What orientation should the North African church have? Like the Berber movement, in an overwhelmingly Eastern- and Arab-facing context, the Algerian church is accused by some of its detractors as being a West-facing movement. How should it respond to this challenge?

This hybridity of national, ethnic, and religious identity of MBBs is understandably resulting in a crisis of identity for some believers. To deal with this crisis, I want to introduce the paradigm of "liberating liminality" in the final and most important phase of our journey.

4. The Fourth Phase: Liberating Liminality

For over one thousand years the Berbers have lived between two realities: their own ethnic identity and universalizing forces within Islam. Therefore "liminality" seems to be a good way to describe some features of Berber identity. As we look in, however, I suggest that it is also important to use this as a lens though which to approach mission in this context. Is there a way to understand the church's in-between, or liminal, status and to use this as a creative context for its identity and mission in North Africa? To do this we must focus on a liberating form of liminality, not the liminality that leads to the marginalization that so often exists between dominant and subordinate groups in society.

Accordingly, consider the power of a positive (self-affirming) approach to liminality, one not defined by the dominant group but rather by those living in this place of "in-betweenness"—an identity of connection rather than exclusion. At heart, this concept is an identity shaped by knowing Jesus Christ and him crucified (1 Cor 2:2). This is the liminality of discipleship described by Karl Barth as a movement "in which man is still, in fact, wholly the old and already wholly the new man" (Barth 1958, 572). The "making" of disciples in this liminal context is an active, intentional process derived from the primacy given in the command of the risen Christ in the Gospels (Matt 28:18–20; John 20:21–23).[9] It will view discipleship across the margins of knowing, being, and doing in Christ.

However, this concept of liberating liminal ministry cannot be merely personal or individual. As disciples called into the body of Christ, the visible church must intentionally take up a place in between church and culture, a radical discipleship that emphasizes God's purpose for transforming society. In a context in which individuals

---

[9] Allen et al. (2009, 115). This is consistent with the latest research on best practices of ministry in the Muslim world, which states that "Fruitful workers are intentional in their discipling" (emphasis mine).

and communities have been marginalized, this requires individual and corporate submission in every part of life to the Lordship of Christ and service under Christ's Lordship in the whole of human life, in a world of fragmented living and thinking (Sugden 1981, 21).

Such a liberated liminal identity might enable us to reconsider the negative influence of believers identifying with the dominant centers of civilization (whether Christian, Muslim, colonial, or other). It might also cause us to become more aware of the "margins" where the mission of God is often most vibrant. In Algeria, the church is highly marginal in this regard. Algerian MBBs are "Christians," but until now they—unlike the historic churches of the Middle East—have no "center." As Christians of a predominantly Berber (Kabyle) ethnicity, they also experience the double marginalization of being non-Arab and non-Muslim in a modern nation state that was built to reflect an Arab-Islamic center.

This perception of the Christian hybrid identity in between two or more margins is graphically portrayed in the words of Berber Algerian Jean Amrouche, whose Kabyle parents converted to Christianity during the French colonial period. Born into a Catholic family, Amrouche was an influential Algerian Francophone writer, poet, and journalist. In the context of the early independence struggle in the 1950s, Amrouche wrote of his identity as an Algerian Christian with these words: "I am a bridge, the arch of which enables a communication between two worlds, but on which one tramples in throngs. And I will remain like this until the end of ends. It is my destiny." Later, after independence in the 1960s, he took up a slightly more depressing image: "I am a cultural hybrid. Hybrids are monsters. Very interesting monsters, but monsters without a future" (quoted in Guemriche 2011, 111).

Amrouche's hybrid identity as an Algerian Christian felt painful and hopeless. Yet I would argue that despite the many challenges facing MBBs in North Africa, this marginalization is neither inevitable nor fatal. Speaking about the same sense of liminality, but with more hope, an Algerian church leader recently spoke to me about this same paradox—that is, of being part of a worldwide Christian community on pilgrimage and yet fully present in the local Muslim family/culture. With a series of powerful metaphors, he described the liminality of his experience as an Algerian Christian in this way:

> I've two faces, two rooms, one opposite the other, which can be opposed one to the other. I've this natural connection, brother with brother, whatever his nationality; but I've also another brother who I need to recover. The presence of one makes the other uncomfortable. I walk on a tight rope ... and I don't want it to break. ... At present I am concerned with the big connection with the large family of Christ, but I have a problem with the local home connection "in my kitchen." It's the connection with my fellow (Muslim) citizens.[10]

---

[10] Interview with Algerian church leader, n.d.

This graphically expresses the liminality of the Algerian church. Nevertheless, the idea of being in between could become a positive, self-affirming understanding that recognizes this tension but moves toward being "in both" rather than merely "in between." This conception looks at liminal space as a potential "creative core" rather than those defined by one or more "centrisms" that create them, whether those be Western Christian, Arab, Berber, Islamist, or any other. This in turn leads to the potential of becoming a liberated liminal person, not only "in between" or "in both," but also "in beyond" a series of margins.[11]

The liminal space in which the Algerian Berber church finds itself today is extensive. It includes the liminality of Christian identity, national (ethnic and linguistic) liminality, interfaith (Christian-Muslim) liminality, and ecumenical liminality. This paradigm of liberating liminality may have the power to unlock these margins as a creative junction in which Algerian MBBs can intentionally perform God's particular *and* universal mission. The power of this performance would not only be in liberating themselves from multiple centrisms (described above), but also to liberate centrists from their obsession to be at the center (Lee 1995, 149). This is liberating for the church and for all Algerians.

The task of adopting a paradigm of liberating liminality that I am proposing here is not primarily about enculturating a foreign Christian dimension into an authentic changeless Algerian, Berber, or Muslim self, but rather "translating" the gospel[12] in the national context so that it facilitates the church's contribution to the ongoing story of *algériennneté* (Algerian-ness). As Charles Van Engen suggests, "Contextualization or inculturation is not the goal but rather an epistemological process of seeking to know God in context" (Ott and Netland 2006, 179).

This paradigm involves the cross-cultural worker and the local MBB recognizing the liminal spaces of Arab-Berber, Muslim-Christian, and East-West, among others. It involves ministry and mission, which inhabits (in between *and* in both) ethnolinguistic, religious, and other worlds. In this way, the presence of the church will not be identified uniquely with just one of Algeria's particularities (such as Kabyle identity). Rather, it will be *in*carnated in the Berber (Kabyle) and the Arab context, yet also in between various contexts, with the ability to critique and not be dominated by each, but through being *in* each and in between each, therefore able to be or go "in beyond" them.

---

[11] Jung Young Lee (1995) develops this concept of "in-between," "in-both," and "in-beyond." (see especially 29–62).

[12] I am using the concept of "translatability" in the sense that Ghanaian theologian Kwame Bediako (1999, 146–58) describes. What I am suggesting here is that the imperative to consciously engage with the context is not primarily about introducing something "foreign" to the Algerian context—which might be called "indigenization"—but rather, in Bediako's terms, "translating" a gospel that to some degree has no native country. See also Van Engen (2006, 164).

One very specific example of the power of such an "in-between," "in-both," and "in-beyond" liberating marginality is in Algeria's plurilingualism. Kabyle Berbers in Algeria have long resisted the imposition of classical Arabic through the post-Independence Arabization process. Undoubtedly the church's growth in Kabylia is occurring in the liminality of this ethnolinguistic particularity, and the freedom experienced by Kabyle Algerians reading the Bible, worshiping, and praying in their mother tongue has been a key context for the church's growth.

However, Kabyle believers are not only competently and confidently using Arabic for pragmatic reasons (for example, to evangelize Arabic-speaking Algerians) but are now seeing its unabashed use in the devotional life of the church (prayer and worship) as a sign of Christian maturity. Given that the church in Kabylia is a socially recognized entity in which a variety of Berber particularities are recognized and celebrated, it has attracted militant Berberists. When new converts are unwilling to sing in Arabic or be around other believers praying in Arabic because of their resistance to Arabization, this is considered an indication of spiritual immaturity. This is how one couple I interviewed expressed this liberating liminality:

> I think that God has known how to work (in our culture). Because there is a kind of wall of separation in Algeria between Berbers and Arabs, for a variety of historical, geographical, and even political reasons. ... And the church, the gospel, has been able to break this barrier. So when a Kabyle chooses to sing a song in Arabic, that is really a miracle. This was impossible before.[13]

They seem therefore to be very aware of the power of language either to alienate or integrate Algerians. While they recognize and celebrate the importance of indigenous languages (especially Kabyle) for both teaching and evangelism in the church, they nonetheless embrace their new identity as believers living in between and in both Kabyle *and* Arabic. This seems to be empowering their mission to go beyond the "Jerusalem" of the Algerian church (in Tizi-Ouzou, the capital of Kabylia) in order to reach other parts of the country and North Africa.

Such a particular-yet-universal liminal vision may facilitate a contribution to what one of my interviewees recently described as a "social dialogue." He suggested the church needed to enter this social dialogue and inhabit the public space in society. The ease with which Algerian Christians will be able to navigate the multiple liminal spaces (described above) will be related to its presence *in* and engagement *with* Algerian society in all its diversity. Any cross-cultural mission in North Africa that does not equip believers to do this is likely to fail. As one of the pastors I interviewed recently explained, "The church needs to make its presence felt, it needs to have its identity, and it needs to have something to say to Algeria. So we need to use all legitimate means for the church to say ... 'Yes, I am here! I am here in Algeria.'"[14]

---

[13] Interview with Kabyle couple, n.d.
[14] Interview with Algerian pastor, n.d.

When it comes to the margins between the gospel and Islam, or more specifically between the visible church and "Muslim" culture, in North Africa, this paradigm of liberating liminality may also pave the way for a more productive and faithful performance of God's mission in this context. For the emerging churches of North Africa, this liberating liminal conception of individual and corporate identity, ministry, and mission will involve drawing a new kind of line: "a line dividing the church and the world but not separating the Christian community from the local culture" (Newbigin 1953, 12). Discerning the church's response to the "world" as distinct from its relationship with local "culture" is *the* challenge.

Conclusion

As we end this tour, if you believe God is calling you to engage in his mission in Muslim North Africa, then I invite you to step onto North African soil and take on this challenge of participating in God's liberating liminal mission. As you do, remember three things. First, keep looking out over the landscape of North African Berber history and anthropology. Observe the variety of ways in which "Islam" has been both acculturated and resisted among North African Berbers and the liminality of the particular-yet-universal nature of Islam in this context. Second, look in at your own particular-yet-universal Christian identity and embrace the liminality of discipleship as a gift to be able to live in between, in both, and in beyond a range of liminal spaces. And finally, look up and pray that the Lord would enable all new believers and those supporting them in North Africa to be faithful to him and the movement of his universal church (in all its diversity) and in tune with the particularism of Berber culture, language, and history.

Reflection Questions

1. What aspects of the Berber context are different than those of more orthodox Islam? How are those differences missiologically significant?

2. Has your own journey of discipleship been liminal? If so, how? If not, why not?

3. How might a "liberated" and "liberating" liminal vision of Christian discipleship facilitate the church's mission *in between*, *in both*, and *in beyond* a range of liminal spaces in Muslim contexts?

References

Allen, Don, Rebecca Harrison, Eric and Laura Adams, Bob Fish, and E. J. Martin. 2009. "A Closer Look at Fruitful Practices: A Descriptive List." *IJFM* 26 (3): 111–22.

Barth, Karl. 1958. *Church Dogmatics*. Vol. 4, *The Doctrine of Reconciliation, Part 2*, edited by G. W. Bromiley and T. F. Torrance. Edinburgh: T & T Clark.

Bediako, Kwame. 1999. "Translatability and the Cultural Incarnations of the Faith." In *New Directions in Mission and Evangelism 3: Faith and Culture*, edited by James A. Scherer and Stephen B. Bevans, 135–52. Maryknoll, NY: Orbis.

Cragg, Kenneth. 1956. *The Call of the Minaret*. Oxford: OUP.

Guemriche, Salah. 2011. *Le Christ s'est arrêté à Tizi-Ouzou: Enquête sur les conversions enterre d'islam*. Paris: Editions Denoël.

Julien, Charles. 1970. *History of North Africa, Tunisia, Algeria, Morocco: From the Arab Conquest to 1830*. London: Routledge and Kegan Paul.

McDougall, James. 2006. *History and the Culture of Nationalism in Algeria*. Cambridge: CUP.

Musk, Bill. 2003. *The Unseen Face of Islam: Sharing the Gospel with Ordinary Muslims at Street Level*. London: Monarch.

Newbigin, Lesslie. 1953. *The Household of God: Lectures on the Nature of the Church*. London: SCM.

Ouerdan, Amar. 1990. *La Question Berbère dans le mouvement national algérien 1926–1980*. Quebec City, Canada: Septentrion.

Sahas, Daniel. 1972. *John of Damascus on Islam: The "Heresy of the Ishmaelites."* Leiden: Brill.

Scheele, Judith. 2009. *Village Matters: Knowledge, Politics and Community in Kabylia, Algeria*. Woodbridge, UK: James Currey.

Shatzmiller, Maya. 2000. *The Berbers and the Islamic State: The Marinid Experience in Pre-Protectorate Morocco*. Princeton, NJ: Markus Wiener.

Sugden, Christopher. 1981. *Radical Discipleship*. Basingstoke, UK: Marshalls.

Van Engen, Charles. 2006. *Globalizing Theology: Belief and Practice in an Era of World Christianity*. Edited by C. Ott and H. A. Netland. Grand Rapids: Baker.

Young Lee, Jung. 1995. *Marginality: The Key to Multicultural Theology*. Minneapolis: Fortress.

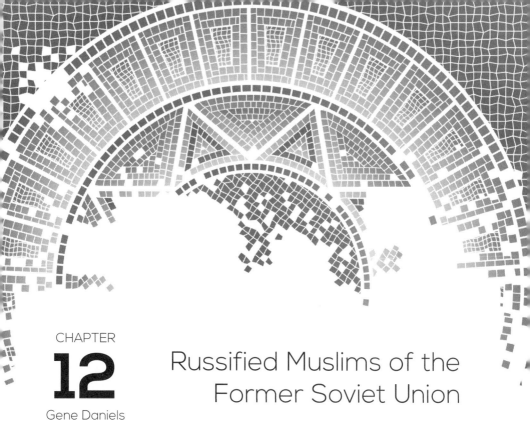

12

Gene Daniels

Russified Muslims of the Former Soviet Union

When people think of the Soviet Union, they seldom think of Muslims. However, one legacy of Russian colonial rule is the tens of millions of Muslims who speak Russian as a first or second language.[1] This is something linguists usually refer to as Russification. Today Muslims live in each of the countries of the former Soviet Union,[2] but the majority live in the Russian Federation, Ukraine, Turkmenistan, Kazakhstan, Kyrgyzstan, Uzbekistan, Tajikistan, and Azerbaijan. This includes millions of Muslim migrant workers from these regions who live and work in Russia—with more than three million in greater Moscow alone. Their experience of Russification is literally the key to their economic opportunities further north and hints at how this phenomenon goes much deeper than language.

Beginning in the Soviet era, a Russified Muslim was not just someone who could communicate with Russians, but someone who was also likely to share some of the same social space withthem. In other words, the Russian language was more than just a vehicle of communication; it has always been a gateway to cultural shift.

---

[1] There is no hard data, but estimates range from a low of twenty million to over fifty million
[2] Only very small numbers live in the three Baltic republics of Armenia, Belarus, and Moldovia.

This combination of interethnic communication and enculturation fit perfectly with the purposes of Soviet authorities who were actively promoting a new vision of the ideal man. However, lest we take a complete turn into arcane academia, this would be a good place to tap into the thoughts and feelings of real people. Fortunately, I have a great deal of interview material to draw from after spending more than a decade as an ethnographer and church planter among Muslims in the former Soviet Union. Here is how a few people described some of their own experience of Russification:[3]

> Of course, my parents were Muslims, but at the same time they were not. Because there was Communism and my father was a Communist, he was a party member, as well as his brothers. Even until now they think of themselves as Communists and party members. Of course at that time nobody even said the word God. There was no mosque in our village. ... We were Communists, nothing about God."[4]

> Our parents were traditional Muslims, like everyone else where we lived. They observed only traditional holidays like Kurban-ayt,[5] etc. Since we were little we were always told that there is God, that there will be the end of the world; but we didn't really have a lot of religious education.[6]

> Here in Central Asia we have a nominal Islam, mixed with traditions. Central Asia was not Islamic before, but when Islam came, it was mixed with traditions. And that's the Islam we still have. ... Here our Islam is very Central Asian. It's like you asked me if I knew the Qur'an [before conversion]. I didn't. Do I know enough Arabic to be able to read the Qur'an? No, I don't. Ninety percent of people in Central Asia do not speak Arabic. They might have learned some verses in Arabic, but they do not understand the meaning.[7]

> My father read the Qur'an and did prayers just to show he was doing it. He didn't really do namaz,[8] but he did some cultural things—saying Omen, etc. Same with my mother. People report that there are several million Muslims in this country. But in actuality there are not so many, because according to their beliefs, whoever says "I am a Muslim" is already considered a Muslim. But they don't practice namaz or read the Qur'an. They are just nominal.[9]

It may be hard for us to reconcile the first word picture—someone being Muslim without ever even mentioning the word *God*—but it offers a glimpse into what people in the region literally call "Muslimness": that is, "a shared community identity which is prioritized over the practice of religion" (Privratsky 2001, 78). In order to

---

[3] All of the interview excerpts in this chapter are drawn from over twelve years that my family spent as church planters among the Muslims of in the former Soviet Union.

[4] Interview with male convert (#414M), Kazakhstan, November 2013. (All interviewees in this study were identified by a number only to protect their identities).

[5] This is the colloquial version of the formal Arabic term Eid al-Kurban, "the festival of sacrifice."

[6] Interview with male convert (#406M), Kazakhstan, November 2013.

[7] Interview with male convert (#206M), Uzbekistan, February 2012.

[8] *Namaz* is used in Turkic languages as the equivalent of the Arabic *salat*, meaning "ritual prayers." It is probably derived from a word for "the place of prayers" (Burton-Page 1993, 947).

[9] Interview with male convert (#203M), Uzbekistan, February 2012.

understand how this happened, we should briefly review some of the history of the Central Eurasian steppe, where Russian and Muslim civilizations have comingled.

A Brief History

Islam has an ancient history on the Eurasian steppe, first entering what we now think of as post-Soviet geography in 751 at the battle of the Talas River.[10] However, unlike further west in the Arabic heartlands, Islam's fortunes in Central Asia have ebbed and flowed. The Mongol armies of Genghis Khan completely devastated Islam in the thirteenth century, but the damage was quite temporary. Within less than one hundred years the great Mongol Empire was crumbling and the Turkic successors to the Khan had converted to Islam, thus causing it to regain status as the religion of the ruling elites (Khalid 2007). Soon afterward Timur (or Tamerlane) created a new high point in world Islamic culture, and eventually the steppe lands became the new center of Islamic civilization, which contemporaries described as comparable to the very seat of the caliphate, Baghdad (Mirza Qazvini, quoted in Juvaini 1958).

However, when the imperial Russians began to push into the region in the early 1800s, they encountered a group of small, weak emirates that fell one after another as Russian soldiers and frontiersmen slowly pushed further south. Many parts of the Islamic world were colonized during that era, but what happened in the Russian world was quite different; and that difference has important missiological implications. During the imperial era, Russian expansion was fairly benign, but after the Bolshevik Revolution the Communists quickly turned it into a massive and prolonged attack against Islam.[11] This Soviet assault transformed Islam in many ways, the importance of which can hardly be overstated.

To begin with, the authorities quickly moved to crush the vital social institution of the *waqf*,[12] confiscating and destroying their properties, such as mosques, madrassas, and shrines. By limiting access to physical sacred spaces, the authorities were making an indirect attack on Islamic knowledge. In that same vein, Soviet authorities changed the script used by the various Muslim languages. For centuries they had, of course, been written in Arabic script, but the Soviets changed them first to Latin and then later to the Russian Cyrillic script (Kreindler 1969). This had a huge impact on practical religion, because it cut Muslims off from the textual sources of their faith as well as interaction with the rest of the Islamic world. Taken together, these actions "destroyed the means through which Islamic knowledge was produced and transmitted" (Khalid 2007, 81–82). However, the actions of Soviet authorities were intended to do more than cut Muslims off from their ties to Islamic civilization; they were also a means to begin binding them to a new one.

---

[10] Modern-day Kyrgyzstan.

[11] The Soviet campaign was against all religions, but their assault was especially pronounced against Islam because they feared the pan-Islamic and pan-Turkic movements that were stirring all across the region at the time.

[12] Peters (2002) explains that the waqf was a tax-free property endowment that could be established for pious benefit or public utility. Some examples of the beneficiaries of waqfs are mosques, schools, graveyards, bridges, poor houses, and public drinking fountains. It was the primary social institution that connected all the parts of public life in Muslim society.

Assimilation

The main reason Soviet authorities encouraged Muslims to use the Russian language was because they theorized that language was the location of ethnic consciousness; thus, linguistic assimilation would lead to deep identity changes (Kholmogorow 1970, quoted in Silver 1974). They believed the end result would be a new anthropological reality, the "new Soviet man," and that this would be the "inter-ethnic bond which could hold a Soviet multi-ethnic society together" (Matuszkiewicz 2010, 213). They also believed this new reality would replace existing ethnic identities and loyalty. While the results were not quite as spectacular as the Soviets had hoped, this campaign did have far-reaching effects—producing what social scientists commonly call Russified Muslims.

Later we will examine the missiological significance of this identity shift, but first we need a firm grasp of how it works out in practical life for Muslims living in Russian territory. A friend once opened a small window of insight into this transformation when he told me about his military experience in the Soviet army:

> I was seventeen when I went to the Russian army. They sent me far up north into Russia somewhere. I could barely speak any Russian at the time. I was cold and alone. I had to quickly learn to understand and speak Russian to survive, because there was no one to translate into Uzbek[13] for me in drill camp. They worked us from early morning until late evening. When they said you could eat, you ran to the dining hall and ate whatever it was they had. I had never eaten pork in my life, but when you are that hungry you don't ask questions about what is in the food.

> After two years I came home. Because I now had a skill [welder] and spoke good Russian, I got a job at the large pump and pipe factory. At lunch we had a dining hall where all the employees ate. I still did not ask questions about what kind of meat was in food.

> So, I have never bought pork to eat, never eaten it at home, but before I really didn't think about it. In those days it didn't matter—food was food.[14]

Here we see the shared experience of military service producing bilingualism, leading to cultural assimilation, producing functional Russification. Another common life experience of the Soviet era—postsecondary education—played a similar role, and impacted both men and women.[15] Like military conscription, college or technical school usually required young Muslims to leave their natal home and live, study, and work in a mixed-ethnic setting. Both required the rapid development of Russian proficiency. And finally, both forced them to eat in common dining halls where they would unwittingly abandon Islamic dietary regulations (Khalid 2007;

---

[13] One of the Turkic nationalities in Central Asia, Uzbeks comprise one of the largest groups of migrant Muslim workers in the Russian Federation today

[14] Interview with carpet trader in central bazaar, Osh, Kyrgyzstan, March 2006

[15] Obviously the Soviet system of higher education is gone, in principle, but much of its structure remains for Muslims who study in Russian-language universities. Certainly the impact on a young Muslim's culture has diminished, but it has not gone away. The Russian educational structure likely now competes with globalization for the greatest impact on many Muslim college students in Russia and the former republics.

Benningsen and Lemercier-Quelquejay 1967). The impact of this should not be underestimated considering the importance Muslims have historically placed on dietary regulations and the emotional value of food. Over time the habits and ceremonies of military or college life became a central node of pan-Soviet identity and collective memory, replacing things like salat or learning the Qur'an. Like some kind of watershed, they left home as Muslim peasants but returned as Soviet citizens.

Keeping our missiological interests in view, however, the weight of these many pressures on Muslims under Soviet rule brought lasting changes that are still felt in their religious life. A survey done in 2011–12 by the Pew Research Center on Religion in Public Life involved Muslims in thirty-nine countries. Below are the results from six countries[16] where Muslims either did or still do live under Russian rule. These help to quantify the point we have been making.[17]

- On average, how often to you attend the mosque for *salat* and *jumah* prayer?[18]
  64 percent answered seldom or never.
- Outside of attending religious services, how often do you pray?
  64 percent answered seldom or never.
- Do you fast during the holy month of Ramadan?
  46 percent answered no.
- How often do you read or listen to the Qur'an?
  56 percent answered a few times a year or never.

Yet these same Muslims answered this way about the *importance* of religion:
- How important is religion in your life?
  81 percent answered very important or somewhat important.

A visiting Turkish scholar said the following about Russified Muslims in the post-Soviet world, "there are Islamic sentiments and feelings, but they lack true knowledge" (Kimmage 2005). That serves as a good point upon which to shift our discussion to matters deeper than behavior—to worldview.

Worldview

So far we have only hinted at issues of worldview. Now it is time to shift gears and focus on how Russification has impacted the worldview of Muslims living under Russian rule, because it is here that we will find the building blocks of missiology.

It may be helpful to briefly remind ourselves that Russification is first a linguistic phenomenon; without language shift there is no cultural assimilation. But once there is a shared language, other things connected to worldview begin to happen. In an interethnic setting, language is both a vehicle of communication and a symbol of

---

[16] Azerbaijan, Kazakhstan, Kyrgyzstan, Russia, Tajikistan, and Uzbekistan.

[17] Of course, we have no way of knowing if every single respondent in these countries was linguistically or culturally Russified. Nevertheless, the statistics do point to a general trend in these Muslim societies that were impacted by Russification

[18] Salat refers to the five-times-a-day daily prayers, and jumah are Friday prayers.

shared identity. First, as a vehicle of interethnic communication, a shared language becomes the conduit whereby the *other* moves closer. People who were strange and alien become knowable. Second, language also functions as a symbol of ethnic or cultural identity—one belongs when one can speak the language.

It is important to point out, however, that the assimilation we are describing was not complete: Muslims did not become entirely subsumed into a Russian identity,[19] something which might be mistakenly implied by the term "Russified Muslim." Rather, the commonality that many Muslims in the former Soviet Union feel toward Russians must be understood as a genuine coexistence of their Islamic and/or ethnic identities within a new Soviet one (Khalid 2007), not as an exchange of their Islamic identity for a Soviet one. Thus we can say that the experience of inhabiting two cultural spaces created a distinctly new worldview, that of a Russified Muslim.

Also, we must recognize that the Soviet pressure on organized Islam attacked the very root of Islamic knowledge, causing a migration of religious identity from scriptural sources to ethnic ones. Across the Russian-speaking world, Islam was transformed from a universal religion with global reach into something that, for most Muslims, is primarily defined by a collection of folk ways and life cycle common across the region—i.e., an ethnic identity marker.

This transformation was supported by what some have called a Soviet-era "parallel Islam"—a reference to the extensive underground Islamic societies that continued to exist even after several decades of government repression (Ro'i 1995). This network of itinerate clerics and unauthorized, underground mosques and simple prayer rooms often included all the religious services a devout Muslim family might need though the cycles of life (Myer 2012, 187). When the Soviet Academy of Social Sciences studied this underground version of Islam in the mid-1980s, they found, to their alarm, relatively extensive practices of Islamic traditions, festivals, and rites among all sociodemographic groups—though they were led by Islamic religious leaders with little or no religious training who clearly based their leadership role on folk practices (Ro'i 1995).

Thus we see two streams flowing side by side: the ethnification of Islam and the strengthening of "Muslim" identity. While these may seem contradictory, both perspectives are necessary to understand the Russified Muslim worldview and how it influences appropriate missiology. Losing access to textual sources caused a loss of content at the same time that the combination of underground Islamic structures and cultural traditions became a bulwark against losing Muslim identity. In other words, Russified Muslims continue to share the same formal structures of Islam with their coreligionists in other areas of the world, but for many of them it has become a form with little overt religious meaning.

---

[19] Soviet-era scholar Vernon Aspaturian argues that many Muslims became so enculturated into Russian culture that they actually became "objectively and psychologically Russian" (1968, 159), which he also develops into a scale. Aspaturian's construction is quite interesting, but far beyond the scope of this chapter.

Another way of thinking about this is that Russified Muslims have developed a "hybrid identity" (Barnett 2013). They were able to keep a sense of belonging in their cultural "homeland" (the Islamic community) while simultaneously building social capital in a new identity "location"—that is, in Russian social/political/economic space. This division of personal identity is a common way of resolving internal-external conflict for peoples living under colonial rule (Werth 2000). Rather than suppressing the tension of cultural ambiguity, this fusing of identity renders the choice between social worlds unnecessary because it *enables* a person to carry markers of both Muslim and Russian identity at the same time and without any sense of contradiction. People with hybrid identities culturally inhabit "an ambiguous third space where the 'incommensurable elements' of multiple belongings are brought into dialogue with each other" (Barnett 2013, 30).

This is precisely where the missiological importance of Russification can be seen. What Barnett calls "an ambiguous third space" is for all practical purposes a new culture, or at the very least a significantly different subculture. It is not really "Russian," nor is it what we commonly think of as "Islamic." In other words, the Muslims living under Russian rule are more than simply bilingual people who can therefore access Christian material in the Russian language. They are people who inhabit an overlapping, yet nonetheless different, cultural space. They possess a meta-identity that goes beyond both their ethnic and Islamic identities; they are very specifically Russified Muslims. Therefore they are significantly different than their ethnic coreligionists in northern Afghanistan or northwestern China, even though they share not only ethnic identity but live in close geographic proximity. Because this mixed cultural background is is so different, it has a huge impact on how we approach people with the gospel.

Missiological Significance

Many missionaries enter the world of Russified Muslims from one of two mistaken perspectives. On the one hand, because of their shared language and social ties, it is easy to assume they are just another kind of Russian—meaning that approaches which work with ethnic Russians will work just as well with Russified Muslims. On the other hand, some missionaries have assumed that Russified Muslims are still primarily *religiously* Muslim, despite the fact that they have been cut off from the sources of their faith for several decades. These misunderstandings lead to foreign missionaries making various kinds of mistakes, many of which have to do with language.

As we have pointed out several times, Russification begins with language shift. For many Muslims, especially those who are highly educated or live in urban settings, Russian is more than a lingua franca; it is their primary or only language of literary communication. For example, today many middle-aged Muslim men in the former Soviet Union speak their ethnic language but read it only with great difficulty—if at all. They use the two different languages in different domains of life. They use the Russian language (written) in technical, professional, or political spheres, but their ethnic language (oral) for community and family interpersonal communication. This domain-specific bilingualism is not uncommon in contexts of colonialism, but it is something few field-workers are aware of. One long-term worker in the region put it this way:

> Within the first few months of arriving in Kazakhstan in the fall of 1990, the first Western workers noticed that many Kazakhs and other Muslims of what was then the Soviet Union did not know their mother-tongues well. Rather, they functioned primarily in Russian, due to their having attended Russian language schools and universities. At the same time, they were deeply attached to their culturally Muslim (non-Russian) ethnic heritage and community. These "Russifed" Central Asians, who were certainly capable of reading the traditional Russian Bible (known as the Synodal Version, a translation from the nineteenth century written in a high literary style), either showed no interest or even displayed genuine fear of reading this Russian version. (Jamison n.d., 1)

This love/hate relationship with the Russian language produces strange problems in gospel communication. For example, since Protestantism is deeply linked to the printed Word, many have assumed that the shortest path to ministry is with the Russian language, which is often true, but only with some important caveats and exceptions. While Russian is many times the best (or only) language through which a Russified Muslim can access printed Scripture, the Russian Bible is an extremely alien world for them.

Many of us have been trained to see gospel bridges in personalities such as Abraham, Moses, and supremely in Jesus himself since they are important figures in both the Bible and the Qur'an. But even though Russian is a shared language, these important figures have very different names for a Russified Muslim than they do for an ethnic Russian. A good illustration of this can be found in the words of a former Muslim who is now an active evangelist. He expressed frustration that his foreign Christian friends do not understand the importance of this issue as it relates to sharing the gospel with Russified Muslims.

> Europeans [Russians and foreign missionaries][20] don't understand the difference between Yesus Christos[21] and Isa Masih.[22] They would ask me, "Why is it so important for you when you know that this is the same person?" So they were worried a bit; they were suspicious of this. They wanted us to leave that completely, and they wanted us [former Muslims] to be just like them. But deep inside I knew the barriers. I knew that only one letter or one word could hinder other Muslims from coming and believing in Jesus. Of course to them, the Europeans, it was not important. Yet it is very important to us.

> Interviewer: So, for a Muslim who speaks fluent Russian, this is not the problem of a language, but it is a problem of culture?

---

[20] Although it may seem strange to us, many Muslims in the former Soviet Union categorize all Westerners the same as local ethnic Russians: "European." In other words, we are all the "other" that really does not belong in their homelands.

[21] *Yesus Christos* is Russian for "Jesus Christ."

[22] *Isa* is the Arabic pronunciation of the name Jesus, and Isa al Masih, Isa Masih, or simply Masih are the Turkified versions of the Arabic term for "Jesus the Messiah"—i.e., *Yesus Christos* in Russian.

Right. I myself was not a real Muslim. I never counted the namaz,[23] was never committed, [and] because I studied in Russian, I had a more globalized thinking. But even despite that, I was surprised, because once I stepped into a European church something began to wake up in me. So I realized that if it happens with me, who had nothing to do with Islam, what will happen to those who worship in Islam? The door will be closed to them. So I knew it was important to address that.[24]

Because of the Russian Orthodox Church, Muslims in the Russian world all grow up knowing that *Yesus Christos* belongs to the Russians, or we might say that he exists in the Russian metaphysical world. But when *Yesus Christos* becomes an Arabic loan term—*Isa Masih*—he also becomes accessible, because he is someone written about in the Qur'an.

> When I heard that Christos is the same as Masih, I liked that there is a different way to pronounce it, instead of saying "Christ."
>
> Interviewer: So to you it made a big difference?
>
> Yes, because it was a real stumbling block. I heard the name Isa from my grandfather, who was a Muslim. He said that Isa was coming back to judge the world. ... Because I heard about Isa before and perceived him as "our prophet," it meant that I did not sell my faith and did not betray the faith of my fathers. So it was important for me to know that it is part of our traditional beliefs.[25]

And this shift of metaphysical location is not limited to personalities; several other loan words are involved. The central text of Christianity, the *Novi Zavet* (New Testament), takes on completely different meaning as the Injil, while Christian gatherings are transformed from a Russian *czerchov* (church) into a *djama'at*.[26]

The premier illustration of this type of approach is the Central Asian Russian Scripture project, or CARS.[27] The purpose of this project was to produce a new version of Scripture, in the Russian language, that would appeal to a Muslim audience. With that goal in mind, the translation team did not start from scratch but rather used a well-known Russian Bible translation published by the International Bible Society. They began with Scripture portions they felt would be of particular interest to Muslims, such as Genesis and Luke, and eventually finished the complete Bible in 2008 (Pritzlaff 2007). At its simplest, the process entailed adapting key, emotionally charged terms like those mentioned above to ones that were familiar and culturally

---

[23] "Counting namaz" is the typical Central Asian way of referring to doing ritual prayers five times each day.
[24] Interview with male convert (#208M), Uzbekistan, February 2012.
[25] Ibid.
[26] *Djama'at* comes from the Arabic root "to bring together, to unite," which expresses an ideal of the bond that unites individuals or groups (Zurayk 1991, 422). Turkic peoples in Central Asia often use it as a generic term for a religious meeting.
[27] The project was originally known as the "Culturally Sensitive Russian Language Scriptures," then renamed "Central Asian Russian Scriptures" or CARS. In the Russian language it is often referred to as simply the *Vostochnie perevod* ("Eastern translation"). This is in recognition a) that the translation reaches a need that spread far beyond Central Asia into most of the Russian-speaking world, and b) that Muslims in the former Soviet Union often refer to themselves as "Eastern" peoples (Pritzlaff 2007).

acceptable to Muslims. Furthermore, they also carefully considered what would be attractive to Muslims as they developed things like page layouts and cover designs.

> Culturally foreign ecclesiastical terminology and Slavic names employed in the traditional Russian Scriptures, which were often bound in a black cover and decorated with a large golden cross (a symbol most Muslims in the region only associate with graveyards or Orthodox Christianity), typically so repelled a prospective Muslim background reader that they would reject the message without even grappling with its contents. (Jamison n.d., 2)

In other words, the CARS approach has harnessed two powerful issues to make itself a strong and secure bridge for the gospel to move across: first, the linguistic adaptation of Russian Scripture to Muslim vernacular terms; and second, changes of physical presentation that took Muslim sensibilities into consideration.

This raises the issue of how far we should go to make the Bible "friendly" to Muslims. Over the past several years there has been significant, and much-needed, debate in the mission world concerning so-called "Muslim idiomatic translations," an approach which the ERSP generally falls under. And thankfully a general consensus has developed.[28] While this discussion is too far afield for us, we should remember the "adaptation" approach above has at least one powerful precedent.

In 1980 the Bangladesh Bible Society released an adapted version of the original Bengali Bible that William Carey translated in 1832. Carey had translated the Scriptures using Hindu terminologies, thus making the book effectively off limits to Muslims for generations. This adaptation, the *Injil Sharif*, proved so powerful in overcoming Muslim emotional resistance to the Bible that it quickly became the all-time best-selling book in the history of the Bengali language[29] (King and McCormick 2013). This is simply a reminder from history that just because a Muslim people may read the same language as a Christian group, the existing Scriptures may not be the best way to reach them.

This points toward the other way Russification impacts successful ministry: the cultural dimension. As we have seen, Russification involves both language and culture, something we must keep in mind as we think missiologically. A Russian Bible is not just a book, nor are Russian churches just places of worship; they are deeply embedded parts of culture, and that culture is the very one that has long epitomized the word *kafir* to the Muslim community.

---

[28] For a succinct, balanced overview of this issue, see Ruth Moon, "Will New Guidelines Solve Wycliffe's Two-Year Bible Translation Controversy? Updated Best Practices Point the Way Forward for Missionary-Muslim Interactions," *Christianity Today*, May 10, 2013, http://www.christianitytoday.com/ct/2013/may-web-only/will-new-guidelines-solve-wycliffes-two-year-translation-co.html.

[29] In 2000 the Bangladesh Bible Society published the *Kitabul Mokaddos* ("Holy Bible"), which contains a significant revision of the 1980 *Injil Sharif*.

One of my dear MBB friends in Central Asia is a very Russified Muslim and a committed member of a very Western-style, missionary-planted church. Yet even after being a Christian for several years, he told me, "I still inwardly accuse myself of being a traitor every time I enter the door of my church," My friend was never, in his own words, a "religious Muslim," so this is not about maintaining connection with Islam per se, yet somehow our approach to ministry has often neglected important cultural symbols for people like him.

We have to find ways to allow culture to still play its important symbolic role. One MBB friend talked about it this way:

> I try to be careful in how I do things. For example, praying after the food, not before. Praying in Islamic way, saying Ameen instead of Amen.[30] … I purposefully choose not to do some things. Not to pray before food or by bowing my head.[31] … This is because I used to tell people I was a Christian, so people would say that I was a betrayer of Islam, a Kafir[32] … but now I tell them I am Masahi.[33] [34]

The necessary cultural adaptation must cut even into our cherished notions of church. Another MBB leader talked about how our cultural meanings have influenced missionary-led churches:

> I kept wondering, "Why do people have to come to church? Nobody knows what you are really like at home or at work. We come, greet each other, and go. No fellowship during the week." So I thought, "This is not a djama'at,[35] because a djama'at should be people in fellowship with one another. My neighbor is my djama'at because they see me, or my sister; that's what djama'at should be like." So I was wondering why the gospel should be only expressed by going to church.[36]

And finally, the reality of Russification forces us to think carefully about the emphasis we have placed on ethnic identities in cross-cultural mission. And while this chapter has focused on one particular context, similar observations could likely be made about certain population segments in other Muslim countries that were previously under colonial rule. This is not to say that ethnicity is unimportant, or even secondary to meta-identities like the Russified Muslim, but it does at least suggest that there are other important identity markers for many Muslims. Discovering and understanding these could be the seedbed of new gospel breakthroughs. These are only a few of the important issues that must be taken into consideration as the gospel flows to more and more Muslims in the Russian-speaking world.

---

[30] This signifies the difference between the way Russians pronounce the same word used as an ending to prayers. Russians say *Amen*, and Muslims say *Ameen*.

[31] Here he is referring to the difference between the way Russian Christians pray before their meals with bowed heads and the common Muslim practice of praying after the meal with upturned head and hands.

[32] In local usage, *Kafir* is a strong pejorative used against those who left Islam.

[33] A follower of *Isa Masih*.

[34] Interview with male convert (#201M), Kazakhstan, February 2012.

[35] Again, *djama'at* is often used by MBBs in place of the Russian word czerkoff, or church.

[36] Interview with female convert (#302F), Kyrgyzstan, February 2013.

Conclusion

By now it should be clear that the Muslim peoples of the former Soviet Union have blended their Islamic heritage with their close relationship with Russians. While this changed what Islam means to them, it did not lessen its importance to them. For many, being a Muslim has very little to do with individual knowledge of sacred material or regular practice of Islamic rituals. It means being part of a community that is Muslim. In other words, ancestors, holidays, and life cycle events slowly took the place of knowledge and adherence to Islamic doctrines (Khalid 2007). These are the Russified Muslims we have talked so much about.

Yet, like all things cultural, the context I have described in this chapter is not set in stone. The shifting sand of the post-Soviet era has seen a proliferation of mosque-building and more people publicly participating in Islamic ritual. Only the future will tell how much of this description will still be true in ten or twenty years. However, what will be the same is that Muslims need to be approached with a studied appreciation for their specific context.

Reflection Questions

1. How has history influenced the worldview of Russified Muslims?

2. What does it mean when the same group of Muslims[37] affirm the importance of religion in their life (81 percent), yet seldom or never attend the mosque (64 percent) and seldom or never pray (64 percent)?

3. How does a hybrid identity like Russified Muslims affect our understanding of "Unreached Muslim People Groups"?

4. In a bilingual environment, how do we determine which is the best language for Muslims to encounter printed Scripture?

References

Aspaturian, Vernon V. 1968. "The Non-Russian Nationalities." In *Prospects for Soviet Society*, edited by Allen Kassof, 144–98. New York: Praeger.

Barnett, Jens. 2013. "Living a Pun: Cultural Hybridity among Arab Followers of Christ." In *Longing for Community: Church, Ummah, or Somewhere in Between?*, edited by David Greenlee. Pasadena, CA: William Carey Library.

Bennigsen, Alexandre, and Chantal Lemercier-Quelquejay. 1967. *Islam in the Soviet Union*. New York: Praeger.

Burton-Page, J. 1993. "Namaz." In *Encyclopaedia of Islam*, edited by C. E. Bosworth, E. van Donzel, B. Lewis, and Ch. Phellat. Vol. 7, Mif–Naz. Leiden: E. J. Brill.

Khalid, Adeeb. 2007. *Islam After Communism: Religion and Politics in Central Asia*. Berkley: University of California Press.

Kreindler, Isabelle Teitz. 1969. "Educational Policies Toward the Eastern Nationalities in Tsarist Russia: Study of Il'minskii's System." Ph.D. diss., Columbia University.

---

[37] Those in Azerbaijan, Kazakhstan, Kyrgyzstan, Russia, Tajikistan, and Uzbekistan.

Jamison, Todd. n.d. "Fruitful Practice Case Study: CARS." Unpublished manuscript.

Juvaini, Ala-ad-Din Ata Malik. 1958. *The History of the World Conqueror*. Translated by John Andrew Boyle. Cambridge, MA: Harvard University Press. Accessed July 10, 2015. <https://archive.org/stream/ historyoftheworl011691mbp/historyoftheworl011691mbp_djvu.txt>.

Kimmage, Daniel. 2005. "Central Asia: Jadidism—Old Tradition of Renewal." *Radio Free Europe/Radio Liberty, Central Asia Report* 5, no. 30, (August), 11.

King, George, and Tom McCormick. 2013. "Muslim Idiom Translations in Bangladesh." *Evangelical Review of Theology* 37, no. 4 (October): 335–48.

Matuszkiewicz, Renata. 2010. "The Language Issue in Kazakhstan—institutionalizing new ethnic relations after independence." *Economic and Environmental Studies* 10, no. 2 (June): 211–27.

Myer, Will. 2012. *Islam and Colonialism: Western Perspectives on Soviet Asia*. New York: Routledge.

Sayid, A. 2006. Personal interview by author.

Peters, R. 2002. "Wakf." In *Encyclopaedia of Islam*, edited by P. J. Bearman, Th. Bianquis, C. E. Bosworth, E. van Donzel, and W. P. Heinrichs. Vol. 11, V–Z. Leiden: E. J. Brill.

Pew Forum on Religion in Public Life. 2012. "The World's Muslims: Unity and Diversity (survey report)." Pew Research Center. Accessed April 22, 2013. http://www.pewforum.org/uploadedFiles/Topics/Religious_ Affiliation/Muslim/the-worlds-muslims-full-report.pdf.

Pritzlaff, Allen. 2007. "Evangelizing Russian-speaking Muslims in Kazakhstan through contextualizing the Scriptures: a case study." *Tren Dissertations*. Paper 5941. Accessed Mar 5, 2015. http://place.asburyseminary. edu/trendissertations/5941.

Privratsky, Bruce. 2001. *Muslim Turkistan: Kazak Religion and Collective Memory*. New York: Routledge.

Ro'i, Yaacov. 1995. *Muslim Eurasia: Conflicting Legacies*. Edited by Yaacov Ro'i. Portland: International Specialized Book Services.

Silver, Brian. 1974. "The Impact of Urbanization and Geographical Dispersion on the Linguistic Russification of Soviet Nationalities." *Demography* 11, no. 1 (February): 89–103. Accessed January 1, 2011. http://www.jstor. org/stable/2060701.

Werth, Paul W. 2000. "From 'Pagan' Muslims to 'Baptized' Communists: Religious Conversion and Ethnic Particularity in Russia's Eastern Provinces." *Comparative Studies in Society and History* 42, No. 3 (Jul): 497–523. Accessed June 12, 2013. http://www.jstor.org/stable/2696643.

Zurayk, C. K. 1991. "Djama'a." In *Encyclopaedia of Islam*, edited by C. E. Bosworth, E. van Donzel, B. Lewis and Ch. Phellat. Vol. 2, C–G. Leiden: E. J. Brill.

CHAPTER

13
Phil Rawlings

The Queen's Muslims?
Muslim Identities in the UK

A man with a heavy beard wearing a *salwar kameez* is probably not what most people expect to see walking out of the London fog, but the religious landscape of the United Kingdom is changing rapidly today. The presence of Muslims has become an increasingly significant influence in the life of the nation. In 2011, there were 2.7 million Muslims in the UK (about 5 percent of the population), a rise from 1.6 million (about 3 percent) in 2001 (ONS 2011). The growth in the Muslim population is due primarily to immigration and higher birth rates in Muslim families. However, since Islam is a missionary religion, conversion has also been a factor. There are an estimated one hundred thousand converts to Islam in Britain, with over half of these being Anglo-Saxons. The majority of these converts are in the 25–29 age bracket, and Islam is firmly established on the religious landscape of the British Isles (Rawlings 2014). This chapter considers the historic and ethnic situation of Muslims in the UK and explores how Christians are responding to God's challenge to the church today.

Who Are British Muslims?

Although the British have had contact with Muslims for centuries, the first mosque in Britain was established in Liverpool in 1887 by William Henry Quilliam, who had converted to Islam while visiting Morocco (Ansari 2004). This mosque was situated in the neighborhood of Woking, near London, to serve Muslims working in embassies and businesses.

Apart from communities of "lascars" (Yemenis and Somalis working for the British Merchant Navy who settled in Cardiff, Liverpool, and South Shields), the numbers of Muslims in Britain remained relatively small until after World War II. Lacing laborers during the postwar boom, British industry appealed to the Commonwealth to staff its factories and mills. In the late 1950s and early 1960s, thousands of migrant workers came from Pakistan, India, and Bangladesh and worked in the cotton and woollen mills in Lancashire and Yorkshire. The largest group came from the city of Mirpur in Azad Kashmir, Pakistan, where in 1960 the British government provided finance to build the Mangla Dam to generate hydroelectricity. Men from the hundreds of villages that were flooded or relocated were given British passports and encouraged to come to the UK. They came as migrant workers to the northern mill towns, sending their earnings back to their families.

In response to alarmist fears about the number of foreigners coming to the UK, in 1962 the government passed the Commonwealth Immigrants Act, which stemmed the flow of additional migrants but gave permission for those in the UK to bring their families. From that time onward migrant workers became settlers, and the development of mosques and madrassas began in response to the needs of these growing communities.

Although people of Indian subcontinent heritage still comprise the largest Muslim communities, an increasing number from almost every country in the Muslim world have found a home in the UK over the last fifty years. In addition to Muslim migrants who fill professional positions, the UK has provided sanctuary for thousands of asylum seekers from every troubled area of the world. In the 1990s, many came from Bosnia and Kosovo, and more recently many have come from Iraq, Kurdistan, Libya, Syria, the Sudan, and Somalia. While all mosques allow any Muslim to worship, in most places a particular ethnic or racial group will be the de facto owners.

Many of these ethnic communities are now into their third or fourth generations, and many are well integrated into British life. Some are well established in employment, sometimes in legal or medical professions, and send their children to local government schools—or even church schools. Overall, they share in the prosperity of the UK while maintaining their Islamic faith. They have a clearly formed "British Muslim" identity. Other Muslims, however, are facing more challenges as they engage with mainstream British culture. Some Muslim communities have even withdrawn into distinct geographical areas, often establishing their own enclaves in the poorest areas of towns and cities. This came to a head in 2001 with "race riots" in the northern towns of Bradford, Burnley, and Oldham. The subsequent government report (the Cantle Report) noted that the affected areas showed a "depth of polarisation" around segregated communities living "a series of parallel lives" (The Guardian 2001). Furthermore, it recommended a number of measures, including the promotion of "citizenship," and warned that further violence was likely unless changes took place.

Where Do British Muslims Live?

Muslims are not evenly spread over the country. Indeed, there are many places, especially rural areas, where the population will never meet a Muslim. Urban areas provide a home for the majority of Muslim communities, with over 40 percent of UK Muslims living in London. Parts of London have very significant Muslim populations, such as the East London boroughs of Tower Hamlets and Newham (next to the financial center of London), where about 35 percent of the residents are Muslims. Some of the outer London boroughs also have significant Muslim populations. Problems of social integration have been at their worst, though, in old industrial communities in the north of England. As the industries that the migrant communities came to support have collapsed, residents are left to deal with poverty, lack of employment, health issues, and substandard housing. Muslim communities have been some of the worst affected.

It is important to understand that these segregated communities often remain tied to their South Asian heritage by the traditional *biradari* systems of patronage (Shalikh 2015) and marriage ties.[1] It is significant that even the fourth generation of migrant families commonly seeks spouses from their heritage homelands on the Indian subcontinent, often with close relatives (first cousins). This inevitably raises questions of identity, loyalty, and the extent to which new immigrants can prosper within the UK, especially where there are serious language and cultural issues. In response, the government has enacted stricter rules concerning proficiency in English and other forms of cultural integration before visas are granted to hopeful migrants.

However, major identity issues remain for those who have grown up in the UK and have been educated in a Western system, yet have continued attending a madrassa where the approach to education is very different. Some might ask, "Am I Pakistani or English? In the UK I am still treated as a foreigner, yet when I travel to Pakistan I don't understand the culture or the language. I'm a foreigner here and I'm a foreigner there. Where do I belong?"

Issues of identity form key questions for many British-born young adults with Asian heritages. They sense a clash of worldviews, a clash between an "Islamic" world of spirit and devotion with that of the rationalistic, Western dependence upon scientific proof and critical thinking. They struggle between the shame-honor culture of their parents and the guilt-innocence culture of the West. Those who attend the mosque are

---

[1] Spouses are the largest single category of migrant settlement in the UK (39 percent in 2008 and 40 percent in 2009 (Charsley, Van Hear, Benson, and Storer-Church 2012).

prescriptively taught to memorize the Qur'an, Hadith, and other aspects of Islamic knowledge. But in the schools they are taught to learn by discovery—to question and critique everything. How very confusing!

This tension creates a serious identity crisis. For some it leads to a rejection of Islam while remaining culturally Muslim. They are assimilated into British youth culture: alcohol, fast cars, fashion, clubbing, etc. Many have become indistinguishable from Western young people; they have a "Muslim" social identity even though they have adopted a secularist worldview and rejected their Muslim heritage.

Others may develop a deeper devotion and practice. Hence we often see young Muslim women adopting Arab dress—the *hijab* and *niqab*,[2] and sometimes the *jilbaab*,[3] and becoming much more serious about their faith. Likewise, some young men become more serious concerning issues around politics and religion;[4] and attendance at the mosque increases, along with a general desire to go deeper into their faith.

A growth in devotion, however, should not be directly equated with radicalization. Governments often make this mistake, which simply aggravates the situation. Academic studies show that radicalization is more common among those who are more ignorant of their faith (Lewis 2007) and hence are more susceptible to influences on the Internet. The majority of mosques in Britain work hard to keep their young people away from radicalizing influences. Nevertheless, young people who have an identity crisis or feel they don't belong anywhere are vulnerable to more sinister influences, especially through the Internet. For example, in 2015 it was estimated that over six hundred UK citizens had travelled to Syria to join ISIS, or "Islamic State," both as jihadi fighters and their brides (BBC News 2015). While this is a tiny fraction of the Muslim population in the UK, it raises serious issues for their communities as they wrestle with these questions of belonging and identity. Furthermore, intergenerational tensions over these issues may lead to alienation and confusion for these young people, especially if and when these jihadi fighters return to their families.

What Kinds of Islam Are Found in the UK?

British representations of Islam are a kaleidoscope. There are those with a very strict Salafi/Wahhabi worldview, Sufi-orientated Berelvis, as well as smaller but significant numbers of Shi'a, both South Asian and Iranian, as well as the Ahmadiyya. In other words, the UK provides a confusing array of Islamic religious diversity that mirrors the wider Islamic world. Not only that, but for a growing number of progressive Muslims in the UK, wrestling with their British identity has forced them to ask questions about how Islam fits with Western democracy and "British values."

Islam is frequently used as politico-religious system to engage with the ruling establishment. Academics such as Tariq Ramadan (2009) who consider themselves to

---

[2] A veil over the face below the eyes.
[3] A full-length garment worn to cover all parts of the female body except the face.
[4] Interestingly, these are the two subjects that white British young people will rarely discuss.

be "European Muslims" are asking profound questions concerning human rights and Islam. A group of academics and thinkers publish a quarterly journal called *Critical Muslim*. This Muslim engagement with British politics, along with a renewed Christian confidence, has led some social commentators to ask whether the UK is becoming "post-secular" (Graham 2013).

One of the earliest and most influential groups to enter the UK were the Deobandi, followers of an Islamic political movement originating in North India in the nineteenth century. Centered around the town of Deoband, they developed a strict form of orthodox Islam that looked to the earliest sources for their authority. Deep devotion and adherence to the basic tenets of their faith characterize the Deobandi, along with a rejection of Sufi influences. As was often the case, their political affiliations in the subcontinent were simply transported across to the UK. The other prominent South Asian stream of Islam in the UK is the Berelvi, which also originated in the Indian subcontinent. The Berelvi defend folk Islam and its Sufi influences, and developed as a reaction to the Deobandi.

The other major movement is the better-known Salafi,[5] who are closely related, theologically, to Saudi Arabian Wahhabism (Esposito 2003).[6] Though they make up a small proportion of mosques (ninety-eight), their influence is significant—with increasing numbers of young people being attracted to their assertive theology and emphasis on rediscovering a "pure Islam." However, it is important to note that neither Deobandi nor Salafi adherents in the UK give automatic support to violent jihad. Many of their affiliated mosques work hard to protect their young people from radical influences. Nevertheless, sympathy for more radical organizations is more likely to come from these movements than others.

Muslims in Britain are a rich mixture of those who integrate well and prosper contrasted with others who segregate themselves (Miah 2015) and often remain poor. In different ways, these give opportunities for Christians to reach out in love with the message of the gospel of Jesus. There are encouraging signs that the church is beginning to rise to the challenge that God has given his people in the UK.

How Is the Church in Britain Responding to the Growing Influence of Islam in the UK?

For the past 250 years, the church in the UK has sent and supported its missionaries to Muslim peoples "over there." Indeed, many churches continue to support mission across the world. Therefore, the immigration of the last fifty years has demanded a paradigm shift with which many churches have struggled to come to terms. In countries that used to be "Christian nations," such as Britain, bewilderment and confusion have often resulted from encounters with people of other faiths, especially another missionary faith like Islam. This has been compounded by an increasing awareness of the persecution of Christians globally, especially in the Muslim world. Organizations such as the Barnabas

---

[5] See *The Week* (2015).
[6] See Crooke (2014).

Fund,[7] Open Doors,[8] Christian Solidarity Worldwide,[9] and Release International[10] have publicized the plight of Christians and encouraged prayer and support for Christian communities under pressure—which can unfortunately lead to the impression that Muslims are our enemy, and hence an attitude of fear can develop.

Over the last ten years or more, however, there has been a growing realization that "over there" has come "over here," and that believers in the UK have a responsibility to share the good news of God's love in Christ with their Muslim neighbors. Many churches in strong Muslim areas of our cities have reached out in love to their Muslim neighbors. In Manchester, for example, ESOL (English for Speakers of Other Languages) classes have been started by churches in different parts of the city for those wishing to improve their English. These classes offer free instruction and education and are sometimes accompanied by knitting and sewing classes. This provides opportunities for Christians to develop strong friendships with Muslim women who often are stuck at home, lonely and feeling powerless. Although not overtly evangelistic, Christians are loving their neighbors; and as friendships develop, questions about faith frequently arise, especially at festival times (Christmas, Easter, and the two Eids). Recently, groups of Christians in our cities have started organizing prayer meetings; and a network has developed nationally, calling itself *Mahabba* (Arabic for "love"), with a vision to motivate and mobilize "everyday Christians to love their Muslim neighbours and to help churches to mentor and multiply dynamic communities of disciples."[11]

Since the Muslims in Britain come in many different shapes and sizes, it is important that each person is understood in his or her unique context. Some are very devout, while others are at best nominal, cultural Muslims. Some have lived in the UK for forty or more years; others have just arrived, possibly fleeing repressive Islamic nations. Many refugees and asylum seekers may be bewildered and confused about their faith and ready to consider alternatives. On the opposite extreme, others may consider themselves British Muslims with a mission to produce an Islamic United Kingdom.

A common question from British Muslim friends goes something like this: "Why are churches becoming mosques, and why are Christians not proud of their faith? We never see Christians protesting or declaring their faith. Don't they really believe it?" We know that recent studies have given a different picture of the church in Britain, which is not simply one of decline (Goodhart 2012). Despite the continued decline of traditional denominations in many areas, new churches, often of a multiethnic nature, are growing at significant rates in many places.

---

[7] Barnabas Fund, https://barnabasfund.org
[8] Open Doors, www.opendoorsuk.org
[9] Christian Solidarity Worldwide, www.csw.org.uk
[10] Release International, www.releaseinternational.org
[11] The Mahabba Network, www.mahabbanetwork.com.

Nevertheless, the picture portrayed is often of a church that has lost confidence in its message and is struggling under pressure from a secular-humanist society that seeks to marginalize it, and now it is under pressure from another missionary faith. The response has been a significant increase in training in apologetics, options ranging from the Oxford Centre for Christian Apologetics[12] to an increasing number of colleges offering courses.[13] This has even reached the grassroots level, with local parachurch groups conducting trainings.[14]

Meanwhile, every Sunday afternoon the Hyde Park Christian Fellowship in London gathers at Speaker's Corner to debate with Muslims. The polemical nature of such debates provides Christians with an incentive to rediscover what we believe, as familiar questions are faced, such as "Christians believe in three gods" and "Christians have corrupted their Scriptures," among others. Led by an experienced apologist, Jay Smith, it is noticeable that while the debates can be noisy and even appear quite aggressive, the combatants usually walk off together at the end.

However, for the average Christian sitting in church on Sundays, whose neighbors are very friendly Muslims from the Middle East or the Indian subcontinent, talk of apologetics seems a long way off. Indeed, rather than trying to convert people to Islam, the majority of Muslims are much more interested in settling down, getting a good job, bringing up their children, and having the freedom to express their faith in familiar ways. Within the church there can be a tendency to develop a culture of fear of Muslims, often related to situations around the world where Christians are experiencing persecution by Muslims. As tragic as this is, such persecution is not common in Britain. And while it is important to support Christians enduring persecution, the local church must focus on following Jesus' twin commands to "love our neighbors" and "make disciples of all nations." In doing so we regain our confidence in the gospel as the power of God for the salvation of everyone who believes (Rom 1:16).

Some within the local church have begun to recognize the issues. Recently the Church of England surveyed its parishes with significant Muslim populations, producing a report and later developing a network of Anglican churches that seek to enable Christian leaders and practitioners to engage Muslims effectively.[15] In 2011 a group of experienced field practitioners produced the book Between Naivety and Hostility (Bell and Chapman 2011), which sought to uncover "the best Christian responses to Islam in Britain." Other examples include Friendship First,[16] Bridges,[17] and *Encountering the World of Islam*.[18]

---

[12] The Oxford Centre for Christian Apologetics (http://theocca.org) was established by Ravi Zacharias and Alister McGrath to "provide a range of training opportunities for all abilities and requirements."

[13] One example is the Manchester Centre for the Study of Christianity and Islam (http://www.mcsci.org.uk) at Nazarene Theological College, which offers an MA module on "Christian Engagement with Islam."

[14] An example of this is AIM, Apologetics in Manchester (http://www.manchesterapologetics.com), which "runs a series of Saturday morning apologetics training sessions designed to equip Christians to respond to these questions in a helpful and effective manner."

[15] See www.presenceandengagement.org.uk: Presence and Engagement—"The Church in a multi-faith society."

[16] The goal of the Friendship First Course (http://friendshipfirst.org) is "helping ordinary Christians to discuss good news with ordinary Muslims."

[17] The Bridges Seminar is produced by the Crescent Project (https://www.crescentproject.org/) in the US. Crescent Project's mission is to inspire, equip and serve the Church to reach Muslims with the Gospel of Christ for the Glory of God. See https://bookstore.crescentproject.org/pages/about-us

[18] *Encountering the World of Islam* (http://www.encounteringislam.org) is a textbook and course designed to help Christians find their part in God's work of reaching Muslims with the gospel.

While some UK Christians continue to stick their heads in the sand, many parts of the church are slowly learning to engage the multi-faith world they now live in. For many this means a radical change in the way they understand the gospel, and it is causing an increasing number of believers to embrace their biblical calling and take opportunities to share with Muslims seriously. An ever further challenge for them, however, is to learn how to provide a true spiritual home for those from a Muslim background who do come to faith in Jesus.

How Are Muslims Becoming Followers of Jesus in the UK?

Within just a few days in November of 2012, Muslims walked into three different churches in the same city and asked how they could become Christians. A young man of Pakistani heritage came into a cathedral, and the retired minister spent time sharing and praying with him before contacting me to ask what to do next. In another church, a Saudi woman walked into the Sunday morning service asking the same question. And on the same day, a young Somali man asked his Christian friend to show him how to become a Christian. All these in one city over only a few days!

Across the whole of Britain there are likely many other such stories. How can we be prepared for this harvest that God is sending, and how will this change the church? What do we need to do to enable believers from a Muslim background to become disciples of Jesus Christ?

It is important to understand that before coming into a relationship with Jesus, people from a Muslim heritage have often already left Islam. For many coming to the UK as refugees, their experience in Muslim countries may have made them ask questions about their heritage. There is a growing movement of "ex-Muslims"[19] who, for a variety of reasons, no longer consider themselves to be Muslims. In fact, there are organizations whose sole goal is to help Muslims leave Islam—for anything else. A good example of this is the Institute for the Secularisation of Islamic Society founded by Ibn Warraq. Under this pen name, Warraq has written several books that are highly critical of Islam, including *Leaving Islam: Apostates Speak Out*. Since this author is now an atheist, the focus of his book is on Muslims who abandon all faith as the rational course of action.[20] However, this same spirit of questioning Islam has helped many carefully consider the claims of the gospel. Two good examples of this are Iranians and refugees.

Since the Iranian revolution in 1979, the exodus of Farsi-speaking people to the West has been considerable. With Western missionaries barred from entering Iran, news of the church there has come via the Internet and refugees fleeing the country. Significant growth is clearly taking place both in the church in Iran and among the

---

[19] See CEMB (Council of Ex-Muslims of Britain), http://ex-muslim.org.uk. Also see Faith Freedom.org, http://www.faithfreedom.org/category/leaving-islam.

[20] Despite Warraq's personal atheism, his writings demonstrate respect for those who leave Islam for Christianity, and he acknowledges the superiority of the Christian conception of God (2003, 92).

diaspora in the West. Organizations in the UK such as Elam Ministries[21] have been at the forefront of seeking to support Iranian Christians, as well as training and equipping them to return to Iran as leaders within the church, where the recent history of martyrdom provides a model of costly discipleship.[22] Through dreams and visions, as well as the testimonies of Iranian believers, many have come to faith in Jesus. Some arrive in Britain as Christians seeking sanctuary from a fundamentalist Islamist regime that actively persecutes Christians; they need to be discipled with appropriate models. Others arrive in Britain without knowing Christ but are quite open to witness, and they encounter Jesus after they have arrived.

Many churches have opened their doors to Iranian believers, with small groups joining Sunday congregations, and often meeting for Bible study in Farsi during the week. When I was leading a church in central Manchester, another church borrowed our baptistery and in one evening baptized over ninety Iranian believers. These new believers struggle with issues of growth, leadership, and identity, but it seems clear that God is doing something special among Iranian/Persian people in which we can rejoice and share.

Another group that has demonstrated openness are refugees. The experience of many is that Muslim refugees are often the most open to hearing the good news. Some are seeking sanctuary in Britain from Muslim countries where they have experienced ethnic discrimination and even persecution. They may well be disillusioned with Islam, and indeed with any religion. But with practical demonstrations of Christian love and friendship their hearts can be opened.

Many Christian groups have sprung up to meet this opportunity. Some offer sustainable solutions to refugee problems through the provision of food, clothing, furniture, training, and enterprise, including ESOL classes. Some even provide legal advice, accommodation, and shelter. Christians with a spare room have invited destitute refugees to live with them, and others have bought or donated houses where groups of refugees can live while their cases are being considered.[23] During the winter some churches provide floor space each night of the week, along with an evening meal and breakfast, for destitute rough sleepers to find a welcome. While never being inappropriately evangelistic, showing such love and care will inevitably lead to questions, and many have come to faith.

---

[21] Elam Ministries, http://www.elam.com.

[22] To name but a few of the martyrs: Rev. Arastoo Sayyah (throat cut in February 1980), Bahram Dehqani (shot dead in May 1980), Rev Hussein Soodmand (hung in prison in December 1990), Bishop Haik Hovsepian-Mehr (stabbed to death in January 1994), Rev Tateos Michaelian (shot dead in June 1994), Mehdi Dibaj (shot dead in June 1994), Mohammad Yusefi (hung in forest in September 1996), and Ghorban Tourani (stabbed to death in November 2005); Iran 30: "Discover, Pray, Transform," Elam Ministries, https://www.elam.com/iran30.

[23] See the Boaz Trust, boaztrust.org.uk.

Conclusion: Unanswered Questions

But what happens when people from a Muslim background turn to Jesus? In many ways, the church in Britain is ill prepared for those from another religion who come to faith in Christ and try to become part of the church. There have been some distressing examples of converts being displayed almost like trophies while others are virtually ignored. There seems to be a lack of understanding of the issues facing these new believers. All who come to faith in Jesus—from whatever background—face considerable challenges, but those from a Muslim background face particular issues that most Christians are unaware of. However, resources are now becoming available to help new believers grow in their faith.

Even in a pluralistic society like Britain, discipling new believers from Muslim backgrounds is deeply impacted by the reality of persecution. While Islamic apostasy law certainly has no de jure force in the UK, the paradigm of honor/shame has great de facto weight in Muslim communities in the country. Just like anywhere in the Muslim world, the act of leaving the faith of your birth is interpreted as betrayal of your whole family, clan, and society; and hence converts are often rejected by their families and disinherited. Families have been known to hold mock funeral services for relatives who have left their faith. In Britain new believers are frequently ostracized by their families, and it is not uncommon for MBBs to have to move away from their family home to a place where they feel safe.

This presents serious issues for local churches, where the new Christian will want to find a place of belonging. Indeed, it raises issues that the church has rarely had to consider in the past. For example, when I moved to serve in inner-city Manchester, the church had welcomed a believer from a Muslim background. Very early in my time there, he came to me and made a request: "Since becoming a Christian, my family has disowned me and thrown me out of the family home. This church has become my family. Traditionally my father would find me a wife and arrange my marriage. You are the head of this 'family,' so would you please find me a wife?"

Three years of theological study and two previous appointments had given me no preparation for such a task!

Issues will be raised that are completely new to a church in the "Christian" West. How can we provide sanctuary for someone in danger? Do we welcome someone into our homes (the aforementioned believer came to live with my family for a time) as an expression of being a genuine community that cares? Many MBBs were used to praying five times a day with their community. Will we only meet with them once or twice a week? Questions will be raised as to which of their previous customs to keep and which to discontinue. What language should they use to talk to God/Allah? Should they dress as Westerners?

There are also cultural differences that have little to do with religion: the patriarchal community they have left; the dress code, particularly for women; food—whether to eat pork. Or even further, does our theology of conversion mean MBBs must be extracted from their Muslim communities? How can we be a church family for those MBBs who desire to remain as salt and light in their Muslim social networks? As Ralph Winter has famously said, "Most of those yet to follow Christ will not fit readily into the kinds of churches we now have."

These are just a few of the many things our churches must wrestle with if we are to become true communities for these new believers. That is because the church will need to help new disciples through many changes, not all of them having to do with faith. The most important will be the sense of belonging they feel; the depth of relationships; time given and commitment to journey with new disciples as they explore their new life in Christ.

The presence of Islam in Britain presents a challenge to the church that will continue to be significant for the foreseeable future. While traditional denominations struggle in the face of secular humanism, there is significant growth in both new churches and ethnic churches (Goodhart 2012). Some of these ethnic-minority churches have been developed by people who are rejecting Islam and seem to wish to have little to do with Muslims. Hopefully this will change as communities become established and more confident. The picture of the church in the UK is one of transition, with "new" churches taking root in many areas and ethnic-minority churches growing rapidly. Although at present this remains within their own monocultural communities, the future is still uncertain.

However, as many Muslims seek to engage in *da'wah* (invitation) and draw people into their Islamic communities, the Christian church will need to adapt significantly. The church will need to rediscover a passion for the gospel and have a renewal of what it means to truly be a biblical "community" that welcomes, loves, and cares for new believers. The next fifty years will see a very different church emerge in the UK, one that is fit for growing the kingdom of God, including effective engagement with our Muslim communities.

Reflection Questions

1. What would happen if a sincere Muslim seeker were to walk into a typical evangelical church in the West today? Would the church be ready to deal with all the complexities of making disciples of people from Islamic backgrounds?

2. Beyond the institutional church, what are possible models of ministry to offer an MBB who is drawn to Christ but not to Western forms of Christianity?

References

Ansari, Humayun. 2004. *The Infidel Within—Muslims in Britain since 1800.* London: Hurst and Company.

BBC News Services. 2015. "What is 'Islamic State'?" Accessed August 20, 2015. http://www.bbc.co.uk/news/world-middle-east-29052144.

Bell, Steven, and Colin Chapman, eds. 2011. *Between Naivety and Hostility.* Milton Keynes, UK: Authentic Media Limited.

Charsley, Katharine, Nicholas Van Hear, Michaela Benson, and Brooke Storer-Church. 2012. "Marriage-Related Migration to the UK." *International Migration Review* 46 (4): 861–90. http://onlinelibrary.wiley.com/doi/10.1111/imre.12003/abstract.

Crooke, Alastair. 2014. "You Can't Understand ISIS If You Don't Know the History of Wahhabism in Saudi Arabia." *Huffington Post*, August 27. Accessed August 20, 2015. http://www.huffingtonpost.com/alastair-crooke/isis-wahhabism-saudi-arabia_b_5717157.html.

Esposito, John L. 2003. *The Oxford Dictionary of Islam.* Oxford: Oxford University Press.

Goodhart, Philip, ed. 2012. *Church Growth in Britain.* Aldershot, UK: Ashgate.

Graham, Elaine. 2013. *Between a Rock and a Hard Place—Public Theology in a Post-Secular Age.* London: SCM Press.

The Guardian. 2001. "Key Points of the Cantle Report." December 11. https://www.theguardian.com/uk/2001/dec/11/race.world5.

Lewis, Philip. 2007. *Young, British and Muslim.* London: Continuum.

Miah, Shamim. 2015. *Muslims, Schooling and the Question of Self-segregation.* London: Palgrave Macmillan.

ONS (Office for National Statistics). 2011. "2011 Census." http://www.ons.gov.uk/ons/rel/census/2011-census/detailed-characteristics-for-local-authorities-in-england-and-wales/sty-religion.html.

Ramadan, Tariq. 2009. *Radical Reform—Islamic Ethics and Liberation.* Oxford: Oxford University Press.

Rawlings, Phil. 2014. *Engaging with Muslims—Building Cohesion While Seeking Conversion.* New York: Grove Books.

Shailkh, Abdul Basit. 2015. "The Influence of Biradari (Caste) System in the UK." *Passion Islam.* Accessed August 20, 2015. http://passionislam.com/articles.php?articles_id=311.

Warraq, Ibn. 2003. *Leaving Islam: Apostates Speak Out.* Amherst, NY: Prometheus Books.

The Week (2015). "What is Salafism and should we be worried by it?" January 19. http://www.theweek.co.uk/world-news/6073/what-is-salafism-and-should-we-be-worried-by-it.

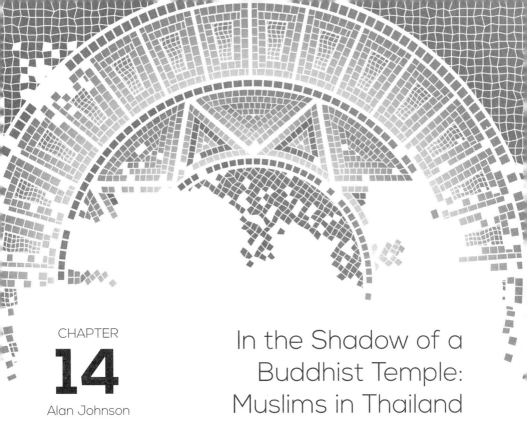

14

Alan Johnson

In the Shadow of a Buddhist Temple: Muslims in Thailand

Muslims in the heart of Thailand?!

My family and I moved to Thailand in the mid-1980s for the purposes of church planting in the central area of the country. I vividly remember driving home one day from a nearby province and noticing a large mosque filled with people. My first thought was *What are all these Muslims doing here in the heartland of Buddhist Thailand?* I knew there were Muslims in the deep south, but I had no place in my mental map for Muslims living in the shadow of temples in the heart of this Buddhist nation. I was so attuned to seeing temples that it was many months before I could even "see" that mosque.

Visitors to Thailand today still find themselves surprised at the public visibility of Muslims. Mosques are clearly visible on the trip in from the airport; the hijab head coverings for women and skullcaps for men are frequent sights, along with Islamic banks; and if you're in the right place at midday on Friday, you'll see numbers of men clad in white heading to prayers. Visitors might wonder if they had suddenly been transported out of Thailand into a Southeast Asian country with a Muslim majority.

Who are the Muslims of Thailand? And how can they be reached with the gospel? This chapter seeks to answer these questions, focusing specifically on the majority of Muslims, who are ethnically Malay and comprised of two groups—one culturally Malay and the other culturally Thai.

The Origin of Muslim Malays in Thailand and Issues of Identity

The history of Muslims in Thailand begins with the Islamization of Patani (a region in the northern part of the Malay peninsula that includes some southern Thai provinces) in the 1500s and the immigration of non-Malay Muslims, continuing with their involvement in the Ayuthaya and Chakri dynasties. This also coincides with Persians coming in the thirteenth century (Yusuf 2006, 9–10). The precise total of all Muslims in Thailand today is debated, but most estimates range from four to seven million, among a total population of sixty-eight million.

Muslims first came to Southeast Asia as a by-product of Arab trade with China, with Arab and Indian merchants settling in the commercial centers, marrying local people, and forming the initial Muslim communities (Che Man 1990, 32). While this pattern of Muslim trade forms the general outline of how Islam came to Southeast Asia, two key ideas provide a more nuanced understanding: "circulating" Islam and "creole ambassadors" (Joll 2012, 27–33).

The idea of circulation challenges the conventional wisdom of a unidirectional transmission from Arab traders. Scholars argue that a more accurate explanation is the existence of "multiple circuits of cultural exchange" in which people moved in both directions, resulting in a cultural adaptation of Islam that was multidirectional. One influence in this cultural circulation came from Muslims of mixed parentage ('creoles'). In the fifteenth century, the Malay kingdom Patani became Muslim in orientation through Shaykh Said of Pasai, a person of mixed parentage who is credited with the conversion of Raja PhayaTu Antara in the year 1457 (Joll 2012, 33; Che Man 1990, 33).

This court conversion sheds light on how Islam is practiced in Thailand today; the shaykh is said to have cured the raja (prince or chief) of a skin disease, resulting eventually in his "conversion." However, the taking of a Muslim identity was a much more pragmatic choice, with both economic and political factors as part of the equation (Che Man 1990, 34). This is seen in the fact that the raja "preserved animist traditions such as worshipping trees and stones and making offerings to spirits" (Teeuw and Wyatt 1970, 155). Those of mixed cultural background actively refracted the Islamic customs passed on to them through their own cultural settings, creating a "range of Islams" as people from Arab, Indian, and Malay communities moved about the region (Shamsul 2005).

In addition to pragmatic choice, two other factors must be joined to the equation. As the raja of Patani was moving his kingdom to the Muslim faith, the Thai were developing an empire based in Ayuthaya. Like many other smaller Southeast Asian political units, Patani found itself in vassal relations with both the kingdoms of Ayuthaya and Melacca.

The Thai state eventually annexed Patani in 1785; and in 1911 what today are the three southernmost provinces were officially brought into the kingdom. The rise of Ayuthaya also saw the immigration of many different kinds of Muslims to trade with the Thai and Malay war captives brought in as slaves for labor in the capital. This latter group settled in the central area around Bangkok, and in the city as well.

This history sets up two very different trajectories for how Muslims among the Thai related to the state. For those rooted in the southern Muslim kingdom (Patani), the move toward national integration was seen as a direct threat to their original Malay ethno-religious identity. This resulted in a palpable fear of assimilation (Abuza 2014). However, for those Muslims whose history is that of relating to the state as individuals—whether as traders, administrators, mercenary soldiers, or the children of war captives who found ways to survive in Thai society—integration was a route to personal or family advancement and prosperity. Thus two distinctly different responses are seen among the Muslims of Malay background: for some, resistance; for others, integration.

This historical material is not just interesting background material on Thai Muslims; these divergent responses have important missiological implications for Christian workers today.

Commonalities and Distinctions between Thai-speaking and Malay-speaking Muslims

Research shows that use of the Thai language rather than Malay[1] is the primary indicator for a positive sense of integration in and loyalty toward the Thai state.[2] In regard to issues of identity, therefore, language provides the primary gateway to creating trajectories that result in different ways of life for Muslims in Thailand. In this section I will use "Thai-speaking" and "Malay-speaking" to differentiate between Muslims in Thailand who are all of Malay ethnic descent.[3]

While the use of Thai language is a helpful starting point for categorizing Muslims, it is not fine-grained enough to do justice to the on-the-ground reality that field-workers will face among Muslims in Thailand. Therefore, following the work of Anderson (2010) and Joll (2012), I am suggesting that it is more useful to look at similarities and differences among Muslims of Malay ethnicity in a rubric that combines language use, geographical location, and level of assimilation. When combining these three factors we come up with at least five distinct groups:

---

[1] The Thai word *melayu* means "Malay," and when used with reference to the Malay language by Muslims in Thailand it refers to a dialect of Malay that is similar to Kelantanese Malay. Local Malay Muslims refer to it as Bahasa Tempatan, or "the local language" (Liow 2009, 17). It is different enough that speakers of the standard Malay taught in schools in Malaysia and a Thai melayu speaker would not be able to fully understand each other.

[2] Research on Muslims in the five southernmost provinces shows language is the primary indicator for assimilation into Thai society. Thai-speaking Muslims in the deep south are generally far more assimilated than their Malay-speaking counterparts (Albritton 2008, 14–15).

[3] See Anderson (2010, 128–130) and Joll (2012, 74–75) for the wide range of terms used to describe Muslims of Malay descent in Thailand.

1. Thai-speaking Muslims on the west side of the peninsula.[4]
2. Thai-speaking Muslims on the east side of the peninsula, on the Gulf of Thailand.[5]
3. Thai-speaking Muslims in central Thailand, primarily in Bangkok and Ayuthaya, whose ancestors are of Malay descent.
4. Muslims who speak Malay as their first language but who are increasingly bilingual and are at home in Thai socioculture.[6]
5. Malay-speaking Muslims in the south.

Despite important differences, a great deal is shared across all five of these configurations. The institution of the mosque is at the heart of both the Malay-speaking and Thai-speaking Muslim communities. Compared to the Buddhist population, they tend to have more family cohesion, a lower divorce rate, and more social aid and assistance among their communities (Gilquin 2005, 26). Key identity markers are the Muslim greeting, halal food, hijab, the skullcap, and various rituals and feasts that are either connected with global Islam or have local roots.

Faith is central to identity for Malay speakers, this being demonstrated in the term for converting to Islam: *masokmelayu*, meaning "to become Malay" (ibid., 51). Most education of children still happens in the traditional Islamic *pondok* schools, where two key social roles are the *tokguru*, those who have religious knowledge to pass on, and the *bomoh*, a kind of shaman who has mastered traditional medicine (ibid., 57). On the other hand, Thai-speaking Muslims are more assimilated into Thai behavior patterns, although in my observation they continue to shift between Thai culture and Islamic culture depending on who they are with. For example, use of their Thai name and the standard Thai greeting is employed when speaking with Thai Buddhists, but they quickly shift back to Muslim speech patterns when conversing with other Muslims.

Thai-speaking Muslims on the southwestern coast have a stronger Thai cultural marker, and they identify themselves as Thais of the Islamic faith. Thus their Malay Muslim neighbors on the opposite coast label them as not being "Muslim enough," or even "not Muslim" (Anderson 2010, 133). However, the majority of both Malay-speaking and Thai-speaking Muslims practice a form of Islam bound up with local animistic practices and little knowledge of the Qur'an. Some can recite a few memorized texts in Arabic but do not have enough facility in the language to actually read the Qur'an with understanding.

Further adding to the complexity of these five categories of Muslims in Thailand are the reform movements that have come to influence all of them.[7] Since the 1920s many waves of religious reform in Thailand have sought to bring a stricter following

---

[4] Including the provinces of Satun, Trang, Krabi, PhangNga, and Phuket.
[5] Including the provinces of Songkhla, Phattalung, and Nakhon Sri Thamarat.
[6] These are located primarily in Patani, Yala, and Narathiwat.
[7] For detailed development see Joll (2012, 42–51, 63–66); see also Liow's chapter 3 on the challenge of Islamic reformism (2009); Braam (2013), McCargo's chapter 1 on Islam (2008), and Gilquin's chapter 7

of the Qur'an and the Sunna of Muhammad to the traditional syncretic practices of the Malay. Traditionalists (*khana kao*; "old school"), reformists (*khana mai*; "new school"), and revivalists (*Tabiligh Jama'at*; society for spreading the faith) (Joll 2012, 64–65) are not rigid positions; rather, there is a good deal of intermixing in understanding and daily practice. McCargo observes that there is not a clear distinction between old and new, and many see themselves as being between the schools, embracing "hybridized beliefs, practices, and identities" (2008, 25).

The Practice of Islam in Thailand: Local Practices and Orthodoxy

While some Muslims in Thailand speak Thai and others speak Malay, they all participate in the central practices of global Islam rooted in the five pillars and the major religious festivals. However, the way in which the pillars are approached, as well as the broader religious life of individuals, varies greatly according to the level of influence from reformist and revivalist movements. I live in Bangkok and experience in my daily interactions with Muslims this wide diversity and mixing of different religious influences. I have friends who are traditionalists, others who are reformists, and some who participate in Tabligh Jama'at. Their lives exemplify the kind of hybridization described by scholars above. In this section I will illustrate some of this variation by following a few of my Thai friends (using pseudonyms) in the practice of their religion.

My friends Sa and Ma both live in Bangkok slums. Their lives typify traditionalist Islam, which includes pre-Islamic traditions: Malay supernaturalism; *phii* (local spirits) worship; and practices influenced by Hinduism and Buddhism, such as the role of shamans (*bomoh*) (Braam 2013, 287; McCargo 2008, 20). Examples of village-specific practices are parading newly circumcised boys through the village, eating three colors of sticky rice at a wedding, kenduri feasts (a pre-Islamic custom) held for life cycle events, *mawlid* events celebrating the Prophet's birthday, differences in qur'anic reading and prayers in the early morning *salat* schedule, and prayers commemorating the dead (Braam 2013, 287–88; McCargo 2008, 20–22).

Kae, raised in the deep south, illustrates this kind of traditionalist practice. When he was on drugs as a teen, his mother took him to the shaman; and they also would go if something was lost, seeking supernatural help to find it. When Kae's father died suddenly, his mother called in the shaman to determine the cause. He had them dig in the front yard until a small bottle was found; and this was ascertained to be a kind of curse, put on him by another person, that caused his death. Curses and spells are common, often involving male-female relationships and love triangles.

Being a traditionalist does not mean that one is not strict about religious practice. This marks the big difference between Sa's family and Ma's family. Ma's extended family, which lives in a mixed Muslim and Buddhist slum, is disliked by everyone.

on the renewal of Thai Islam (2005).

They sell drugs, and numerous relatives are serving jail sentences (including Ma at the time of writing), leaving children to be cared for in a kind of group fashion by whatever relatives are left. On the other hand, Sa's mother was a very observant Muslim, praying regularly and fasting during Ramadan, even in her old age.

When Sa's mother died, we were invited to attend a ceremony forty days later in their home province. We learned many interesting beliefs about the presence of the deceased's spirit among the family. We were told that Sa's mom was able to visit and be with the family for thirty-nine days, but then she would have to go before Allah on the fortieth day. This transition was accomplished by two hours of chanting the Qur'an in the time period of two hours from the time of day that she died. This activity was explained as making merit for her (*tham bun* in Thai), but there was no detail as to how that merit helped her. The family even produced a photograph on their smartphone that showed a white spot by a window during Sa's burial, explaining that it was her watching the ceremony.

Others I know, like Ahmad, are influenced by the reform stream. They try to shape their practice, to varying degrees, around the Qur'an, Hadith, and Sunna. When I told Ahmad of my experiences at the after-death ceremony and explained how I was trying to learn more about how my Muslim friends like Sa practice their religion, he was appalled and told me that none of these things are "Islam." Reformists want to stop things that are seen as "un-Islamic," as well as promote new practices related to dress, strict observance of prayers, and personal morals.

Revivalists associated with Tabligh Ja'maat seem to be the most strict and vocal. They are the most aggressive in their opposition to my Christian faith. My friend Ali claims that I worship three different gods and likes to tell me that I am going to hell. Ya Ya attends a mosque influenced by this movement and has taken several short-term *da'wa* trips to invite Muslims to more devout practice. Adam refuses to listen to any kind of music except an unaccompanied version of religious singing called *nasheed*.

Despite their fervor, I have found that revivalists are often looked down on or avoided by the other Muslims in the area where I live. Those who are lax in practice try to avoid them, while others resent that these poor urban men leave their families to struggle while they go out on missions funded through the propagation center, and they speak harshly to them and tell them to leave.

With all this diversity in both belief and practice among Muslims in Thailand, are there any unifying elements no matter what religious stream a person is involved in? At this point in my experience, I have identified two major areas present among every kind of Muslim. First, in regard to Muslim identity, I have found that the Muslims of my acquaintance, across the board—whether highly educated or uneducated, whether rich or poor, and whichever stream of Islam they belong to—will have the same set of stock objections to the Christian faith. My sense is that due to their minority status in Thailand, Muslims often feel the need to define themselves against the Buddhist majority. Therefore the common person will sometimes know more about what they are *not* than the actual tenets of their religion. Even for those who maintain virtually no Islamic religious practice, their identity is Muslim because they were born into Islam. I personally have never met anyone who expressed being unhappy with Islam or wanting to leave it.

The second commonality, which really confused me when I first began to interact with Muslims in Thailand, was their use of the Thai term *tham bun* (to make merit). This was familiar ground for me from my ministry with Buddhists, but quite unexpected with Muslims. At first I wondered if it was due to influence from the Buddhist environment and thus represented a kind of syncretistic practice, as some scholars have proposed. However, Joll's work on Muslim merit-making challenges the assertions of some who see it as an accommodation to the influence of Buddhist society. Joll shows that while increased bilingualism has led to more Malay Muslims expressing Islamic ideas in the Thai language, "Their religious rhetoric is also replete with Islamic ideation" (2012, 197).

It is much too simplistic to try to account for the use of *tham bun* among Thai-speaking Muslims as a borrowing from Buddhist concepts. Joll's research shows that when you dig deeper, the Thai terminology for merit-making often serves as a cover term for several different kinds of ritual activity, some of which are merit-making and others which are not. In addition to this, Islamic cosmology also undergirds the practices of merit accumulation for the living and merit transference to the dead with the architecture of *dunio* (this world), *alam al-barzakh* (the world of the grave, where people await resurrection and judgment), and *akhirat* (the afterlife). Knowing that the Muslim practice of merit-making in Thailand is not simply borrowed from Buddhist surroundings but driven by key Islamic concepts is important as we learn how to share the gospel with our Muslim friends. To assume their use of merit-making terminology means they are not serious or strict about their personal faith and that, therefore, we don't need to be attentive to understanding their worldview can lead to a way of framing our witness to the gospel in a way that misses issues that are central to the practice of their faith.

Context-appropriate Ministry among Muslims in Thailand

In the history of Christian mission in Thailand, ministry to Muslims has been neglected for two primary reasons. First, my own blindness to seeing Muslims illustrates how the focus of the majority of expatriate workers on the Buddhist majority pushes Muslims in Thailand off the strategic radar. The second reason is that, for various unfortunate reasons, Thai Christian believers from Buddhist backgrounds typically have not reached out to their Muslim neighbors. This final section will look at some potential ways that expatriate missionaries can move from the natural relationships of their ministry and service platforms toward the goal of working with new believers to develop communities of faith that can be faithful to Jesus in their sociocultural setting.

The uniqueness of the Thai Muslim experience, which presents great challenges to the spread of the gospel among Thai Muslims, may also hold within it a key for planting churches among Muslims in the deep south—in both Thai-speaking and Malay-speaking communities. The trajectory of their history and relationship with the Thai state as a minority has caused a hardening of their boundaries around their religion and Malay culture. Their fear of the loss of ethnic and religious identity increases the already natural suspicion against Christians who are perceived as wanting to "snatch" (*yaeng* in Thai) them from their religion. Scholars trying to understand the reasons for the insurgency and violence in the southern three provinces point out that it is not rooted in Islamic ideology but is related instead to Malay identity and the political legitimacy of the Thai state, which concerns issues of power, participation, and accountability (McCargo 2008; Liow 2009, 22; McCargo 2012, ix, 11; Jory 2007, 273).

Since the perceived loss of Malay identity is the greatest obstacle to reaching these Muslims, the key to developing context-sensitive ministry should allow believers from this background to follow Christ within their social setting. If those who begin to follow Jesus develop ways of living out their faith that are expressed through forms associated with Malay identity, it could help create social space for them to live among their people. Expressions of following Jesus that are not seen as a threat to Malay identity may mitigate the local community's natural reaction to persecute and expel those who are perceived to betray this identity.

The dream of a believers of Muslim Background (MBB) Church with a Malay cultural identity

In order to explore and suggest some tentative ways in which communities of faith could be seen by their society as maintaining Malay identity, I will begin by briefly describing what typically occurs when Thai Muslims become Christ-followers. With that background, we will then discuss key cultural elements for the development of a community of faith embedded in Malay socioculture.

Kathryn Kraft, in her work on conversion in the Arab world, found that converts, for the most part, thought that abandonment of one's culture was the only option and were hopeful when other possible models for living out their faith in Jesus were presented to them (2012, 111–12). From my research with those working with Thai Muslims, and also with pastors of Thai churches in the south, two general patterns emerged. The first is clearly a type of abandonment, where new believers physically leave their community and integrate completely into a Thai church. They also take a Thai name and no longer use their Muslim name or relate to their Muslim community at all. The second pattern is that new believers remain in their community but, due to either existing or expected social pressure, must go out of the community to study

Scripture with someone or meet in a house group. They either live as secret believers and don't reveal their faith in Jesus or only talk with a very limited group of people whom they trust when they are home in their residential community.

Two unfortunate consequences stand out in both of these scenarios. First, there is little or no gospel witness to the immediate family and social network of the new believer. Second, there is no gathering of believers where they can express their faith in ways that maintain their Malay identity. It should be little wonder why so few Muslims have come to faith in Christ in this kind of ministry context. Instead, my goal here is to envision ways in which communities of believers are able to share Christ organically in word and deed in the midst of Thai Muslim communities. I suggest that intentionally developing gatherings of Christ-followers so that Malay identity markers are visible among the new believers may be the best way to see this happen.

Developing a "dual-belonging" community of faith in a Malay cultural environment

Warrick Farah's (2015) rubric of different types of "insiders" linked to the cultural, social, communal, ritual, and theological dimensions of religious contexts helps situate the kind of approach I am advocating. In his model of "Five Expressions of Insiderness," those MBBs discussed previously who extract from their Malay Muslim communities into the Thai church, for whatever reason, are functionally "exiles" from their community. And those MBBs who continue to live in Muslim communities and gather discreetly in neutral locations away from their homes are "cultural insiders" who have very little interaction and witness with their society at the community level.

In terms of Farah's rubric, I feel that a gathering of believers having a visible Malay identity is best achieved by what he calls the "dual-belonging" (*not* dual-allegiance) level of insiderness. These are believers who belong to the church as full members and somehow also belong to their local Muslim community as affiliate members. The power of such a gathering of dual-belonging MBBs is twofold. First, even when their worship meetings are not located specifically in a Muslim village due to social pressure, believers have a gathering that is clearly culturally Malay—they can easily invite friends from their personal networks. While faith in Jesus will be theologically deviant in the eyes of their Muslim community, the style of the gatherings will be Malay and not seem foreign. Second, dual-belonging MBBs will intentionally connect with the social life of their community and be able to minister to others through their relationships. These relationships are the bridges that carry a faith which would now be expressed in Malay cultural forms.

Critical Malay cultural elements for reappropriation

In this final section, I use Farah's categories of cultural, social, communal, and ritual aspects of religious contexts as a starting point for thinking about four arenas where cross-cultural laborers can work with local believers to build a fellowship of dual-belonging MBBs at the corporate level of a community of faith.

1. For expatriate workers, the first step will be immersion in the language and culture of the group they are working with, either southern Thai-speaking or Malay-speaking Muslims. While Thailand has four major regional dialects, Christians mostly use the central Thai dialect, which is taught in the public school system. This dialect is used in their public worship, preaching, and Bible translation, regardless of the regional dialect that believers first learned in their home. If we are going to see contextually sensitive communities of faith arise among Thai Muslims in the south, it will require the hard work of learning a dialect or language beyond central Thai, along with a deep understanding of such things as food, dress, music, customs, forms of worship, ritual life, and social structure. This sociolinguistic competency will be necessary to develop culturally relevant expressions of the faith that express the identity of that particular language group.

2. As noted previously, a central part of the collective life of Malay communities is the pre-Islamic tradition of ritual feasting called *kenduri*. From the perspective of anthropologists, this is a form of wealth redistribution and is one type of charity in Malay Muslim societies (Siapno 2013, 127; Scott 1985, 172). It has also become an Islamicized form of making merit. The three major categories of these feasts include religious events, life cycle crises and transitions, and happy events or fulfillment of wishes (Frisk 2009, 142). Three things stand out that make this an important ritual to adapt into the new community of believers to show their communal identification. First, the preparations require intense collective social work, and there is the expectation of reciprocation. If MBBs participate in the *kenduri* feasts of others, then when they as a community of believers hold their own feasts, they can invite the participation of people in their social networks. Second, the wide range of reasons for putting on a feast allow for MBBs to choose non-Islamic events, which creates the space to shape the ceremony around prayer for blessing in Isa's name. Another critical element is the role of the prayers in the ritual. Normally there is prayer and Qur'anic recitation, but in smaller *kenduri* where no one with religious training is present, anyone can lead the prayers. This makes it natural for MBBs to use the Bible in the ritual and follow the ritual components involving the food as closely as possible, so that participants feel that it is a true *kenduri* event but with the unique expression of their faith in Christ.

3. Another cultural piece that could be adapted for use in various group settings for explicit gospel communication is shadow puppetry. This kind of puppetry uses flat, two-dimensional figures placed against a screen illuminated from behind. The first mention of this art form is tenth-century Javanese poetic forms of Indian epics (Yousof 1991, 6). The dramas include either multi-character or single-character plots. This art form is used by southern Thai Buddhists, but also in folk Islam on both the Thai and Malay sides of the border (Wright 1981; Smithies and

Kerdchouay 1972). While the modern cinema has greatly diminished the use of shadow puppetry, it is worth exploring whether the single-character versions could be utilized as a means of sharing the gospel in various venues.

4. Southern Thailand has specific kinds of musical genres for different occasions performed by traditional Muslims, which is predominantly in a Java-Malay style (Sumronthong 2008, 100). Sumronthong identifies five different kinds of entertainment performances, each with a different purpose that is a central part of the Thai Muslim lifestyle (ibid., 112). Taking time to explore which of these could best be used for singing the gospel message and praising God corporately, accompanied by local instruments, could yield great benefits. Expressing the gospel message in a song with a Muslim Malay flavor will open the door for a hearing far more easily than a foreign form. Praising God in local language through local music will also help in the discipleship of new believers by increasing the impact of the message through a familiar medium.

Conclusion

If new believers are going to find ways of living out their faith in a Thai Muslim Malay fashion, they are going to need friends who can walk with them through the process of thinking and engaging Scripture and their culture. The likelihood is that those who will come to faith are most often going to see their choice to follow Jesus as entailing rejection, not only of the creedal tenets of Islam but of virtually all of their birth culture. Loving friends can help them see from the Scriptures that it is possible to have a gathered life in Christ that entails full allegiance to Jesus while also being deeply embedded in the social world of their society. For the cross-cultural worker, this approach involves a steep learning curve, but that effort will be critical to furthering the dream of a vibrant community of faith following Jesus among their own people.

Reflection Questions

1. How might the fact that Thai Muslims in part define their identity against the Buddhist majority influence the way Christians should approach them with the gospel?

2. How can being aware of the background of a Muslim (traditionalist, reformist, or revivalist) help us in find appropriate ways to share the gospel?

References

Abuza, Zachary. 2014. "Religion in the Southern Thailand Conflict," *The Interpreter*, October 10. http://www.lowyinterpreter.org/post/2014/10/10/Religion-in-the-southern-Thailand-conflict.aspx.

Albritton, Robert B. 2008. "The Muslim South in the Context of the Thai Nation." The 10th International Conference on Thai Studies, Thammasat University, Thailand, January 9–11.

Anderson, Wanni W. 2010. *Mapping Thai Muslims: Community Dynamics and Change on the Andaman Coast.* Chiang Mai, Thailand: Silkworm Books.

Braam, Ernesto H. 2013. "Malay Muslims and the Thai Buddhist State: Confrontation, Accomodation and Disengagement." In *Encountering Islam: The Politics of Religious Identities in Southeast Asia*, edited by Yew-Foong Hui, 271–312. Singapore: ISEAS Publishing.

Che Man, W. K. 1990. *Muslim Separatism: The Moros of Southern Philippines and the Malays of Southern Thailand*. South-East Asian Social Science Monographs. Oxford: Oxford University Press.

Farah, Warrick. 2015. "The Complexity of Insiderness." *International Journal of Frontier Missions* 32 (2): 85–91.

Frisk, Sylva. 2009. *Submitting to God: Women and Islam in Urban Malaysia*. Copenhagen, Denmark: NIAS Press.

Gilquin, Michel. 2005. *The Muslims of Thailand*. Translated by Michael Smithies. Chiang Mai, Thailand: Silkworm Books.

Joll, Christopher M. 2012. *Muslim Merit-Making in Thailand's Far South*. New York: Springer.

Jory, Patrick. 2007. "From 'Melayu Patani' to 'Thai-Malay': The Spectre of Ethnic Identity in Southern Thailand." Asia Institute Working Paper Series. Singapore: Asia Research Institute.

Kraft, Katherine Ann. 2012. *Searching for Heaven in a Real World: A Sociological Discussion of Conversion in the Arab World*. Oxford: Regnum International.

Liow, Joseph Chinyong. 2009. *Islam, Education and Reform in Southern Thailand*. Singapore: Institute of Southeast Asian Studies.

McCargo, Duncan. 2008. *Tearing Apart the Land: Islam and Legitimacy in Southern Thailand*. Ithaca, NY: Cornell University Press.

———. 2012. *Mapping National Anxieties: Thailand's Southern Conflict*. Copenhagen, Denmark: NIAS Press.

Scott, James C. 1985. *Weapons of the Weak: Everyday Forms of Peasant Resistance*. New Haven, CT: Yale University Press.

Shamsul, A. B. 2005. "Islam Embedded: Religion and Plurality in Southeast Asia as a Mirror for Europe." *Asia Europe Journal* 3: 159–78.

Siapno, Jaqueline Aquino. 2013. *Gender, Islam, Nationalism and the State in Aceh: The Paradox of Power, Co-Optation and Resistance*. Oxford: RoutledgeCurzon.

Smithies, Michael, and Euayporn Kerdchouay. 1972. "Nang Talung: The Shadow Theatre of Southern Thailand." *Journal of the Siam Society* 60 (1): 379–90.

Sumronthong, Bussakorn. 2008. "The Blending of Thai-Muslim Musical Performances in Southern Thailand." *Manusaya* 16: 99–113.

Teeuw, A., and D. K. Wyatt. 1970. *Hikayat Patani*. Vol. 5 of Bibliotheca Indonesica (5) 2. The Hague: Nijhoff.

Wright, Barbara S. 1981. "Islam and the Malay Shadow Play: Aspects of the Historical Mythology of the Wayang Siam." *Asian Folklore Studies* 40 (1): 51–63.

Yousof, Ghulam-Sarwar. 1991. "The Shadow Plays of Southeast Asia: Relationships between Various Forms." *SPAFA Journal* 16 (2): 5–16.

Yusuf, Imtiyaz. 2006. "The Southern Thailand Conflict and the Muslim World." In Public Seminar on "Southern Violence and the Thai State" and "Nonviolence, Violence, and Thai Society." Research Project. Room 407, Princess Maha Chakri Sirindhorn Anthropology Centre.

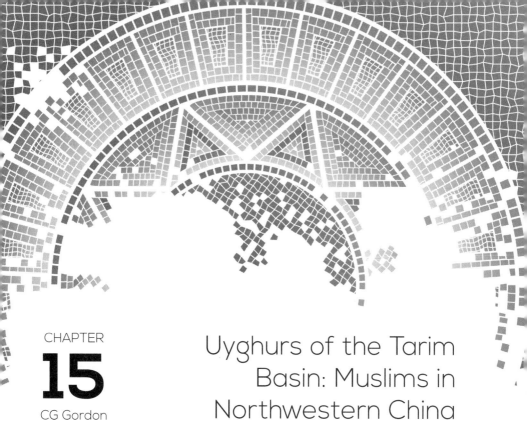

CHAPTER

15

CG Gordon

Uyghurs of the Tarim Basin: Muslims in Northwestern China

What do you find when East Asian animism, Buddhism, Manichaeism, and Zoroastrianism are mixed together with a major dose of Islamic identity? The Uyghurs of the Tarim Basin in China. This chapter offers a case study on how Islam adapts as it enters new territories and also explores ways in which Christian workers can be effective ministers of the "power of the gospel" (Rom 1:16). The case of the Uyghurs provides valuable lessons beyond the context of northwestern China.

History of the Tarim Basin

In the center of the Asian continental land mass is a desert cul-de-sac—the great Taklimakan Desert. Adventurers, merchants, armies, migrants, and missionaries have traversed this dry and desolate place since the beginning of time. Those who entered and exited these shores along this landlocked "Sea of Death" often had great stories to tell, which in turn compelled others to travel to this foreboding place. A few of these travelers decided to make this difficult land their home, and they carved out a livelihood within the patches of fertile soil interspersed along the shores of the Taklimakan Desert.

Over the centuries, these patches of fertile land developed into unique and independent city-states. These city-states have historically been referred to as the Altishahr, or "six cities," and settlers were grounded in an animistic worldview of traditions and practices, despite having contact with "axial age"[1] religious philosophies and later with the introduction of Islamic religious thought and practice. While these people have cloaked themselves in Islam, underneath their religious exterior is the soul of a devoted animist. This reality is evident in many cultures around the world where people were forced to adopt a lifeless set of doctrines and rituals.

Other Religions at the Core of the Uyghur Worldview

The people of the Tarim Basin have been something of religious chameleons, changing their belief system many times in their long history. They first adopted a major world religion before the time of Christ, during the Maurya dynasty in India (c. 268–239 BC). This occurred after Ashoka, one of the greatest emperors of the ancient Indian subcontinent, became a Buddhist and promoted his new religion far beyond the borders of his own empire, including the Altishahr region (Strong 2007, 137.

In the seventh century AD, a Chinese Buddhist pilgrim named Xuanzang retold a legend of Buddha appearing in the sky before the king of Khotan and of the subsequent conversion of the king and his kingdom (Stein 1907, 231). The kingdom of Khotan then became an important center for Buddhism and its propagation eastward, even playing a role in the religion's spread as far as China, Korea, and Japan (Foltz 2010, 48–49). As a result, Buddhism thrived in the Tarim Basin for almost a millennium and had a lasting influence on the beliefs, practices, and art of the people there.

However, during the centuries of Buddhist dominance throughout the Tarim Basin, Buddhist rulers were very tolerant of other religions and allowed them to expand within their realms. It was during this time that Sogdian traders of the ancient Syriatic church[2] brought Christianity to the region while traversing the ancient Silk Road. In 650 AD, the Tarim Basin's most western city-state of Kashgar became the furthest eastern bishopric of the Syriatic church. Later, Sogdian missionaries were joined by Uyghur Christians and took the good news even further, seeing several mass conversions of Turks and Mongols. In fact, early Uyghur missionaries from the Syriatic branch of the church were responsible for giving the Mongol language a written form, and one of their scribes produced the first written copy of the ancient law code of Genghis Khan, the *Yasa* (Brose 2005).

---

[1] "Axial age" is a term coined by German philosophers to characterize a pivotal age of ancient history from about the eighth to the third century BC. This period is without parallel in that it contained striking developments in religion and philosophy across the cultures of the Eurasian continent.

[2] In the past, the Syriatic church was referred to as the "Nestorian church." However, scholars have moved away from this term because it was commonly used as a pejorative that implies that the church was, in its entirety, heretical. Today the more common terms are the "ancient Syriatic church" or the "great church of the East."

These Christians developed a liturgy that included hymns, psalms, and portions of the New Testament with commentaries. Many of these Christian texts were discovered between 1902 and 1914 in the Turpan oasis by four different German expeditions to the area.[3] However, Christianity was always weak in the Tarim Basin and was eventually extinguished by the Muslim Turkic ruler Tamerlane in the fourteenth century.

The religion of Manichaeism[4] also had a significant impact on the people in the Tarim Basin. The Manichaeism chapter of the Uyghur story began when one of their kings met a number of Sogdian traders and took four of them back to his capital in Mongolia in 762. These Manichaean missionaries were such effective communicators that within a few months the Uyghur king was converted to their form of quasi monotheism. Subsequently the king officially banned all shamanistic practices. Manichaeism prospered among the Uyghurs until approximately 840, when they were forced out of their homeland in Mongolia by another Turkic people. They migrated into the Tarim Basin, a Buddhist stronghold; thus Manichaeism slowly began to dwindle until it completely died out, probably in the thirteenth century (Doniger 1999, 689–90).

Another influential religion in the Tarim Basin was Zoroastrianism. Once again, it was Sogdian traders who shared this faith while traveling to and through the Tarim Basin. Many of the basic tenets of Zoroaster are very similar to Christian ideas, such as the belief in one supreme God who created all things, the sinfulness of man, the importance of righteousness and the need for the expatiation of sin, the final judgment, and belief in the afterlife (Jayaram V n.d.). Thus Zoroastrianism easily syncretized with teachings of the Syriatic church. Since Zoroastrianism is of Persian origin, it is not surprising that one of the most visible reminders of it today in the Tarim Basin is the celebration of the Persian New Year festival called Nowruz. This celebration of the vernal equinox has continued for thousands of years in Iran and for the past millennium among the Uyghurs.[5]

Islamization of the Uyghurs

As we have seen, the Tarim Basin long held a diversity of religious communities, but this pluralism among the Uyghurs began to change with the Islamization of the region beginning around the end of the first millennium. Nevertheless, because of their long history of adopting and discarding various religions, it was easy for the Uyghurs to continue with their underlying animistic beliefs and practices intact, as well as to maintain residual beliefs from their earlier religions.

The Islamization of the Uyghurs can be attributed to several factors. First, Islam spread through the employment of the political force and influence of the ruling class.

---

[3] A large number of explorers from many different countries traveled to the Tarim. The most well known were Marco Polo, Sven Ander Hedin, Albert von Le Coq, Nikolai Mikhaylovich Przhevalsky, Sir Marc Aurel Stein, Paul Pelliot, and Sir Francis Edward Younghusband.

[4] For a general overview of Manichaeism, see Encyclopaedia Britannica Online at https://www. britannica.com/topic/Manichaeism

[5] Nowruz is widely celebrated in the Muslim world in a band from Turkey to nortwestern China

More often than not, the people would eventually adopt the religion of their leaders. The local ruling class and lower-level functionaries were willing to embrace the religion of the newcomers so that they might keep their former positions of authority. There was also an economic factor, which included offering fellow Muslims business opportunities and preferential treatment upon conversion to Islam. And another often forgotten factor was the simple matter of population assimilation. Non-Muslim men could not marry Muslim women, but Muslim men were permitted to marry non-Muslim women, and the children of these marriages were raised Muslim. So with every succeeding generation there was a slow reduction in the number of non-Muslims in the Tarim Basin, until eventually the whole population became Muslim.[6]

Yet in the midst of all these very practical factors, it was the preaching of charismatic Sufi missionaries that connected most to the animistic heart of the Uyghurs. And because of the mystical, nonlegal nature of Sufism, these missionaries naturally facilitated the incorporation of many non-Islamic beliefs and practices into the local expression of Islam that emerged (Tang 2005, 73). Sufi missionaries from Yemen, Iran, and Central Asia adopted older local non-Islamic narratives and changed them for Islamic narratives, giving Islam greater acceptance and legitimacy within the local populace. As a result of these historical dynamics, the Islam practiced today in the Tarim Basin is a complex amalgamation of various belief systems mixed with an animistic foundation. Over the passing centuries, a religious system developed—*a form of Islam localized to the Uyghur people*—where special places, persons, periods, and paraphernalia together express the Islamic religious life of the people of the Tarim Basin.

As we begin our look at the aspects of Uyghur belief and practice that are not part of orthodox Islam, a brief discussion of animism might be helpful. Animism is not a discrete religious system; rather, the term describes people who generally believe the problems they experience in life are the result of spiritual forces that can be controlled by special people using special techniques during special times and in special places. The animist's guiding religious principle is to manipulate these spiritual forces to gain peace, happiness, security, and success. The Uyghurs of the Tarim Basin have long followed this pattern of seeking to influence unseen spiritual forces, regardless of their official religious affiliation. The following examples will illustrate the way animism influences their society.

Places of Power

The animist believes there are places where spirits dwell, particularly in prominent features of terrain like mountains, rivers, trees, caves, or other unusual topographical features. These local spirits can be either benevolent or malevolent. The animist will placate these spirits so as to live in peace with them and to seek favor from them when

---

[6] That said, these non-Muslim mothers often played a unique role in passing down non-Islamic traditions to their children. Nawruz is probably an example of this (Poliakov 1992, 59–75).

necessary. There are many places in the Tarim Basin where people encounter the spirit world. Generational narratives tell stories of spirits and *numen*, or divine powers, who have demonstrated supernatural authority over circumstances, things, and places. It is important to note that these places of power anchor people to their historical past and reinforce this significance for potential of blessings in the present.

Considering this, it is important to note that many former Buddhist religious sites were converted into Islamic ones. These places of power during Buddhist times continue to be places of power for Muslims today. In order to preserve the significance of these Buddhist sites, Buddhist narratives were edited into Islamic ones. For example, the Pigeon-Mazar located outside Khotan was once a site that celebrated victory over an invading Hun army. The legend asserts that large rats once lived in Khotan and that the Uyghur king prayed to these rats for help. When the day of battle arrived, the enemy was unable to fight because the rats had gnawed apart all the leather horse straps, armor, and bowstrings of the Hun army so that the king of Khotan easily defeated the Huns. On this site they erected a temple where all the people would come and pay homage and bring offerings to the rats.

However, when Muslims took over Khotan, the narrative was modified. The new version told of a great battle between the Muslims and the Buddhists in which so many people died on both sides that it was difficult to distinguish between the faithful "Shahids" and the "Kafirs." Then, through the prayer of one of the surviving Muslim fighters, the bodies of those who were martyred were miraculously collected to one side. The Muslim commander Imam Shakir Padshah also died during the battle, but miraculously two doves emerged from his dead heart. Today, faithful Uyghur Muslims feed the pigeons that gather at the Pigeon-Mazar.

The explorer who first uncovered this historical layering, Aurel Stein, commented that this was only the first of many other instances where Buddhist sacred history was reworked to remain a part of the folklore of the Tarim Basin peoples (1904). It is quite likely that the same could be said for many of the hundreds of other sacred shrines, or mazars, surrounding the Tarim Basin.

All the shrines in the Tarim Basin are burial sites for supposedly departed Islamic saints who during their lifetimes did some meritorious act for the Islamic faith. Ross and Papas (2013) write:

> Throughout the history of Islam in the region (Tarim Basin) believers have venerated the heroes of this religious heritage, that is to say convert kings, great proselytizers, holy fighters, learned men, pious zealots, mystical figures and so on. These saints of Islam in Western China (Tarim Basin) not only aroused the devotion of the masses but receive material as well as spiritual support from the elite. Considered "friends of God" they became for the people powerful intermediaries and the spiritual world. Those who came and help with the upkeep of the shrine would also receive the Baraka of the saint.

The many hundreds of *mazars* dotting the Tarim Basin each have a history of some saint. The Uyghur people have a deep and abiding connection with these places of power, specifically because they also have a connection to those people in Uyghur society who are people of power.

People of Power

As in many parts of the world, among the people of the Tarim Basin are those who promote the traditional narratives and provide important spiritual services for the community—the shaman, the sheikh, the Sufi, and the storyteller. More often than not, these different roles are intertwined.

Like all the formerly nomadic people of the Tarim Basin, Central Asia, and Mongolia, the Uyghurs have a long history of shamans: those who have access to, and influence in, the world of benevolent and malevolent spirits through the use of magic words, incantations, and music. Uyghur shamans use trance-like states to act as mediums, practice divination, and heal those who are sick. All in all, there are sixteen different categories of shamans among the Uyghurs. Women have their own shamans who perform an important role within the community among the women and children.

Some shamans prepare and prescribe herbal medicines, while others are adept at preparing powerful talismans and amulets to protect people from evils spirits. Some are even known for their practice of curses and spells. In Uyghur society, shamans particularly function as a connection point between the "Muslim" life of people today and the old ways—to nature and to their totem, or sacred symbol, the wolf[7] (Chan 2013).

Sheikhs are guardians and custodians of a particular local shrine. This responsibility is normally passed down within the family, and much spiritual authority is gained from being a descendant of a long line of sheikhs who possesses the baraka (power) from the venerated saint. The sheikh is responsible for maintaining the grounds and tomb and assisting pilgrims in their prayers and rituals. More importantly, the sheikh is the official keeper of the shrine's tazkirah, the historical narrative connected to the veneration of that saint and their shrine. These textual histories retelling past events are also considered living histories, where the content can be annotated, edited, abbreviated,or become a composite with another narrative (Thum 2014).

Sacred histories are the local community's understanding of the past and mutually accepted "truth." This "truth" is the community's sanctioned meaning of a particular narrative, not the veracity of the events that might have actually happened. More often than not, the *tazkirah* of a shrine most likely was not factual; or if it did happen, it represents a gross distortion of any actual historical event. The importance of these tazkirah for the Uyghur community is not in the factual truth of the narrative. Instead, their shared history functions to provide community cohesion. Thus, as guardians of the shrine and its narrative, the sheikh guards the community's past, present, and future.

---

[7] Even well-educated, secular Uyghurs considered it good luck to carry a wolf claw in their pocket.

Whereas the shaman and the sheikh represent connection to the non-Islamic past, the Sufi represents the connection to Islam itself. The role of Sufi missionaries and the presence of Sufi brotherhoods in the Tarim Basin cannot be underestimated. The most common and widespread *taraqah*, or Sufi religious order, found in the Tarim Basin is the Naqshbandiyya, which emerged at the end of the fourteenth century in Bukhara and is the only Sufi order that supposedly traces its linage back to the prophet Mohammad through Abu Bakr. This order of Sufis began in Yemen but reached Central Asia and the Tarim Basin in approximately the fourteenth or fifteenth century (Fletcher 1995). The preaching of the Sufi had much appeal to the people of the Tarim Basin because it was quite similar to the Buddhists' message of following a master who will guide them on the path toward union with the divine.

The Sufi orders continue to have a huge influence on the people through their message of detachment from the world and union with the divine, but their greatest influence among the Uyghurs is through *pirs*, or holy men, who have become a kind of living ancestors to the people. There are hundreds, if not thousands, of different colored cloths tied to the fences and poles surrounding the tombs of the saints in the Tarim Basin. Those making petitions believe power is associated with the spirit of the saint in the shrine. In this way, in both life and death, Sufis continue to hold sway over the daily life of Uyghurs.

The "historical" narratives of the shrines have always been meaningful to the Uyghurs, and they have arranged these to music in order to effectively communicate Islamic values, history, and traditions to each succeeding generation. In this tradition, a storyteller sings *dastans*, a Persian form of ornate retelling of oral history. These sung narratives recount the lives of famous Islamic heroes and saints. The storyteller can use various instruments, such as the stringed instruments of a *dutar* or *rawap*; the tambourine-like dap; or the sapaya, a piece of wood or an animal horn with a couple of large metal rings attached to smaller metal rings. Sufis particularly like the rattling sound of the *sapaya*, which is said to induce altered states of consciousness when shaken close to the ear. Also known as "the beggar's instrument," the *sapaya* is used by Sufi dervishes who wander around and live off of the alms given to them (Qian 2016).

These four different types of roles in the life of Uyghurs reinforce the past while maintaining the health of the present.

Periods of Power

There are special times throughout the year when people will gather together at one of the local shrines. For example, in the early spring when the mulberries begin to ripen and before the wheat harvest, large crowds will begin to gather at the shrine of Imam Asim near the city of Khotan. Every week during this time, from Wednesday to Friday, people visit this shrine. Most pilgrims are locals, but others travel long distances to this festival. The gathering is much like a county fair, where people from different villages come together and hold wrestling, cock-fighting, and ram-fighting contests. Food and various religious paraphernalia are for sale. Storytellers reciting *dastans* will retell Islamic folk epics and stories of Sufi saints and Islamic heroes in song.

Those who attend these gatherings can observe colorfully dressed Sufis and even naked hermits in chains shaking their *sapaya*. Much like the naked sophists of ancient Greece, this later class of Sufis have renounced the world and its attachments. They are respected and held in great esteem in the eyes of ordinary folk. During the day, people will visit the shrine to pray and petition the shrine's saint for health, wealth, and happiness. Barren women will come swearing vows of alliance to the saint for the gift of children. They will bring small homemade cloth dolls and lay them at the shrine and will also roll themselves down the sand dunes to activate their reproductive organs. In the evenings, many people gather together in a large circle and begin chanting while they wait for people to become ecstatic and overtaken by the spirit of the shrine. These large community events provide the people with entertainment between harvest times, but more importantly they reinforce, validate, and reignite the community's religious devotion.

There are other times of power when smaller groups will gather together for entertainment, which will include food and music. Some gatherings might only be for males and others only for females, while others might be mixed gatherings. All in all, thirteen different types of smaller social gatherings have some kind of relationship to those seeking spiritual power. One of the better-known gatherings is the meshrep, which combines food with someone performing portions of the twelve *muqams*, a series of epic stories and poems arranged to melodies specific to the Uyghurs. Each *muqam* can last two hours, and it could take up to twenty-four hours to finish all twelve, although normally only portions are played at any one time.

Another important community event among the people of the Tarim Basin is the *helqe-sohbet*, which literally means "circling and talking" and includes chanting the names of God (*zikr*), singing, playing instruments, dancing, ritualized crying, and entering into altered states of consciousness. The Uyghur version of the Sufi tradition of *Samā*, it is intended to bring the listeners into union with the divine. In recent years these rituals have been forbidden in any public place; therefore they are now held in private homes.

Life has not been easy for the Uyghurs living in the Tarim Basin. There are presently many powerful factors putting pressure on the Uyghurs to change.

Power versus Force

In his book *Power versus Force*, David Hawkins (1985) develops a pair of concepts; it is the distinction between them that is particularly important for understanding the reasons behind the longevity of animism among the people of the Tarim Basin. Hawkins' detailed analysis of the determinants of human behavior include two primary influences on people: "Power" and "Force." Power simply exists. It is much like gravity. It is not explained; it is just to be reckoned with. In Hawkins' schema, Power energizes, supplies, and supports life (ibid., 149). Power can be explained as the life-giving principles of the pursuit of happiness, freedom, and love. Power is then contrasted with the other influence on people—Force. Force is an external influence that comes from outside and must be exerted on people in order to change and control them. While Power *is*, Force must find energy from outside itself in order to influence and control others.

A good example of Power versus Force is Gandhi and the British Empire. The British Empire had to use Force to keep the Indians under their control. Gandhi, however, did not use Force to defeat the British Empire; rather, he used Power—the power of the innate desire for freedom—to ultimately overcome Force.

To extend the metaphor to Islam, Islam has striven to use Force to influence and maintain control over the peoples and territories of its expansion. However, people seek after a sense of Power that will give them life; and many have felt that the official teachings and duties of orthodox Islam do not carry true Power. This is why the people of the Tarim Basin continue their ancient folk religious practices; the spiritual power in the animistic parts of their worldview is, to them, more real than Islamic doctrines.

As is commonly the case when Islam enters a new territory, the early Islamic missionaries and teachers allowed the people of the Tarim Basin to repurpose their existing practices and beliefs. They reworked the old religious narratives, practices, and beliefs into an Islamic framework that, in turn, legitimized and promoted the new Islamic narrative. Thus they took existing places of power and converted them into Islamic sites. They also gave the shaman a quasi-official role within society and offered responsibilities to other Islamic religious leaders to preserve, perpetuate, and promote the places, narratives, beliefs, and traditions of past generations. They adapted Islam into the ancient annual cycles of life of the people in the Tarim Basin to gather people together to further reinforce Islamic narratives. Sufi missionaries and the new Islamic hierarchy kept the forms and functions of power the Uyghurs were accustomed to, simply changing the non-Islamic meanings to Islamic ones.

The Dynamic Equivalence for Power in the Tarim Basin

As gospel workers, we certainly don't want to mimic the Islamization of the Tarim Basin in our approach to mission. We must ask ourselves, however, if there are there any lessons in that history for us. A helpful framework might be what Charles Kraft (1979) has called "dynamic equivalence." Originally this term was used exclusively in the area of Bible translation to refer to translations that were thought-based (translating the meanings) rather than word-for-word-based (translating the words literally). Then, in 1979, Kraft suggested that the idea should be broadened to many areas of cross-cultural mission. He argued that rather than starting churches as a "word-for-word" replication of the missionary church into a new setting, the new church must express apostolic ideas through appropriate equivalents in the local culture.

With this in mind, let's consider how the gospel relates to the three dimensions of power discussed previously: places, people, and periods.

In the earlier discussion about "places of power," we saw that the Uyghurs connect power to a place by use of narrative—often ancient historical narratives that have been reworked to support Islamic themes. These narratives connect the living to divine blessing based on actions in the past. When we step back from the details, we see how this fits well with many biblical teachings, most supremely in the story of the atoning work of Christ. By intentionally framing the gospel presentation in this way, the missionary can connect with a deep part of the Uyghur worldview.

The second power issue has to do with people—that is, special people who are seen as stewards of supernatural power. One way we might connect with this is in the public profile of the gospel messenger. Might Uyghurs in the Tarim Basin respond better to a gospel worker who fits the profile of a mystic rather than the more typical scholar or humanitarian? And more personally, what would an authentic, modern Christian mystic look like? These questions don't even begin to cover all the issues this idea raises, but they do point us in an interesting direction.

And lastly, we saw that in the Tarim Basin periods or seasons of power are an important part of communal life. This is perhaps the easiest of the three for which to find dynamic equivalence, because the church has its own long history of following "periods of power"—commonly referred to as the liturgical calendar. Whether it is the angelic appearances at Advent or the elements of cosmic war running through Lent and culminating at Easter, perhaps an emphasis on these times of power would be as meaningful to modern-day Uyghurs as they were to our ancient ancestors in Europe. Or to dream even further, could the gospel be presented as a melodious series of stories and poems in the style of their beloved *muqams*?

Conclusion

The Tarim Bain has been crisscrossed by many a world religion: Buddhism, Manichaeism, Zoroastrianism, and even Syriatic Christianity. Each has left its footprints on the fundamentally animistic Uyghurs who live there. Cross-cultural workers who desire to see real transformation of that society must be aware of the underlying reasons why these Muslims continue to connect with their animistic practices and rituals. As Christians, we know the gospel is the true power of God for salvation to everyone who believes (Rom 1:16), but we often have a difficult time expressing this in forms that have meaning for people very different than ourselves. However, since the people of the Tarim Basin intuitively seek for life-giving power, missionaries among them must find ways to teach, demonstrate, and live out the gospel as the very power of God.

Reflection Questions

1. Like Muslims in many other places, the Uyghurs have remained animists after they accepted Islam. What implications does this have for the Christian worker who seeks to address the whole person with the power of the gospel?

2. The Uyghurs are an expressive people who enjoy gathering together to sing and dance. How can we use music and dance to begin to communicate a biblical worldview to them?

References

Brose, M. C. 2005. "Uyghur technologists of writing and literacy in Mongol China." *T'oung Pao* 91 (4–5): 396–435.

Chan, Elsie Yuen Ching. 2013. "The Worldviews of the Uyghurs of Urumqi, China." PhD diss., Western Seminary.

Doniger, Wendy. 1999. "Manicheaeism." In *Merriam-Webster's Encyclopedia of World Religions*. Springfield, MA: Merriam-Webster Inc.

Fletcher, Joseph. 1995. *The Naqshbandiyya in Northwest China*. London: Variorum.

Foltz, Richard. 2010. *Religions of the Silk Road: Premodern Patterns of Globalization*. 2nd ed. New York: Palsgrave Macmillan.

Hawkins, David. 1985. *Power versus Force*. Carlsbad, CA: Hay House.

Jayaram V. n.d. "Zoroastrianism—Important Beliefs of Zoroastrianism." Hinduwebsite.com. Accessed October 15, 2016. http://www.hinduwebsite.com/zoroastrianism/beliefs.asp.

Kraft, Charles. 1979. *Christianity in Culture*. Maryknoll, NY: Orbis Books.

Poliakov, Sergei P. 1992. *Everyday Islam: Religion and Tradition in Rural Central Asia*. New York: M. E. Sharpe.

Qian, Mu. 2016. "Islamic Soundscapes of Khotan." Sounding Islam in China website. April 1. Accessed May 16, 2016. http://www.soundislamchina.org/?p=1430.

Ross, Lisa, and Alexandre Papas. 2013. *Living Shrines of Uyghur China*. New York: The Monacelli Press.

Stein, Aurel. 1904. *Sand-Buried Ruins of Khotan: An Archaeological and Geographical Exploration in Chinese Turkestan*. London: Hurst and Blackett Limited.

———. 1907. *Ancient Khotan: Detailed Report of Archaeological Explorations in Chinese Turkestan*. Oxford: Clarendon Press.

Strong John. 2007. *Relics of the Buddha*. Delhi, India: Motilal Banarsidass Publishers.

Tang, Li. 2005. "A History of Uighur Religious Conversions (5th–16th Centuries)." Asia Research Institute. Working Paper Series No. 44, June. http://www.ari.nus.edu.sg/wps/wps05_044.pdf.

Thum, Rian. 2014. *The Sacred Routes of Uyghur History*. Cambridge: Harvard University Press. Kindle edition, chap. 2.

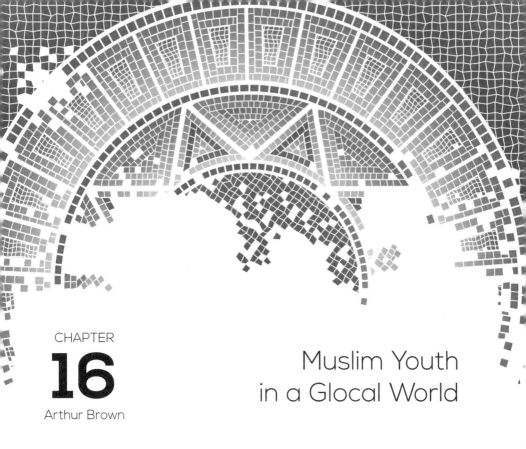

16

Arthur Brown

Muslim Youth in a Glocal World

What is the gospel of Jesus Christ for a girl-child in a Muslim country and context,
who is still living with her family, unable legally [to] go to church, or become a
Christian without upsetting her parents, her extended family, and her community?
What, if anything, does the gospel mean, in essence and in practice, for this child?
(Keith White 2014, 3).

Trying to define what we mean by the term "youth" is challenging enough. Adding
to this the notion of "Muslim youth" increases the complexity exponentially. A
Muslim young person could be thirteen, sixteen, twenty, twenty-five years of
age, or older.[1] They could be British, Bengali, Syrian, Thai, Nigerian, Palestinian,
Brazilian, Australian, Pakistani, Tunisian, Chinese, Canadian, Lebanese, or from
anywhere else in the world. They could be "secular," "somewhat religious,"
"devout," "salafi jihadi," "agnostic," and even struggling to work out how their
faith relates to some very "un-Islamic" parts of their lives.

---

[1] In many contexts, including many Islamic ones, the concept of "youth" often lasts until marriage,
at least in the eyes of the community. And with changing demographics, this transition from youth
to adulthood is stretching later and later into life. However, the focus of this chapter will be on
those between the ages of approximately thirteen and twenty-five.

Yet despite this stunning diversity, what they do have in common is that many, if not most, of them are spending significant amounts of time on Facebook, Twitter, Snapchat, WhatsApp, Instagram, YouTube, Pandora, Google, or whatever is the latest social media platform. This creates a confusing cacophony of globalized voices, as many Muslim young people search for an identity that is integrated, authentic, and holistic—one that makes sense within their specific local context as well as a global context. Diverse potential sources of authority include "religious authority, state, national or secular ideologies, family and kinship groups, peer subculture, popular and cyber culture, and, as of late, the seductive global allures of commodified consumerism, virtual images, and life styles" (Khalaf and Khalaf 2011, 9).

So, unlike the other chapters in this volume, my task is to reflect not on a particular ethnolinguistic or geographically specific Muslim context, but rather on a broad social context. The themes and issues in this chapter confront a wide spectrum of young Muslims; therefore it is important to consider how they impact our missiological thinking in relation to this often-neglected demographic.

Islamic Faith in a Glocalized World

This amalgamation between the local and global contexts is what sociologists are now calling "glocal."[2] This clashing potpourri of cultures is never uniform from person to person, but it does tend to unfold along certain themes. And while this struggle often results in antagonism and discord within their own community, it also has the potential to create highly innovative expressions of faith and culture that resonate with the local and global youth subcultures they relate to.

As adherents of diverse expressions of Islam become more adept at spreading their own interpretations and ideologies to an increasing global audience, it is young people who are the target of these groups' messaging. Groups such as the so-called "Islamic State" (*Daesh* in Arabic) use social media effectively to draw young people into their narrative because they are aware of the struggle so many Muslim young people face. They struggle to find an identity that is able to cope with a world in which their faith has been marginalized, scapegoated, and ridiculed by governments and significant parts of the media.

And yet at the same time there are other Muslims around the world who are offering a different narrative for the young Muslim—one that seeks to integrate global youth culture and religious piety into an expression that is attractive to young people who

---

[2] British sociologist Roland Roberston is credited with coining the term "glocal" in the English-speaking world in the early 1990s. He stated that glocalization "means the simultaneity—the co-presence—of both universalizing and particularizing tendencies." Other sociologists using the term include Keith Hampton, Barry Wellman, and Zygmunt Bauman. The origin of the concept is from Japanese agriculture and specifically the term dochakuka—global localization—which referred to the adaptation of farming techniques to local contexts. More commonly the concept has come to mean the ways in which multinational companies adapt or customize their global brand items (or business practices) to suit local tastes, customs, and demands. For example, a McDonald's menu in Beirut or Seattle will look slightly different than one in Manila or Dubai.

want to be both pious and "cool" at the same time. For example, the Deen Squad are Canadian Muslim rappers who take popular songs and augment them with religiously pious lyrics. Another is the blog site hijabaliciousforever.blogspot.com, which was set up "for the average modern Muslim teen … a style guide to help Muslim teen girls stay stylish and cute yet modest and hallal!!! :)."

Then there are the numerous Facebook pages with "cool imams" or preachers presenting Islamic teaching in a way that is attractive and relevant to their ever-increasing audience.[3] This glocal Islamic outreach extends even to books, such as the fantastic teen novel *Does My Head look Big in This?*—about Amal, a seventeen-year-old Australian-Palestinian Muslim who is trying to discover who she is in the world, how her faith interacts with the rest of her life, and the challenges of "going full-time" in regard to wearing the hijab (Abdel-Fattah 2005).

Three Diverse Muslim Youth: Amena, Rana, and Abdullah

Now might be a good time to introduce the stories of a few Muslim young people, each of whom represents a different expression of the contemporary Muslim youth scene. Amena is from the Philippines; Rana is a Palestinian living in Beirut; and Abdullah is a Bengali-British young man from East London.

Amena is eighteen years old and has just started her postsecondary schooling. She leaves home each morning in her school uniform, with a hijab covering her hair. Once on the train she removes her hijab, replacing it only on her way home in the afternoon. During the weekend, she goes out with other female Muslim friends. She leaves home dressed conservatively, but changes into non-Muslim attire at a friend's house. Amena and her friends are extremely fashion-conscious, but this forms an identity carefully hidden from their parents.

Like most of the young people she knows, Amena is glued to her cell phone. She is either on WhatsApp or sending Facebook messages. She attends Friday noon prayers with her family, but otherwise portrays a life that seems to be far more connected with global youth culture than Islam. Although she attended the madrassa during her primary school years, when she entered her teens she stopped attending. She speaks positively of her religious allegiance and of being a Muslim. She has both Muslim and Christian friends. She flirts with Christian boys, but is very careful how others perceive her relationships with Muslim boys. Her father is quite strict regarding how she portrays herself in their community. Schooling is her lifeline outside the strict confines of her Muslim community. It is also her primary source of stress, as her Christian friends have more money and perceived freedom than she does, so she often feels inferior in comparison.

Rana is seventeen and has lived all her life in a Palestinian refugee camp in Beirut. She was educated in the camp until she was seven and then moved to a UN school

---

[3] For examples of such sites, see https://www.facebook.com/MustafaHosny; https://en.wikipedia.org/wiki/Moez_Masoud; https://en.wikipedia.org/wiki/Ahmad_Al_Shugairi.

just outside its boundaries. She attends a mosque inside the camp, shops inside the camp, and expects to marry a man from within the camp. To please her fiancé's family, she has recently started wearing the hijab. Ahmed, her fiancé, comes from a religious family—unlike Rana. Rana has never questioned Islam—it frames her life—but at the same time, she is not devout. Her prayers are sporadic and she does not see Islam solving any of her problems. She does not see any solution to the challenges she faces as a young female refugee in Lebanon. She has quietly accepted this fact and has a very fatalistic view of the world.

Rana enjoys listening to Western music and spends a lot of time on Facebook. She is aware that she will not enjoy the freedoms that many young people in Lebanon take for granted. The nightclubs, expensive shops, and restaurants of Beirut seem like another world to her. Most of her friends are in the same position, so she accepts this reality. Rana is not political; she has no more faith in politics as an answer than she does in Islam.

It is not hard imagining Rana uttering the following words, which were actually taken from Shelina Janmohamed's *Generation M: Young Muslims Changing the World*, in the chapter entitled "Forgot to Be Oppressed, Too Busy Being Awesome."

> I'm tired of being the token "omg-look-such-an-articulate-awesome-non-stereotypical hijabi!"
> … I realized being thought of as "amazing" was actually insulting.
> Because the assumption was that being veiled meant I was stupid and very non-amazing. …
> I'm tired of the hijab taking so much space in my life.
> I'm tired of speaking about it.
> I'm tired of explaining it.
> I'm tired of defending it.
> I'm tired of being treated differently.
> I'm tired of having to prove I'm normal.
> I'm tired of being thought stupid and backwards.
> I'm tired of the judgments—from both sides.
> I'm tired of the opportunities denied.
>
> I'm tired of expectations.
> I'm tired of hijab. (Janmohamed 2016, 221–22)

Abdullah is fifteen and the second of six siblings. A second generation British-Bangladeshi living in East London, until recently Abdullah attended the local Islamic school. He has just been expelled from this school because of his extremist sympathies and is now at the local Church of England school. Academically he is doing well, but socially he struggles. He is very vocal about the evils of drugs, alcohol, smoking, gang culture, women not covering, and dating. This puts him at odds with many of his classmates, including the other Bangladeshi Muslims.

At home, Abdullah views his parents as Western sympathizers for leaving Bangladesh to come to England. His parents are not well educated and practice a form of folk Islam. This causes Abdullah great difficulty because he was taught, at the Islamic school, a strict Hanafi interpretation of Islam. He spends a lot of time away from the home with his older friends who share his convictions. He dreams of leaving London to join *Daesh* as a graphic designer, but in his heart he knows he won't do so. Despite his difficulties at home, Abdullah loves his family and wouldn't hurt them in that way. Nevertheless, he feels like a failure, which is expressed in angry outbursts at home and school. He attends a local mosque each day and regularly joins the religious classes they offer.

Being Young and Muslim in a Glocal World

In a book about Arab youth, Johanna Wyn suggests, "Youth is a social process—a way of defining individuals that is linked to complex social, political, and economic processes" (2011, 35). These processes lead to a sense in which specific generations develop personalities or traits of their own. Young people in the millennial generation have been shaped by a world that Anthony Giddens describes as a "post traditional order"; and therefore the consequences of globalization and connectivity loom large for this group (1991, 28).

This "millennial generation" has been described as "confident, self-expressive, liberal, upbeat and open to change" (Pew Research Center 2010). In addition to being the most connected generation of all time, they are also the most educated. All these factors provide them with the skills and attitudes to play a significant and increasing role in the formation of societies. In essence, this is a generation that is striving to become creators rather than consumers.

But what does this mean for the Muslims who are part of this group? How do they make sense of their "Muslimness" at a time when Islam in general is under intense scrutiny, both from within and without? Many young Muslims are becoming increasingly embarrassed by "their religion" because of how it is being represented in large parts of the global media.

As is the case for many Christian young people, there is also an increasing mistrust of large and powerful institutions, be they political, financial, or religious. The religious establishment—often represented by the local mosque or church—becomes, for many, disconnected from and irrelevant to the everyday life and challenges faced by young people. Friday sermons, like their Sunday equivalents, rarely address the hopes, fears, challenges, and opportunities faced by young people. As we have seen within many Christian contexts as well, a growing generation is choosing to vote with their feet.

However, a disconnect with official religious structures does not necessarily imply the loss of faith or spirituality. In fact, many Muslim millennials are looking for something worth living for, a deeper spirituality expressed as an individualistic "mix and match" preference that is unimaginable to previous generations. It is within this atmosphere that diverse expressions of religion compete for the allegiance of their young. And it is for this reason that, for some, *Daesh* (ISIS) is an attractive option—inviting glocalized young people to belong to something larger and more meaningful than themselves and their localized socio-religious community. Essentially, they are being invited to play their role in creating a new world—a new "Islamic" state—despite the fact that the majority of Muslims from around the world, including the main centers of Islamic religious authority, categorically refute the Islamic basis of *Daesh's* activities and motivations.[4]

At the same time, young people, including young Muslims, may be less inclined toward wholesale religious allegiance on the terms that their parents knew and have laid out before them. With such choice, in a very real sense many young people are moving toward hybridity when it comes to their faith and how they apply it to their identity and sense of belonging. Thus it is important to make a clear distinction between the notions of hybridity and syncretism, to which we now turn.

One Faith?

Young people today are less interested in binary identity markers that place them in one box or another. How does this provide an opportunity to help young people, from whatever religious background, grow in Christlikeness through the use of Scripture and engaging with relevant social issues that help them put their emerging faith into practice, particularly in ways that may be viewed positively by their parents? Might this generation of young people be the ones who are more likely to follow Christ in a way that is "supra-religious"—refusing to be pigeon-holed into one particular religious system yet living in ways that create authentically biblical Christ-centered faith?

When someone comes to faith in Christ from a non-Christian background, a sense of dual belonging is almost inevitable, at least in the early stage of identification with Christ as Lord and Savior. By "dual belonging" I mean that while they belong to the body of Christ, they also simultaneously belong culturally and socially to their Muslim community. This is not dependent on whether or not the person deliberately desires to dis-belong to their religious/faith and cultural heritage. Instead, it is the result of a deep, worldview-level connection to their Muslim cultural and religious heritage. This heritage includes their beliefs about God, practices associated with these beliefs, and long-held relational ties and a sense of belonging within the ummah. It is implausible for such a worldview to be discarded so easily and quickly that the new believer avoids any sense of hybrid or dual belonging. Whether short or long, they are very likely to wrestle with both their Islamic traditions and their new Christocentric

---

[4] See Martin Accad's post on the Institute of Middle East Studies blog, IMES.BLOG [URL says Arab Baptist Theological Seminary]—"ISIS and the Future of Islam"—for a helpful discussion on this issue and links to key reports condemning the actions of ISIS; https://imes.blog/2015/11/06/isis-and-the-future-of-islam/.

sense of belonging. This blending of past and present realities can result in a healthy, genuine model of discipleship when syncretism is avoided.[5] Thus the critical question becomes, "How may this young person develop an authentic, integrated expression of faith in Christ within both their private and public worlds?"

This line of thinking moves us closer to the reality of many postmodern yet religious young people who may assume "that the good, true and holy is not confined to one's own religious tradition" (Schmidt-Leukel 2009, 48). Whether we agree completely with this or not, it is the reality many Muslim youth live in today. Muslim, Christian, Hindu, Jewish, agnostic, etc., young people "meet" constantly, both online and off-line; thus, it is quite likely they will encounter the teachings of other faiths. But rather than despairing of this inevitably leading to syncretism, can we imagine that some of this will influence their faith and practice in some positive way?

For example, a Christian young person may be inspired by the modesty or prayer life of a Muslim friend, or a Muslim may discover a new sense of beauty and authority in Jesus that they had not previously considered. In such interfaith practical dialogue, we see ways today's religious young people may feel less "religiously constrained" than their forbearers.

What is essential, however, is that young people develop an authentic, if not traditional, personal narrative of faith in Christ—even if this may stem from a range of sources of authority and influence. This does not mean that the core elements of the gospel are lost or in any way diluted. In fact, the gospel may be more faithfully expressed by those paying careful attention to it through a process of developing an authentic, Christ-centered faith narrative within their own multi-faith experience and reality.

While reflecting on Christian faith formation in an interfaith world, Marcia Bunge makes an important point, which I think has resonance for adherents of other faiths, including the emerging faith of Muslim young people.

> As children grow and develop, they will certainly have to assimilate, publicly confess, and "own" their own faith. Yet as they develop and grow, they are already exposed to values, beliefs and commitments around them. Thus, the burning question regarding faith-formation is not "will our children have faith?" but rather "what kind of faith will they have?" We live in not only a religiously pluralistic world but also a highly consumer-orientated global economy. ... They will certainly be shaped by other values, whether in the market-place of religions or the shopping mall. (Bunge 2014, 202)

In this kind of environment, it is inevitable for children to be shaped by the values of others. Thus the goal of discipling young Muslim millennials moves beyond the idea of simplistically "purging" them of other influences, moving instead to distilling these influences through the Word of God.

---

[5] There are many definitions of syncretism. Phil Parshall (1980) helpfully and succinctly says that syncretism occurs when "critical elements of the gospel are lost in the process of contextualization" (46).

Within the context of uprisings and revolutions in the MENA (Middle East/North Africa) region, Miriam Gazzah suggests that despite the fact that "Islam is often seen as standing in tense relation to many aspects of pop culture," certain expressions of Islam are indeed able to provide a powerful inspiration for creative, provocative, and politically motivated expressions, most of it expressed through Muslim youth subcultures (2011, 320).

As one Lebanese student laments,

> My society is full of contradictions: a society that dissolves the identity of the individual into the identity of the group, a society that is afraid of change, a society that praises freedom of expression but ultimately suppresses it. ... There is no logic in our society. We must live up to the expectations of the family, the community, our religious sect, and political party but I have no intention of doing so. (Khalaf 2011, 166)

As we have shown, the lived experience of young Muslims is far from homogeneous or straightforward. How they respond to the diverse and mixed messages they receive from uncountable sources will depend on an equally uncountable range of factors and worldviews. Given this, how might the church respond to its responsibility to make Christ known to such a diverse and numerous demographic?

The Challenge of Mission

Recall the important question posed at the beginning of this chapter:

> What is the gospel of Jesus Christ for a girl-child in a Muslim country and context, who is still living with her family, unable legally [to] go to church, or become a Christian without upsetting her parents, her extended family, and her community? What, if anything, does the gospel mean, in essence and in practice, for this child? (White 2014, 3)

Lebanon provides Christians with many opportunities to witness to people from multi-faith backgrounds. It is legally possible for adults to change their religious affiliation and legal identity in Lebanon—although socially this is often fraught with complexity. Lebanon also provides numerous contexts for Christians to witness to Muslim young people, whether in schools, universities, youth organizations, or churches. This is even more prevalent given the present refugee demographic in the country.

However, despite the relative religious freedom enjoyed in Lebanon, significant challenges remain when considering mission to young people of a different faith—particularly when they are under the age of eighteen.[6] These include notions of religious freedom for children, which are quite ambiguous in international law, as well as many ethical, missiological, and social considerations.

---

[6] In international law, a child is defined as anyone under the age of eighteen.

One Example: Hiba's Changing Faith

An example of some of these challenges can be found in the story of Hiba and Maria, two young women from Lebanon. Hiba is a fifteen-year-old Sunni Muslim girl who lives in a religiously mixed community in Beirut. She attends a Catholic school and also has friends who are evangelicals. Hiba and her friends participate in a youth event, run by a parachurch evangelical youth organization, that meets twice a month. Hiba feels welcomed by this group, is intrigued by their teaching, and enjoys the fun activities and worship songs.

Though her family is not particularly religious, Hiba is interested in spirituality and has many questions. She has observed differences between what she understands of her Muslim faith, the beliefs of the Catholic school she attends, and the beliefs of the evangelical Christianity of her friends. She has also noted that many of the moral teachings from each appear similar. Hiba is attracted to the faith and freedom she sees within the evangelical community, and this increasingly informs her personal spirituality. She once attended a youth meeting at a local evangelical church, but didn't enjoy it as much as "her" youth group.

Maria is an evangelical Christian and volunteer leader at the parachurch youth group. Since she lives in the same area, she knows Hiba's family, though not very well. Hiba's parents are aware of Maria and her involvement at the youth meeting. Despite being an evangelical Christian, Maria is well respected in the Muslim community. Maria has mixed feelings about Islam, but has Muslim friends—some of whom are devout. She respects them, although she feels it is important for the young people she works with to know that Jesus alone provides salvation.

Maria is eager to see young people like Hiba "come to faith in Jesus," but she is aware of the problems this might cause. Due to pragmatic and legal considerations, as well as an awareness of the potential conflict religious conversion may cause, Maria continues to encourage Hiba toward faith in Christ but advises her not to talk about this with her family at this stage.

After some months, Hiba expresses a desire to accept Jesus as Lord, and she wants to get baptized, as she has read about this in the Bible. She is less interested in attending church services. Maria explains that it would be best for her to wait until she is significantly older before telling others about her developing faith, but she encourages Hiba to continue attending the youth group and to model good behavior to her family as her act of witness. Maria also invites her to various other Christian activities, which does not seem to cause a problem with Hiba's family. Maria is intentional in her support of Hiba's new faith, though she is nervous about Hiba's parents finding out.

Wanting to see her faith make a more significant impact on her family, Hiba asks how she might be a good witness. While taking Maria's advice seriously, she starts asking her parents questions about their faith journey and highlighting some of the positive things she has been learning at the youth meetings. Though careful not to push ideas on her parents that will make them uncomfortable, Hiba is aiming to help develop an environment in which faith and personal spirituality is discussed openly. She has heard of people who came to faith in Christ in their youth but later suffered rejection when they told their parents—something she wants to avoid.

Hiba seeks to be respectful of the Muslim tradition in which she has grown up, but also to ask questions of it. She finds the fact that her parents were willing to send her to a Catholic school helpful as a basis for faith-based discussions within her family. Hiba hopes that as time progresses she will be able to be more explicit about what Jesus means to her. While she understands that baptism probably needs to wait, she hopes that this will be possible in the future—although she is uncertain what this might look like or mean for her and her family.

Approaching Young People in Diverse Religious Contexts

The youth ministry "industry" is good at developing programs and curriculum to support the spiritual growth of young people—typically from a Western or "global youth culture" perspective—but not so good at giving consideration to ministry among young people from different cultures or faith backgrounds. Clearly it is naive to think there is a "one-size-fits-all" approach to ministry with Muslim young people.

Youth ministry is about relationships, not programs! It is unhelpful to have a set of prescribed or expected "outcomes." We must walk the journey of faith with young people. Vincent Donovan, an extraordinary American missionary to Masa tribes in Tanzania from 1955 to 1973, expressed this well when he suggested, "In working with young people do not try to call them back to where they were and do not try to call them to where you are, beautiful as that place may seem to you. You must have the courage to go with them to a place that neither you nor they have ever been before" (1982, xiii).

Transparency, integrity, honesty, and sensitivity must be foundational elements of any activity with young people, regardless of their faith or cultural background. In participating in the lives of Muslim young people, we must recognize that we need to walk sensitively, as the place where we are walking is holy ground. Young people's faith, values, beliefs, and practices may differ considerably from our own, but we must have the humility and desire to see that even in those differences God may be at work in their lives.

It is not in the least "universalistic" to believe that God is at work in a Muslim young person's life long before they meet a Christian worker or hear the gospel. As David Bosch contends, we do not

> have God in our pockets as the haves, the beati possidentes standing over against spiritual have nots, the massa damnata. We are all recipients of the same mercy,

sharing in the same mystery. We thus approach every other faith [or paradigm] and its adherents reverently, taking off our shoes, as the place we are approaching is holy. (Bosch 1991, 484)

The process of becoming a new creation in Christ is complex and multidimensional. Adolescence already involves a complex process of change and development involving identity formation. It is important that young people are supported through this process in a way that empowers and equips them to develop their own faith narrative. We need to accompany young believers on their long but necessary journey toward mature faith, rather than telling them what and how to believe. Yes, we are guides and mentors; but within such complex and often sensitive relationships, we must come alongside rather than lead from ahead.

Conclusion

The context in which Muslim young people live and practice their faith is complex and diverse. They experience many mixed messages, as do all young people, and must make sense of their spiritual and religious lives within connected and noisy environments. Considering their somewhat pluralistic world, it is important to ensure that our practice of mission lives up to the standards we profess in our own faith. As we meet young people, of any faith—or none—we must take with us the words of Peter: "But in your hearts revere Christ as Lord. Always be prepared to give an answer to everyone who asks you to give the reason for the hope that you have. But do this with gentleness and respect, keeping a clear conscience, so that those who speak maliciously against your good behavior in Christ may be ashamed of their slander" (1 Pet 3:15–16 NIV).

Reflection Questions

1. What potentially negative consequences could you foresee if a Muslim young person wanted to convert to Christianity publicly? Are there ways to alleviate some of these potentially avoidable consequences?

2. In what ways can you encourage the young person to grow in faith and wisdom in Jesus/Isa, while at the same time seeking to ensure a healthy and positive witness within their family that is unlikely to cause conflict and tension?

References

Abdel-Fattah, Randa. 2005. *Does My Head Look Big in This?* London: Scholastic Children's Books.

Bosch, David. 1991. *Transforming Mission: Paradigm Shifts in Theology of Mission.* London: Orbis Books.

Bunge, Marcia. 2014. "Faith Formation in an Interfaith World: Passing on the Faith to Children Amidst the Realities of Religious Pluralism." In *Theology, Mission and Child,* edited by B. Prevette, K. White, R. Velloso-Ewell, and D. J. Konz, 201–14. Oxford: Regnum.

Donovan, Vincent. 1982. *Christianity Rediscovered: An Epistle from the Masai.* London: SCM.

Gazzah, Miriam. 2011. "European Muslim Youth: Towards a Cool Islam?" In *Arab Youth: Social Mobilisation in Times of Risk,* edited by Samir Khalaf and Roseanne Saad Khalaf, 319–36. London: SAQI Books.

Giddens, Anthony. 1991. *Modernity and Self-Identity: Self and Society in the Late Modern Age*. London: Polity Press.

Janmohamed, Shelina. 2016. *Generation M: Young Muslims Changing the World*. London: I. B. Tauris.

Khalaf, Samir, and Roseanne Saad Khalaf. 2011. "On the Marginalization and Mobilization of Arab Youth." In *Arab Youth: Social Mobilisation in Times of Risk*, edited by Samir Khalaf and Roseanne Saad Khalaf. London: SAQI Books.

Parshall, Phil. 1980. *New Paths in Muslim Evangelism: Evangelical Approaches to Contextualization*. Grand Rapids: Baker.

Pew Research Center. 2010. "The Millennials: Confident. Connected. Open to Change." Report, February 24. Accessed April 21, 2015. http://www.pewtrusts.org/en/research-and-analysis/reports/2010/02/24/the-millennials-confident-connected-open-to-change.

Schmidt-Leukel, Perry. 2009. *Transformation by Integration: How Inter-faith Encounter Changes Christianity*. London: SCM Press.

White, Keith. 2014. *Introduction to Theology, Mission and Child*, edited by B. Prevette, K. White, R. Velloso-Ewell, and D. J. Konz. Oxford: Regnum.

Wyn, Johanna. 2011. "Youth as a Social Category and as a Social Process." In *Arab Youth: Social Mobilisation in Times of Risk*, edited by Samir Khalaf and Roseanne Saad Khalaf. London: SAQI Books.

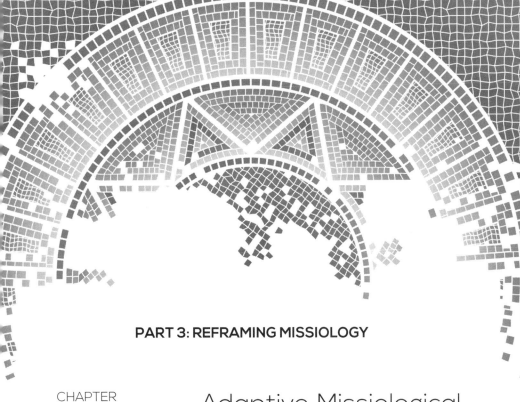

PART 3: REFRAMING MISSIOLOGY

CHAPTER

17

Warrick Farah

Adaptive Missiological Engagement with Islamic Contexts

As the chapters in this volume demonstrate, developing appropriate missiology in a Muslim context takes wisdom, patience, and skill. So how can we, as practitioners who love Muslims, deal with the diversity of approaches to lost people in the New Testament, on the one hand, and the diversity of approaches to Muslims in the mission community, on the other?[1] Why does God seem to be blessing so many drastically different approaches to working with Muslims today, sometimes even in the same context?

This chapter builds upon the blueprints for understanding Islam in the introductory chapters and the thirteen case studies in the book to propose an "adaptive" approach to mission. That is, mission in a world full of multifaceted

---

[1] See, for instance, "The 'W' Spectrum: 'Worker' Paradigms in Muslim Contexts" (Farah and Meeker 2015).

challenges must adapt to the issues it faces within Muslim contexts, following the example of how Jesus and his disciples engaged complex situations in the New Testament. Adaptive missiology is a reflective process that enables us to deal with complexity while discerning gospel-centered responses appropriate for specific contexts.

Changing Understandings of Muslim Contexts

Significant shifts in recent decades have influenced how we conceptualize Muslim contexts and approach reaching them with the gospel. Reactions against colonialism and the influence of postmodernism led to changes in anthropology and religious studies that have played a large and often unexamined role in how we as Christians understand our biblical calling to engage Muslims in Islamic contexts. This section offers a brief survey of these influences as they relate to missiology.

Postcolonial studies: "The Muslim world" versus "the West"

Several decades ago, Edward Said published a highly influential critique of Western scholarship on Asia titled *Orientalism: Western Conceptions of the Orient* (1994 [1978]). Even if Said's arguments were at times polarizing (or if he, ironically, negatively stereotyped Western scholarship), he exposed the prejudicial and monolithic thinking of some Western scholars in their descriptions of the "Orient" during the colonial period. We cannot provide a full summary of his arguments here, but would highlight how persuasive he is in framing the way some European and American scholars describe Arabs, and especially Muslims, in a generally pejorative construct. The Orientalist narrative created a discourse in the *West of a civilized Western "us" versus an uncivilized Eastern "them,"* which was subsequently used to reinforce Western colonialism and imperialism over parts of Africa and Asia.

This is relevant to us in mission studies because some traditional missionary discourse was a form of Orientalism (Swanson 2004, 108). Muslims were often described in a way that dichotomized the world into two antagonistic and incompatible realms—Christian and non-Christian. "Like Orientalism, missionary discourse traditionally has been aggressive, and derogatory in its treatment of Asians of other faiths, expressing attitudes that have frequently also included negative views of indigenous cultures" (ibid., 109).

Said's insights offer critical reflection upon our approaches to understanding Muslims, leading us to ask if we describe Islam in overly negative ways, failing to also see the problems in our own cultures as well (Matt 7:5). When seeking to describe unknown and seemingly threatening contexts, do we resort to a simplistic "textual attitude" (ibid., 110) by cherry-picking our descriptions of Muslims from the worst texts found in the Qur'an and Hadith? Do we feel superior to Muslims? Or do we approach them with humility and with the attitude of a learner? This kind of missiological reflection is an important antidote for biased and injurious theologies of mission.

Another common assumption challenged by postcolonial studies is the very idea of a unified geopolitical entity called "the Muslim world." This idea does not come from the Islamic teaching of ummah, but instead emerged in the nineteenth century.

> Mistaken is the belief that Muslims were united until nationalist ideology and European colonialism tore them apart. This is precisely backward; in fact, Muslims did not imagine belonging to a global political unity until the peak of European hegemony in the late nineteenth century, when poor colonial conditions, European discourses of Muslim racial inferiority, and Muslims' theories of their own apparent decline nurtured the first arguments for pan-Islamic solidarity. (Aydin 2017, 3)

The "Muslim world" construct is a racial (racist?) product of the colonialist narrative and has been embraced by both Muslims and Westerners to homogenize "Muslims" and the "West" in (often antagonistic) political discourse. In mission, we can learn to recognize the phenomenon without being biased by this worldly understanding of Muslims.

Unfortunately, Orientalism and neocolonialism are still alive and well in some streams of missiology. Two recent articles published in the journal *Global Missiology* highlight this fact. For example, one author displays the objectivist, "textual attitude" to Muslims when he claims, "The one who rationalizes away jihad and other illiberal ideas from the Qur'an is also likely to rationalize away the virgin birth, the resurrection, and other key doctrines of Christianity" (Anonymous-Three 2017, 7). He further states that only very liberal Muslims infected with Western rationalism will reject the true, violent nature of Islam, thus enforcing the stereotype that faithful Muslims are incapable of successfully integrating into democratic societies. Placing himself in the seat of Islamic authority, he laments, "Who is going to tell our political leaders, as well as the general public, the true, classical nature of Islam?" (ibid., 9).

Another author advances this same totalizing rhetoric, saying, "Evangelical Christians must understand Islam 'as it is,' not as they imagine it to be … a medieval and unreformable totalitarian religio-political system that masquerades as a religion" (Anonymous-Two 2017, 7–8).[2] Michael Rynkiewich notes the tragedy of when this kind of thinking creeps into the mission world:

> Unlike anthropologists, missionaries and mission scholars have been slow to be self-reflective and to rethink what missionaries are doing. Both anthropologists and missionaries have been entangled in colonialism, but missionaries have resisted admitting the entanglement, and slower to do something about it. (2011, 172)

---

[2] Both authors are also unaware of the nuanced role religion plays sociologically in communities and could benefit from the "bottom-up" approach to understanding Islam discussed in chapter 2 in this volume, "How Muslims Shape and Use Islam: Towards a Missiological Understanding."

While most current scholarship on Muslims and Islam have been able to move on from this simplistic and prejudicial thinking toward Muslims, some Christians, unfortunately, have not. If we cannot recognize this in our missiology, "We end up being ethnocentric and colonial in ways that we are often unaware" (Greer 2017, 93).

Cultural anthropology: Modern essentialism and postmodern relativism

The influences of neocolonialism also call us to reflect critically on our models of anthropology in understanding Muslim contexts. The Bible teaches certain things about humankind and how we relate to God; in systematic theology, this is called anthropology (the study of humanity). Just as everyone has a framework for understanding theological anthropology, everyone also assumes a cultural anthropology—whether consciously realized or not. One outdated understanding of mission (based on an outdated and inaccurate modernist cultural anthropology) assumed that the missiological task of communicating the gospel was a simple exercise like this: A messenger (evangelist) encodes a message (the gospel) to a receiver (an unbeliever), like sending a letter in an envelope. In this view, individuals within a culture are well integrated and nearly identical to other members of their culture. Thus, one simply interprets the gospel for the "others" in a static process.

This modernist model of anthropology taught that cultures were homogenous and that people in each culture were objectively understandable, basically spoke only one language, and were virtually unaffected by peoples around them. However, "Neither culture nor the missiological situation is like this anymore, and it seems questionable that it ever was" (Rynkiewich 2008, 33). Unfortunately, many missionaries are still attached to this outdated anthropology, and their missiology remains stuck in the 1960s (ibid.). Today we should realize that people in their contexts are much more complex and quite different from the simplistic way modernist anthropology often described them.

Postmodern anthropology developed precisely to correct the errors of modern anthropology, but it was an exercise in pendulum swinging and made many mistakes of its own. The objectivity and certainty of modernity was replaced by subjectivity and skepticism in postmodernity. If modernity is characterized by essentialism, then postmodernity is marked by relativism. Unfortunately, both modernity and postmodernity are insufficient for framing our understanding of mission. One way forward is "a post-postmodern missiology" (Yip 2014) that tries to handle the complexity of understanding contexts while rejecting the pluralist theology of religions. George Yip's proposal for a polythetic and progressive contextualization[3] helps us deal with the variations and cultural exceptions that exist within religious settings, and especially the diverse manifestations of Islam, even within the same context.

---

[3] For more on polythetic and progressive contextualization, see http://muslimministry.blogspot.com/2017/06/polythetic-and-progressive.html.

Religious studies and the fog of "religions"

Related to this postcolonial reframing of how we understand the "other" and the challenges of our assumed model of cultural anthropology is the shift found in religious studies. The current consensus in the field is that there is no timeless, transcultural definition of "religion" that is not also a function of political power (Cavanaugh 2009), and that the ability to frame a distinct category in society as "religion" has more to do with the Enlightenment and Protestant Reformation than with how people understand themselves (Nongbri 2013). The "religious" category also fails to adequately tie together dissimilar ritualistic practices in different faith traditions.[4]

However, this critique of the concept of religion does not mean that religion is not real, only that religion itself is socially constructed—it would not exist if there were no people (Schilbrack 2010). Islam, as it is lived and practiced, repeatedly transforms to match the realities of different contexts. Classifying all Muslims (or Hindus, Christians, etc.) into a single category in the "world religions" paradigm obscures many of the most crucial defining characteristics specific to their respective contexts. Martin Accad proposes a way beyond this limitation:

> The "world religions" approach has a tendency to view people of faith as prisoners of theological systems, whose every move can be predicted by their communities' sacred scriptures. Whereas the "sociology of religions" approach offers a dynamic vision of mutually-influential forces between theology and the practice of religion. I would argue that the latter vision offers us a far richer field of inquiry, engagement, and action than the former. From a missional perspective, therefore, it is far more useful, far more empowering and energizing; it invites us to new possibilities in terms of creative and constructive action required for the mission of God. (2016)

Therefore, as Christians who long for Jesus to be embraced as Lord and Savior in Muslim contexts, we desperately need to be alert to how we use the category "religion" in mission, because "missiology as a discipline has not yet adequately engaged discussions and controversies in the field of religious studies" (Richard 2014, 214).

These monumental changes in postcolonial theory, anthropology, religious studies, and especially with Muslims themselves in our globalizing world demand that today's cross-cultural worker reject one-size-fits-all strategies for working with Muslims and become able to adapt with the context. But how?

A Call for Adaptive Missiology

The introductory chapters in this volume provide theoretical foundations to explain the diversity of Islam as it is found in various settings around the world, which is further exemplified through the case studies in this book. At this point, it is perfectly natural

---

[4] Evangelicals often reduce religion to a system of beliefs (e.g., Keller 2008, 15), yet one of the major problems in this approach is that "social and psychological research shows that people tend to hold a collection of contradictory beliefs that cannot be put together into a coherent system. In addition, research shows that people's behavior is often based on something other than their beliefs" (Martin 2014, 7). Additionally, in Muslim contexts beliefs often take a back seat to practices: "For Islam, orthopraxy is more important than orthodoxy" (Ess 2006, 16).

for us to disagree over the supposed "true nature" of Islam, both historically and ideologically. I do not pretend that we can adequately address that issue in a volume like this. Instead, the topic at hand is specifically about our *missiology of Islam*. That is, how should the church attempt to understand what Muslims in their context believe, love, and do? And how should that contextual understanding inform our missional impulse, in light of God's mission in Christ to redeem all nations back to himself?

Toward a missiology of Islam(s)

Considering all that we have learned about "Islam," this book demonstrates that mission must deal with the plurality of islams and the diversity of Muslims around the world. In the personal-missional encounter, Islam, simply put, *should be whatever our Muslim friend says it is*. This is not to deny that our friends could be further or nearer to what certain "mainstream" Muslims throughout history have decreed as authentic Islam. This is also not to deny that something called Islam exists, and that our friends could be somewhere on the margins of Islam. Instead, what this means is that we must primarily deal with how Muslims shape and use Islam in their context. This approach moves us closer to an appropriate missiology of Islam. If we don't begin with the local expressions of Islam,[5] we end up assuming something other than what our friends hold to be true, and therefore miss the vital and necessary connection for the power of the gospel to do its transformational work specifically in that context.

Furthermore, in mission through mass media or writing is it is important to be informed through cultural anthropology that there are great variations among individuals in cultures. Even when looking for the broad-based values in a people group, it is still doubtful that one could determine an approach that is properly contextualized for the "Egyptian culture," for example. Any approach focusing on a large grouping of people will have to acknowledge such inherent limitations. This is especially important at a time when the understanding of ethnicity is evolving and peoples are losing the sense of "groupness" in ethnic identity, which questions the very idea of "people groups" common in evangelical missiology (Gill 2014, 90). This further illustrates the need for adaptation.

Consider the biblical support for adaptation according to context. One important observation is that we have no records of Jesus nor his apostles defining and dealing with paganism or Judaism (which were both diverse in the first century), and we have no record of a biblical call to overthrow the Roman cult. Instead, Jesus engaged *people* in their situations. Moreover, concerning debating the true nature of Islam (or any other religious system) and quarrelling over whose understanding is the most accurate, mission historian Andrew Walls makes an important point:

---

[5] Studying the Qur'an and the history of Islam is also vital for missiology; beginning with our friends' understanding will only enrich our understanding of the interpretations of the Qur'an and the diversity of Islam throughout history.

Argument about which is correct, or the more correct, picture of "Hinduism" is beside the point in the light of Romans 1:18ff., for Paul's concern here is not with systems at all, but with men. It is people who hold down the truth of unrighteousness, who do not honor God, who are given up to dishonorable passions. It is upon men, who commit ungodly and wicked deeds, that the wrath of God is revealed. (Walls 1996, 66)

Biblically based ministry in the Islamic world is not about engaging Islam per se, but rather about engaging Muslims.[6] Furthermore, Walls continues that our message must not be a religious system in return, for it is "not Christianity that saves, but Christ" (ibid.). If it is best to view "Islam" as simply being what people who profess it actually believe and do (Bates and Rassam 2001, 89), then we begin our missiological engagement by understanding their worldview in the light of Romans 1:18ff, not some supposed orthodox Islam. We should indeed be good students of Islam, but we should be even better students of Muslims.

To deal with the elastic concepts of religion previously discussed, one possible proposal is to be "supra-religious" in our missiological engagement (e.g., Accad 2012) and attempt to rise above the fray of worldly religiosity. This is not to say that religion is unimportant, but to ensure that we are gospel-centered in our approach instead of clouding mission with flexible concepts like religion. However, instead of bypassing religion in our missiological approaches, I propose that a more fruitful way of engaging Muslims is to deal with idolatry, which, depending on the context, may be a much more specific topic than Islam.

Idolatry and mission

Any discussion of idolatry necessarily begins with the theology of God and worship:

As God eternally outpours within his triune self, and as we are created in his image, it follows that we too are continuous outpourers, incurably so. The trouble with our outpouring is that it is fallen. It needs redeeming, else we spend our outpouring on false gods appearing to us in any number of guises. Salvation is the only way our continuous outpouring—our continuous worship—is set aright and urged into the fullness of Christ. (Best 2003, 10)

In this concept of idolatry, as continuous and habitual worshipers in need of redemption, we find a missional hermeneutic that leads toward an adaptive approach to Muslims. In this sense, religion is of no redemptive benefit. No matter what religious identity people claim—Christian, Muslim, pagan, atheist, etc.—they are all lost apart from the gospel (Rom 3:22–23), and are left clinging to various types of idols instead of Christ alone.

The central theological theme in the Bible is the refutation of idolatry (Rosner 1999, 21), yet expressions of it are quite diverse. In his seminal book *The Mission of God* (2006), Christopher Wright teaches that biblical monotheism is necessarily

---

[6] I do not intend to imply that the scope of the gospel is merely individualistic, but that it is deeply personal in nature. Indeed, "The goal of God's rescue operation, the main aim of Jesus coming and dying in the first place, is *the restoration and transformation of all creation*" (Wright 2015, 72).

missional and biblical mission is necessarily monotheistic. The biblical concept that keeps people from honoring God as God[7] is not the wrong religion, but idolatry. Wright describes the motivations behind our idolatrous worship:

> Having alienated ourselves from the living God our Creator, we have a tendency to worship whatever makes us tremble with awe as we feel our tiny insignificance in comparison with the great magnitudes that surround us. We seek to placate and ward off whatever makes us vulnerable and afraid. We then counter our fears by investing inordinate and idolatrous trust in whatever we think will give us the ultimate security we crave. And we struggle to manipulate and persuade whatever we believe will provide all our basic needs and enable us to prosper on the planet. (2006, Kindle 2216–19)

Biblically speaking, idolatry is a broad concept that plays a large role in our engagement with lost people. Unfortunately, this concept is often neglected in missiology. But this begs the question—What is the relationship between religion and idolatry?

The idea that religion can be separated from culture or simply reduced to a theological system is an assumption heavily influenced by the Enlightenment, not by biblical theology. Therefore, it is a mistake to assume that the totality of one's so-called "religious heritage" is something that must be "renounced" in all cases and times and contexts as disciples are made. This is akin to equating the ambivalent, modern concept of religion with the biblical category of idolatry. It also ignores some of the positive virtues that religion provides in structuring societies (Netland 2001, 329). It is critical to bear in mind that there are various dimensions to religious contexts, and religion is not monolithic (Farah 2015a; Smart 1996). So instead of "Islam," what should be abandoned, biblically speaking, are idols. Additionally, there are times when people need deliverance from demonic influences—this is true in every context (but too far afield from the topic at hand for us to explore further).

I am not defending Islam nor being naïve to the powerful influence of Islamic ideologies. There are indeed times and contexts in which Muslims who turn to Christ will need to reject the majority of their religious heritage. In that case, the supra-religious approach may be inappropriate and religious change may be a clear way to deal with idolatry. An example of this is that salvation for many Muslims is a "prophetological concept," meaning "the logic of salvation has everything to do with one's relation to the Prophet Muhammad" (Pennington 2014, 198). In this case, Muslims will indeed need to turn from Muhammad as an idol (as previously defined).

---

[7] The related issue, "Do Muslims and Christians worship the same God?" is a fallacious and unanswerable question that creates many pseudo arguments in missiology. Instead, I argue that the "only way to know God is through Jesus. A genuine personal relationship with God can only be Christological and Trinitarian. All other worship of God outside of Christ is 'in vain' (Mk 7:7). So, whether or not Muslims believe in a different God is somewhat of an irrelevant issue, because in fact no one knows God apart from Jesus. All conceptions of God, whether they are American, Muslim, Asian, Agnostic, Pagan, Mormon, or even 'Christian,' all of them are incomplete and inaccurate without the gospel revelation of the Son (Heb. 1:2)" (Farah 2010).

However, not all Muslim-background believers (MBBs) feel that they must categorically reject Muhammad, or that they must view him as some sort of antichrist.[8] MBBs who have come to faith have widely diverse opinions about Muhammad, just as they have different experiences of their religion. Some MBBs view Islam as a form of spiritual bondage, some as a culture or set of politics, with many others somewhere between these two poles (Farah 2015b, 73–77). Missiologist L. D. Waterman also testifies to the diverse spiritual experiences that Muslims have of Islam:

> In the Bridging the Divide network,[9] through numerous case studies from scholar-practitioners with a wide range of perspectives and experiences, we have learned of the incredible diversity of contexts within "the Muslim world." We have noted not only differences of social and political contexts, but also of diverse spiritual alignments and experiences among Muslims. Within these very different contexts, God is working in a variety of creative ways to shine the light of the gospel. (2017)

If we come to accept the varieties of the MBB experience with Islam, we can see that there are many diverse journeys on the one way to God, through Christ alone (Greenlee 2007). This strongly suggests that we do well not to assume that all Muslims must reject their "religion"—whatever that means to them. This is too vague to be meaningful, in many cases, and can also erroneously lead some MBBs to abandon their cultures and social networks.[10] Instead, we learn to exegete the context and be adaptive in our approach.

Idolatry can take many forms. As we have seen through the chapters in this volume, potential idols in Muslim contexts (other than those discussed above) can include merit-seeking through good works to appease God, nationalism,[11] pride, intercession of saints, materialism, "prophetolatry," personal reputation, folk religious practices, strict adherence to ritual, or any combination of the above. (Christians are equally prey to such idols.) In the midst of the context-specific encounter with Muslims, adaptive missiology requires Christian workers to discern the form of idolatry in which they are entangled and then offer the appropriate gospel-centered response. Yet this is a dynamic process; we will frequently cycle between our response, the Bible, and the context. "Combating idolatry can take many forms. The Bible itself prepares us to recognize that different approaches may be relevant in different contexts. Wisdom in mission calls us to be discerning and to recognize that what may be appropriate in one situation may not be so helpful in another" (Wright 2006, Kindle 2337–39).

---

[8] Space prohibits more discussion on the understanding of Muhammad. But to share one approach, John Azumah tends not to characterize Muhammad as a "false prophet," but more like a "fallen prophet." He also demonstrates how various Protestant missionary attitudes in recent decades have "moved away from calling Muhammad an impostor or the anti-Christ to appreciating his positive and admirable qualities and sincerity as a religious figure" without also ascribing to Muhammad a positive "prophetic" role (2016, 211).

[9] http://btdnetwork.org.

[10] Space prohibits from going further, but I have previously argued that there are various dimensions to religious contexts, which different MBBs relate to differently (Farah 2015a).

[11] Olivier Roy argues that nationalism is a greater motivating force than Islamism in places like Iran and in groups like Hamas (2003).

Taking our cues from the previous discussion on postcolonialism and anthropology, and realizing there is more than one way to deal with idolatry, we recognize how unwise it would be to respond apart from relationships with those who know their own contexts far better than we do.

Transforming relationships

Adaptive missiology recognizes that all people everywhere who embrace the gospel experience both a continuity and a discontinuity with their past (Netland 2001, 327). Earlier approaches to contextualization taught that previous practices and beliefs can be either retained, rejected, or repurposed (Hiebert 1986, 188). This reflects how Paul saw his ministry of becoming all things to all people (1 Cor 9:19ff), while avoiding harmful syncretism (2 Cor 6:14ff). Yet there are clearly limits to the usefulness of contextualization when it is a one-sided exercise, done by the worker for the local community. In such cases, the valuable ways in which indigenous people contribute to the process and the ways in which God is already at work may be overlooked, even before the unique and sufficient message of the cross of Christ is proclaimed (1 Cor 2:2).

Our focus should not be on envisioning what the church looks like in a context as an end result, and then prescribing a static mission praxis from that assumption. Instead, we need continual missiological inquiry into the nature of the dynamic relationship between ourselves, Muslims, and God revealed in Christ (cf. Shaw 2010, 209). Transforming relationships are key in this process, and will require us to be vulnerable in a postcolonial spirit while walking in humble confidence in the authority of Jesus. It is, after all, God's mission, and we often get in the way. "The Bible shows that God's greatest problem is not just with the nations of the world, but with the people he has created and called to be the means of blessing the nations. And the biggest obstacle to fulfilling that mission is idolatry among God's people" (Lausanne Movement 2011, 145).

Adaptive missiology aims to get at the heart of how Jesus and the apostles approached "the other" in the New Testament. No single evangelistic address was identical, and they always took the context into account in their witness (Flemming 2005). By understanding the New Testament itself as a missiological document (Wright 2011), we can see Jesus and the apostles taking time to humbly reflect and give an appropriate consideration to their audience; they were continually adapting to the challenge of seeing lives and communities transformed by the power of God.

Conclusion: An Apostolic Challenge for Our Day

The world adds another thirty-two million Muslims each year, mainly through high birthrates, but some by conversion. The numbers of Muslims coming to Christ in our time are indeed unprecedented, but we are only talking about *thousands* of new believers each year, while *millions* more are born as Muslims. With all the great things happening in mission to Muslims today, the world is actually getting more and more unreached (Parks 2017). So not only do we need to do more, we also need to do better; and this requires fresh reflection on our missiology.

Yet, in this vein we also need to recover the apostolic spirit of Jesus and the apostles if we want to see our Lord receive the worship he alone deserves among Muslims. One way is to call the church to a renewed *apostolic imagination.* I use "apostolic" in two senses: 1) *extending* the kingdom, and 2) *innovating* in mission praxis.[12] The spirit of adaptive missiology is to take up residence among unreached Muslims in humble relationship and seek to discern how they use Islam, what their idols are, and what a pioneering Christ-centered engagement requires.

Adaptive missiology, like this book, is a conversation and a communal exercise. We need each other. And new contexts need innovative approaches, not quick fixes. As ministers of the gospel, we must adapt to people in the complexity of their contexts. Our job is not to define Islam, but to make disciples. Though decontextualized approaches to Muslim ministry are commonplace, engaging people *as they are* requires embracing their complexity and the complexity of their contexts.

Although great things are happening in mission to Muslims these days, we still have not learned how to reach most Muslims with the love of Christ. Islam is perhaps the greatest challenge the church has ever faced. Yet it is not simply that we do not know the answers; we are also unsure of the nature of the problem. Through seeking to extend and innovate, adaptive missiology stirs up the church, in prayerful dependence on the Holy Spirit, to help Muslim communities discover God in Christ and to see him glorified, even "to the ends of the earth" (Acts 1:8).

Reflection Questions

1. Describe adaptive missiology in your own words. In your view, what are some of the possibilities and limitations of this approach?

2. Integrating insights learned from this book, write out some practical and specific steps you could take to develop an approach to Muslim ministry in your Islamic context.

References

Accad, Martin. 2012. "Christian Attitudes toward Islam and Muslims: A Kerygmatic Approach." In *Toward Respectful Understanding and Witness among Muslims: Essays in Honor of J. Dudley Woodberry*, edited by Evelyne Reisacher, 29–47. Pasadena, CA: William Carey.

———. 2016. "Mission in a World Gone Wild and Violent: Challenging the Monochromatic View of Islam from a Silent Majority Position." *IMES* (blog). Accessed July 21, 2017. https://abtslebanon. org/2016/07/08/mission-in-a-world-gone-wild-and-violent-challenging-the-monochromatic-view-of-islam-from-a-silent-majority-position.

Anonymous-Three. 2017. "Why I am an Essentialist about Islam and Why is that Important?" *Global Missiology* 3 (14).

---

[12] I intentionally mirror these two themes with Walter Brueggemann's concept of biblical "prophetic imagination," which involves both criticizing and energizing (2001).

Anonymous-Two. 2017. "Essentialism and Islam." *Global Missiology* 3 (14).

Aydin, Cemil. 2017. *The Idea of the Muslim World: A Global Intellectual History*. Cambridge, MA: Harvard University Press.

Azumah, John. 2016. "Mission in the Islamic World: Making Theological and Missiological Sense of Muhammad." In *The State of Missiology Today: Global Innovations in Christian Witness*, edited by Charles Van Engen. Downers Grove, IL: InterVarsity.

Bates, Daniel G., and Amal Rassam. 2001. *Peoples and Cultures of the Middle East*. 2nd ed. Upper Saddle River, NJ: Prentice-Hall.

Best, Harold. 2003. *Unceasing Worship: Biblical Perspectives on Worship and the Arts*. Downers Grove, IL: InterVarsity.

Brueggemann, Walter. 2001. *The Prophetic Imagination*. Minneapolis: Fortress.

Cavanaugh, William T. 2009. *The Myth of Religious Violence: Secular Ideology and the Roots of Modern Conflict*. New York: Oxford.

Ess, Joseph van. 2006. *The Flowering of Muslim Theology*. Cambridge, MA: Harvard University Press.

Farah, Warrick. 2010. "Is Allah God? A Relevant Issue?" *Circumpolar* (blog). Accessed November 28, 2014. http://muslimministry.blogspot.com/2010/09/is-allah-god-relevant-issue.html.

———. 2015a. "The Complexity of Insiderness." *International Journal of Frontier Missiology* 32 (2): 85–91.

———. 2015b. "Factors Influencing Arab Muslims to Embrace Biblical Faith That Inform Adaptive Evangelism in Islamic Contexts," Doctor of Intercultural Studies diss., Fuller Theological Seminary.

Farah, Warrick, and Kyle Meeker. 2015. "The 'W' Spectrum: 'Worker' Paradigms in Muslim Contexts." *Evangelical Missions Quarterly* 51 (4).

Flemming, Dean. 2005. *Contextualization in the New Testament: Patterns for Theology and Mission*. Downers Grove, IL: InterVarsity.

Gill, Brad. 2014. "Global Cooperation and the Dynamic of Frontier Missiology." *International Journal of Frontier Missiology* 31 (2): 89–98.

Greenlee, David. 2007. *One Cross, One Way, Many Journeys: Thinking Again About Conversion*. Downers Grove, IL: InterVarsity.

Greer, Bradford. 2017. "Starting Points: Approaching the Frontier Missiological Task." *International Journal of Frontier Missiology* 33 (3): 93–100.

Hiebert, Paul. 1986. *Anthropological Insights for Missionaries*. Grand Rapids: Baker.

Keller, Tim. 2008. *The Reason for God*. New York: Penguin Group.

Lausanne Movement, The. 2011. *The Cape Town Commitment: A Confession of Faith and a Call to Action*. Peabody, MA: Hendrickson.

Martin, Craig. 2014. *A Critical Introduction to the Study of Religion*. New York: Routledge.

Netland, Harold. 2001. *Encountering Religious Pluralism: The Challenge to Christian Faith and Mission*. Downers Grove, IL: InterVarsity.

Nongbri, Brent. 2013. *Before Religion: A History of a Modern Concept*. New Haven, CT: Yale University Press.

Parks, Kent. 2017. "Finishing the Remaining 29 Percent of World Evangelization." *Lausanne Global Analysis* 6 (3).

Pennington, Perry. 2014. "From Prophethood to the Gospel: Talking to Folk Muslims about Jesus." *International Journal of Frontier Missiology* 31 (4): 195–203.

Richard, H.L. 2014. "Religious Syncretism as a Syncretistic Concept: The Inadequacy of the 'World Religions' Paradigm in Cross-Cultural Encounter." *International Journal of Frontier Missiology* 31 (4): 209–15.

Rosner, Brian S. 1999. "The Concept of Idolatry." *Themelios* 24 (3): 21–30.

Roy, Olivier. 2003. "Islamism and Nationalism." *Pouvoirs* 104 (1): 45–53.

Rynkiewich, Michael. 2008. "A New Heaven and a New Earth? The Future of Missiological Anthropology." In *Paradigm Shifts in Christian Witness*, edited by Charles Van Engen, Darrell Whiteman, and Dudley Woodberry. Maryknoll, NY: Orbis.

———. 2011. *Soul, Self, and Society: A Postmodern Anthropology for Mission in a Postcolonial World*. Eugene, OR: Cascade Books.

Said, Edward. 1994 [1978]. *Orientalism: Western Conceptions of the Orient*. New York: Random House.

Schilbrack, Kevin. 2010. "Religions: Are There Any?" *Journal of the American Academy of Religion* 78 (4): 1112–38.

Shaw, Daniel. 2010. "Beyond Contextualization: Toward a Twenty-First-Century Model for Enabling Mission." *International Bulletin of Missionary Research* 34 (4): 208–15.

Smart, Ninian. 1996. *Dimensions of the Sacred: An Anatomy of the World's Beliefs*. Berkley, CA: University of California Press.

Swanson, Herb. 2004. "Said's Orientalism and the Study of Christian Missions." *International Bulletin of Missionary Research* 28 (3): 107–12.

Walls, Andrew. 1996. "Romans One and the Modern Missionary Movement." In *The Missionary Movement in Christian History: Studies in the Transmission of the Faith*. Maryknoll, NY: Orbis.

Waterman, L. D. 2017. "Different Pools, Different Fish: The Mistake of 'One Size Fits All' Solutions to the Challenge of Effective Outreach among Muslims." *Global Reflections* (blog). Accessed January 28, 2017. http://sparks.fuller.edu/global-reflections/different-pools-different-fish-the-mistake-of-one-size-fits-all-solutions-to-the-challenge-of-effective-outreach-among-muslims.

Wright, Christopher J. H. 2006. *The Mission of God: Unlocking the Bible's Grand Narrative*. Downers Grove, IL: InterVarsity.

———. 2011. "Truth with a Mission: Reading All Scripture Missiologically." *Southern Baptist Journal of Theology* 15 (2): 4–15.

Wright, N. T. 2015. *Simply Good News: Why the Gospel Is News and What Makes It Good*. New York: HarperCollins.

Yip, George. 2014. "The Contour of a Post-Postmodern Missiology." *Missiology* 42 (4): 399–411.

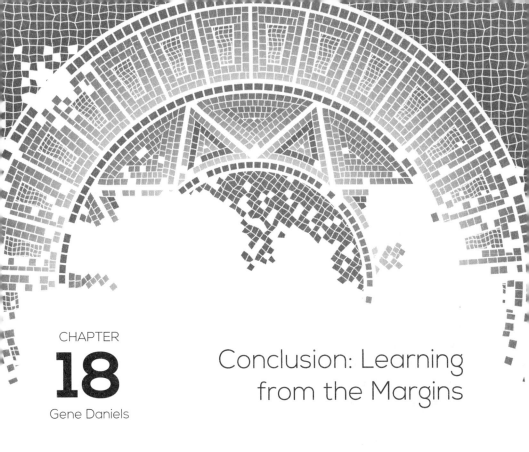

18

Gene Daniels

Conclusion: Learning from the Margins

Hopefully you have enjoyed this journey across the Muslim world over the preceding chapters. We visited widely diverse contexts, yet these were by no means exhaustive. The simple religion of the Bedouin Muhammad has produced quite a kaleidoscope of practice as it has spread and rooted in different cultures. It would take an encyclopedia to explore them all. But the goal of this volume was never to document the innumerable margins of the Muslim world that do not fit stereotypical images of Islamic orthodoxy. Instead, our purpose was more practical, and falls along three lines.

First and foremost, the point of this book is to show that even in our age of globalization and mass-marketed mission methodologies, context still matters. Effective gospel ministry to Muslims requires us to look beyond sometimes surface commonalities and dive deep into the nuances created by the social, cultural, and historical dimensions of a context. Second, we hope to have moved beyond simple persuasion and into demonstration. In the preceding pages, experienced field-workers have painted detailed, practical pictures of some of the many "margins" of the Muslim world. While some of these portraits may seem, to us, mismatched to the term "Islam," they reflect the way many Muslims actually live their lives. And finally, our goal is to help you apply these insights to your own ministry—which is where we are at now.

A Framework for Learning

If you happen to find yourself now, or someday in the future, in a context similar to one presented in this volume, the application may be fairly direct. The lessons learned by that particular scholar-practitioner could be easily adapted. But even then, very few will be in *exactly* the same setting and have *exactly* the same spiritual giftings and ministry style, thus exact copy of their approach may not bear abundant fruit. Imitation may be the sincerest form of flattery, but it makes a poor mission strategy.

And what of the thousands of other contexts on the margins of Islam that we have not explored? How does this book help workers in such settings? Or what about those reading this who don't yet know where they will serve in the Muslim world—How can they learn from these examples? The first step is to think of each chapter as a missiological case study.

Case studies have long been used in business, law, and the social sciences, where they are approached with inductive, rather than deductive, reasoning. Case studies teach us to reason from the starting place of a real, concrete example and then move on to the principles that can be derived from them. Unfortunately, many missionaries are not familiar with this style of learning. More than we're likely to admit, we attend seminars or read books that teach us to follow a prescribed pattern that someone else has developed. Sometimes this is a missiological theory and other times it is complete methodology; but what both have in common is that they do not teach you to reason and reflect on the concrete—something we believe is infinitely more important.

Social Sciences in Dialogue with Scripture

In this book we have focused on the social sciences side of missiology—the social, cultural, and historical dimensions of the contexts—and for the most part we have steered clear of secondary theological issues. There are several reasons for this, including three that are worth noting briefly. First, considering the wide range of theologies represented in the evangelical mission world, we would have been foolish to write this book narrowly to fit into one stream. Second, using a theological lens to understand Muslims tends to emphasize the essentialist view of Islam (or the "top-down" approach discussed in chapter 2, something that is antithetical to the philosophy of this volume. Third, and most important, we assume that our readers came to this text already possessing a solid, and hopefully growing, knowledge of the Bible—since it is the foundation of everything we do in mission. The problem for most missionaries isn't a poor understanding of Scripture, but rather that they don't know how to integrate their knowledge of Scripture into the context of their ministry. Thus our goal has been to help readers learn how to exegete a context so that they will properly apply their existing Bible knowledge to it. We need to read Scripture *in light of* the context God has sent us to, as well as reflect on that context *in light of* Scripture—a two-way conversation. All missionaries read Scripture in dialogue with something; unfortunately, all too often it is in dialogue with Western logic or philosophy, which contributes terribly to the gospel because it seems alien and irrelevant to many Muslims.

And one final point before exploring some of the themes from the chapters. When I make reference to "Scripture," I very much *do not* mean theology. We inevitably bring our existing theology to the mission field with us; nevertheless, Scripture needs to be carefully and thoroughly examined anew as we do missiology in each new frontier setting. When missionaries think in terms of theology rather than Scripture, their cultural and denominational biases often blind them to many things they need to see.

With these things in mind, I would now like to walk through a process of inductively learning from the previous chapters—specifically by connecting the dots between different authors and their practices—in such a way as to develop some key concerns that flow through the different contexts.

Popular or folk Islam

Without a doubt, contexts involving folk, or popular, Islam are the most widespread form of non-orthodox Islamic practice. In the preceding chapters we saw a sampling of folk Islamic practices from contexts across the entire breadth of the Muslim world, from Indonesia (chapter 10) to North Africa (chapter 11). These practices run the gamut from wearing charms and amulets, to visiting the tombs of holy men, to using incantations. What these behaviors have in common is that they are all motivated by the belief that life's difficulties are always the result of spiritual forces which can be controlled and manipulated by "special people using special techniques during special times and in special places" (see chapter 15, p 174)

Missionaries must be careful lest they fall prey to the common misperception that "popular" and orthodox Islam are mutually exclusive—which is simply not the case for millions of people. Furthermore, folk Islam is not limited to "backward," unsophisticated, or tribal Muslims. Even well-educated Muslims who otherwise seem quite Western may be involved with popular Islamic practices, although they may be loath to discuss the fact openly. Larson put it eloquently: "The line of separation between folk and traditional Islam is often thin. 'People of the shrine' are usually also 'people of the mosque'" (chapter 8, 82).

Whether these occultic practices are rooted in Muhammad (as per Samuel Zwemer) or are strictly localized later additions, they are classic examples of syncretism—the blending of two or more religious systems. While missionaries are usually concerned about the incidence of Christian syncretism, and rightly so, it is missiologically important for us to know when, and with what, Muslims have syncretized their own faith.

For example, let's take a situation where a gospel worker diagnoses that the "popular" version of Islam she is facing is actually a case where the line between Islam and Hinduism has become blurred. What should she do? To begin with, since at least part of the local worldview is rooted in Hinduism, she should take time to learn about that religion and the general contours of a worldview shaped by it. Furthermore, she would be wise to consider the life strategies that Hindus use for interacting with multiple powerful supernatural beings—all at the same time—because this would differ greatly from a classic orthodox Islamic worldview rooted in absolute monotheism.

On a more personal level, Western missionaries facing folk Islam need to confront their own assumptions about the nature of the supernatural world. We often have a hard time wrestling deeply with anything outside our scientific-materialistic worldview, and the occultic behaviors of popular Islam certainly lie far beyond the pale for most of us. Not that gospel workers should uncritically adopt a Muslim view of the supernatural in their context, but we very much need to embrace a biblical one. Any intentional steps in that direction will probably bring us much closer to our Muslim friends than we are now and help us stop dismissing their beliefs as mere "superstitions."

The impacts of colonialism

The next stream of thought winding through many of the chapters and that we should explore reminds us how important it is for missionaries to learn the history of their context. When I began ministry in the former Soviet Union, I had almost zero understanding of the region's unique history and was completely unaware of the huge shadow that colonialism cast over that context. And this is actually quite widespread; at least nine of our chapters specifically raise issues related to colonization. This is not surprising since most of the Muslim world was under colonial rule until the mid-twentieth century. These contexts reflect a past history of Western "Christian" powers, such as the French in North Africa, the Dutch in Indonesia, or the Russians in Central Asia.[1] However, we also have two chapters about contexts where the colonial power is current and non-Western—that is, Chinese colonialism over the Hui (chapter 9) and the Uyghurs of the Tarim Basin (chapter 15).[2]

Taken together, this demonstrates that the vast majority of the world's Muslims have struggled under the yoke of a colonial power within living memory. And as with most

---

[1] Although we normally associate Russian domination of Central Asia with Soviet policy, the region was already colonized before the end of the Russian imperial era, which clearly considered itself Christian as much as any other European empire.

[2] Most of us do not think of the situation of Muslims in China as a case of colonialism. Nevertheless, Chinese acquisition of, and policy toward, Muslim homelands now incorporated into western China are every bit as colonial as were British and Russian geopolitical moves in Asia, and sometimes were in response to them (see Peter Hopkirk's classic, *The Great Game*).

things that touch the issue of worldview, there are two sides to the story. In addition to deeply affecting many Muslims, colonialism has also colored how many missionaries think about the Muslim world. But since my coeditor, Warrick Farah, has already done a great job of dissecting that in the preceding chapter, now we will focus on unpacking some of the ways this colonial legacy directly impacts our Muslim friends.

One result that many expatriate gospel workers miss is that Muslims often perceive them as part of a new colonial intrusion into their lives and culture. This can be the case even when the gospel messenger is from a completely different culture than the one that formerly ruled over them. Workers need to be aware of and sensitive to this issue. Expatriates obviously cannot pretend they are not foreign, but they can minimize the degree to which they are associated with the negatives of colonial rule. For example, when new MBBs become "cultural converts"—visibly changing their culture to that of the missionaries—this plays right into the fear of renewed colonialism, because it mimics the way colonial masters extracted people from their culture and integrated them into the ruling cultural paradigm. Conversely, we saw among the Berbers (chapter 11) that when the gospel is "culturally translated" into the context of a proud culture, the resulting church sees itself as contributing to both the universal body of Christ *and* the history of their people.

We should also consider the impact colonialism has had on religious practice among the Muslims who experienced it. Usually there is a long, slow decline of public religious expression under colonial rule (see chapters 4 and 12 for examples). However, that same trend often makes a noticeable reversal during the postcolonial era in many of the same places. As a result, a widespread Islamic "revival" in many postcolonial contexts has important missiological implications.

When a people are experiencing a resurgence of their ancestral religion, the atmosphere is quite different than when they are in either a steady state of religious practice or when religion is in decline. For example, there is an increase in public displays of Islam, which is often, at least partly, an expression of nationalism. Also, even nominal Muslims may feel compelled to "defend the faith" from any offense by the gospel worker.

A final important insight about colonialism is that it generally causes biculturalism, which can be a doorway for the gospel. But since this was one of the strongest themes running through many of the chapters, it deserves to have a section all its own.

Biculturalism[3]

Many of the Muslims in the contexts we have examined have their feet firmly planted in at least two distinctly different cultural spaces. Sometimes they are aware of this precarious position, such as the Muslim youth living in the "glocal" culture that Brown

---

[3] Since the majority of the contexts we explored are primarily bicultural, we will use that term. However, much of what follows in this section also applies to "multicultural" contexts.

describes (chapter 16).[4] Other times bicultural Muslims have so completely blended their worldviews that they seem oblivious to the cultural syncretism they practice (see chapters 4, 7, and 15 for examples). A gospel worker in this kind of environment must realize that both cultures matter and we need to pay careful attention to both dimensions of a bicultural Muslim's context. A missionary may find that one or the other cultural world provides a better entry point for the gospel, but that doesn't mean the other is irrelevant.

Kim unpacks this well in his chapter on the Hui (chapter 9). He writes about the way Chinese urban culture sits superimposed as an "outer layer" over a deep core of Hui traditional culture. He goes on to explain how this outer layer creates space for "cultural common ground" between Muslims and outsiders, thus opening opportunities for the gospel naturally to pass person-to-person.

In this urbanized Hui context, Kim looks at points of contact such as education or similar preferences for hobbies and media. At the same time, he cautions us to remember that despite these important commonalities, the Hui, as Muslims, still have "unique traditional values and patterns … that do not translate across cultures." This reminds us that while Muslims in postcolonial, or colonial, contexts are often truly bicultural, we cannot afford to ignore the significance of their core Muslim cultural identity. This comports well with what Esler noted in Bosnia (chapter 4). He demonstrated that even when dealing with secular Muslims (as many postcolonial Muslims tend to be), the gospel worker should have a clear understanding of how to answer standard Islamic objections to the gospel, because they will surely come up.

After considering biculturalism, it quite naturally follows that we should turn to a closely linked linguistic phenomenon.

Multilingualism

Most readers were probably already aware that a multitude of languages are spoken across the Muslim world and that only about 20 percent of Muslims speak Arabic. However, many workers enter the field unaware of an important related phenomenon: the fact that many of the world's Muslims are multilingual. While this includes many different situations, it is of particular missiological interest when Muslims speak their mother tongue *and* the language of a non-Muslim people.

The relationship between language and effective ministry is much too broad to explore thoroughly here. One key takeaway, though, is that a shared language can be a strong bridge to carry the gospel across. There are many reasons for this, but what we saw rather concretely in some chapters was that it creates a hybrid identity that enables a Muslim to carry cultural markers from both their birth and adopted cultures without any sense of contradiction. This is extremely important in an era of globalization that has allowed millions of Muslims to migrate to other countries.

---

[4] The youth culture Brown describes is probably better understood as multicultural since Muslim youth often paint with many colors on their globalized cultural palate.

For example, Muslims in the UK are more than simply English-speaking; they are "British Muslims" (chapter 13), in a very similar way to Russified Muslims being so much more than people who speak Russian (chapter 12). This bilingualism relates to biculturalism and results in shared social spaces that can lead to effective engagement by the local CBB[5] church and keeps Muslim ministry from being a domain only specialists can enter.

The idea of Muslims living in Christian cultural contexts makes a fine segue to our next topic.

Globalization

The effects of an ever increasingly interconnected world appeared in several of the chapters. In the chapter on the Nurcu Gülen movement in Turkey (chapter 6), we saw how this is facilitating the movement's spread into other countries through private schools. Even in geographically remote places like China's Tarim Basin,[6] globalization is bringing life-changing technologies from the outside into contact with Muslim peoples (chapter 15). The key to engaging globalization *missiologically* was strongly hinted at in Brown's chapter on the global Muslim youth culture (chapter 16), where he explains and explores the concept of "glocal." This slightly unusual term refers to how people interact with elements from a truly global cultural menu yet transform them as they integrate those elements into their local context.

This is critically important, because it keeps us from the common misconception that globalization is simply making Muslims "more Western"—that is, being drawn into the dominant culture of our era. The truth is much more complicated than that. We often find that Muslims, particularly younger ones, are assimilating parts of other cultures[7] into their own, which is a very different scenario. Field practitioners can often find points of contact produced by globalization that can help reach Muslims, but they must remember that it is a chaotic, multi-vectored form of cultural appropriation that changes people, but not in simplistic or binary ways.

Innovative approaches to Scripture

Evangelicals affirm a strong commitment to Scripture in the practice of mission because it is a deep part of our Protestant heritage. However, if the way we use Scripture does not really speak to people in our context, then we are falling back into the same kind of traditionalism the Reformers struggled against so long ago.

There were several instances in which our scholar-practitioners pointed toward the need to think creatively in the way we use Scripture. For example, some chapters

---

[5] The term "Christian Background Believer" (CBB) can be a helpful distinction, particularly in contexts where Muslims and Christians of different cultures live side by side.

[6] A monument on the north edge of the Tarim Basin marks the point on earth that is furthest from an ocean. It is technically called the "Eurasian pole of inaccessibility."

[7] Globalization is providing access to many other cultures, not just Western. The worldwide popularity of "Bollywood" movies is a perfect example of the global reach and impact of Indian culture, and is itself an example of the phenomenon we call *glocal*.

(12 and 14) caution gospel messengers to consider carefully how they might use terms that are more friendly to Muslim ears, particularly in evangelism and early discipleship. This is a reminder that even a shared language is much more than a neutral set of symbols; it can carry a great deal of emotional baggage—both good and bad.

Related to this is the fact that even people who are completely fluent in multiple languages often use different languages in different domains of life. They may use a regional or trade language in the technical, professional, or political sphere, but their ethnic language for community, family, and interpersonal communication. As I saw firsthand in the former Soviet Union, this domain-specific bilingualism is not uncommon in contexts of colonialism, though it is something few field-workers are aware of. When considering language choice, or even the use of Muslim-friendly terms, we must remember that the gospel is not a technical message that someone learns as if a formula; it is a call for a heart-level change of allegiance.

Another creative way of using Scripture was suggested by Higgins (chapter 3), when he reflected on the way Sufis use and understand stories. Whereas we typically want biblical storying to give *information* that leads to a decision for Christ, Sufis think of stories as a means to cloak meaning and provoke thought. Could it be that our approach to Scripture, as facts and information, has more to do with our scientific-materialist worldview than with the actual nature of God's self-disclosure? Perhaps rather than seeking to bring about information-based decisions, we could think of Scripture as a means of changing the feelings Muslims have toward faith in Christ, which is a vitally necessary part of their journey.

In Kilgore's chapter on Indonesia's Java island (chapter 10), we were challenged by another area in which we may need to approach Scripture innovatively—choosing what script to use. Because of the multiple overlays of culture, ruling government, and education systems, many Muslims in our margins have been exposed to a bewildering confusion of scripts through which to read their own language. The government may use one script in their schools, but often the same language is taught at the madrassa using an Arabic-based script.[8]

A final example of innovative and very appropriate use of Scripture comes from Hadaway's chapter on Sufi-oriented African traditionalists (chapter 7). He observes that such Muslims would be more likely to understand the gospel if it was presented around the themes of fear and power. "Elements of the shame-honor worldview, as well as portions of the guilt-inno-cence value system, persist as secondary themes in their culture. Thus gospel messengers to the Beja must understand all three, but probably focus their presentation on the area of fear-power" (page 78).

---

[8] For a great article on this topic see Decker and Jiniru, 2012: "Living Letters: The Arabic Script as a Redemptive Bridge in Reaching Muslims," International Journal of Frontier Missiology 29 (2): 75–82.

This points toward the need to consider carefully how our own worldview influences the way we interpret and apply Scripture. We must be quick to recognize when it is our worldview, not theirs, that causes Muslims to misunderstand Scripture. This means that gospel tracts and related evangelistic programs from the West are best kept where they were developed.

Social interaction as a gospel bridge

Another theme well worth exploring is something we might call "the importance of normal social interaction as a gospel bridge." This was most obvious in contexts where Muslims are routinely living side by side with non-Muslims, such as in the UK, France, or the Hui in Chinese cities (chapters 13, 5, and 9). Meaningful, consistent, and genuine human interaction are important raw materials for building a strong bridge for the gospel. Kronk pointed out that recent research in France has shown that one of the most significant catalysts for conversion was having a Christian friend or family member.

Finding better ways to harness this could be a key to wider gospel advance in some Muslim contexts. Perhaps gospel workers have put too much effort into constructing structures that we like—NGOs, microenterprise, etc.—and not enough time looking for ways to engage deeply in already existing social structures.

Also, it is important to note that this social interaction takes a slightly different shape in Brown's chapter on Muslim youth culture (chapter 16). The shared experience of common media platforms and content creates bonding and friendship among youth across both geographic and cultural distances. Thus we see that it is not just the mechanical application of new technologies that will bear gospel fruit; rather it is using them to facilitate new forms of meaningful relationships that will lead to transformed lives.

Learning from and with MBBs

Several chapters referred to MBBs and their churches—and before doing any analysis of this theme we should first simply stop and rejoice before the Lord!

In the current climate of God's work in the Muslim world, most workers eventually become acquainted with men and women who have turned from Islam to faith in Christ. And these MBBs have much to teach us about effective ministry to Muslims.

One thing we must learn from them, which came out most clearly in the Berber context (chapter 11), concerns the difficult "no-man's land" that MBBs inhabit. Most of us realize MBBs take great risks—persecution, rejection by family, etc. But we are quite unaware that they often feel a tension between being part of the worldwide Christian community and preserving meaningful connection to their own people. The words of an unnamed Algerian church leader are worth repeating:

I've two faces, two rooms, one opposite the other, which can be opposed one to the other. I've this natural connection, brother with brother, whatever his nationality; but I've also another brother who I need to recover. The presence of one makes the other uncomfortable. I walk on a tight rope ... and I don't want it to break." (page 127)

As outsiders, foreign gospel workers can never truly understand the heartrending difficulty of this tension. If it comes up, we must remember the issue is not about us, but about how to help our MBB friends find ways to be fully loyal to Christ while at the same time maintaining an active witness to their community.

Another significant insight concerning MBBs comes from looking beyond the details and thinking about the chapters in aggregate. As we reflect on the wide diversity of the Muslim contexts we have considered, we must remember that all of our MBB friends are themselves the product of a particular context. Before their conversion they may have been devoutly orthodox, traditionally folk Islamic, or even secular to the point of being functional atheists. This means that while their insights are deep and meaningful, our friends are also limited in ways they are probably unaware of. For example, a brother from post-Soviet Central Asia may have solid ministry advice as it concerns fellow nominal Muslims somewhere like the Balkans, but it would be almost meaningless for dealing with Sufis in Africa. And despite the best of intentions, strategies learned from MBBs coming out of folk Islam in Bangladesh will be much less helpful when the audience changes to North African migrants in France.

Like all followers of Christ, the ministry experience of our MBB friends is not universal, no more so than the Orientalist image of a Muslim being a camel-riding Arab. In their own particular context, their insights have great clarity; but the value of those insights decreases as we moves into other contexts. Unfortunately, many MBBs will tell you that since they are themselves former Muslims, they know the right way to reach other Muslims—even those very different from themselves. Thus missionaries must carefully listen to local MBBs as it concerns the immediate context of ministry, but just as carefully discern the limits of those insights.

The preceding topics were only a few of many we could have teased out of the various contexts explored in this book. You may have noted others that you can explore later. Taken together, they remind us that although each context is unique, they share common threads that should be picked up and carefully considered. This act of careful consideration is a perfect segue to the next practical aspect of learning from this book.

Becoming "Reflective Practitioners"

Now that we have gathered our thoughts and observations from the fourteen case studies in this book, what do we do with them? How do they help practically? I would like to suggest something based on what I have observed over the past several years as part of the Fruitful Practice Research taskforce, a team of missiologists from various agencies who have studied the best practices of ministry in the Muslim world.[9]

---

[9] For more information on Fruitful Practice Research, please contact info@fruitfulpractice.org.

Aside from the many specific practices gleaned through that research, several general principles have emerged. One that I find most enlightening is that fruitful missionaries tend to be "reflective" missionaries. Repeatedly our research team has seen that gospel workers who are successful in the Muslim world are those who have moved past the rote learning of methods and into the practice of missiological reflection. They carefully consider a wide range of inputs—their existing knowledge, contextual information, new ideas, etc.—and then contemplate how all these pieces inform each other.

Over the years of my own involvement in Muslim world ministry, I have had the privilege of interacting with missionaries from a wide range of nationalities, backgrounds, and agencies. And I must say that "reflective practice" remains more of an ideal than a practice for most of us. We seem to be much more likely to attend a seminar learning a prepackaged evangelistic technique than "wasting time" doing some nebulous activity called "reflecting." Perhaps this is because of the time constraints that so many missionaries feel, a pressure to produce and therefore be worth the support they receive. Be that as it may, any time spent reflecting on our context and personal practice will indeed pay good dividends. Besides the many things we can learn through reflection, by slowing down we might also give the Holy Spirit more latitude to work in the lives of the Muslims around us.

Conclusion

In chapter 10, Kilgore recounted an incident from early in his ministry when a mission expert questioned his call to Indonesia, because "they're not even real Muslims over there." Unfortunately, this kind of ignorance still exists in the missions community. Some veterans of Muslim ministry act as if those at the margins of the Islamic world are not "real" Muslims because they are not strictly orthodox. I have never understood exactly what such comments are supposed to mean in terms of mission—but that is beside the point. The living experience of hundreds of millions of people argue otherwise. True, many of the Muslims you have encountered in these chapters do not practice a pure Qur'anic version of Islam, but then again most Muslim sects say the same about each other anyway, so that hardly disqualifies them from being Muslim for missiological purposes.

I believe this is representative of a systemic problem in the Muslim-ministry community. There are, unfortunately, many loud voices advocating an "essentialist" or "reductionist" approach to Islam. They argue that Islam can and should be reduced to its essential doctrines and practices, and that these are the things which need to shape appropriate ministry to Muslims. Of course, by now you are well aware that this is not the philosophy of the writers and editors of this volume. We believe that although Muslims share many things in common, the diversity of their social, cultural, and historical contexts is of greater practical meaning for ministry—particularly in the type of contexts described in this book.

Furthermore, as missionaries it is not our place to decide the boundaries of what is and what is not Islam—and more importantly, it is not to our benefit. Whether our Muslim friends' beliefs are orthodox, heterodox, or completely heretical has little bearing on their need for Christ. These things do have a huge impact on how we approach them with the gospel, however, and that is the reason for this book. We hope that as you have read the preceding chapters you have given up the pursuit of a "pure Islam," which you will likely never find, and have realized that we are called to reach Muslims just as they are, with all their quirks and peculiarities.

It is our sincere desire that this volume becomes one of the practical things God uses to, "equip you with everything good for doing his will, and may he work in us what is pleasing to him, through Jesus Christ, to whom be glory for ever and ever. Amen" (Heb 13:21, NIV).